Luminos is the Open Access monograph publishing program from UC Press. Luminos provides a framework for preserving and reinvigorating monograph publishing for the future and increases the reach and visibility of important scholarly work. Titles published in the UC Press Luminos model are published with the same high standards for selection, peer review, production, and marketing as those in our traditional program. www.luminosoa.org

The publisher and the University of California Press Foundation gratefully acknowledge the generous support of the Robert and Meryl Selig Endowment Fund in Film Studies, established in memory of Robert W. Selig.

Publication of this open monograph was the result of Cornell University's participation in TOME (Toward an Open Monograph Ecosystem), a collaboration of the Association of American Universities, the Association of University Presses, and the Association of Research Libraries. TOME aims to expand the reach of long-form humanities and social science scholarship including digital scholarship. Additionally, the program looks to ensure the sustainability of university press monograph publishing by supporting the highest quality scholarship and promoting a new ecology of scholarly publishing in which authors' institutions bear the publication costs.

Funding from Cornell University made it possible to open this publication to the world. www.openmonographs.org

Publication was also supported by the Hull Memorial Publication Fund of Cornell University and by the Jewish Studies Program at Cornell University.

Togo Mizrahi and the Making of
Egyptian Cinema

UNIVERSITY OF CALIFORNIA SERIES IN JEWISH HISTORY
AND CULTURES

Edited by

Todd Presner, Ross Professor of Germanic Languages and Comparative
Literature, UCLA

David Myers, Professor and Sady and Ludwig Kahn Chair in Jewish History, UCLA

In partnership with University of California Press's Luminos program, the University
of California Series in Jewish History and Cultures publishes cutting-edge scholarship
in Jewish studies, with a particular ability to highlight work that relies on digital
media. The series promotes interdisciplinary work that opens new conceptual and
methodological horizons and has the potential to make a broad impact on diverse
fields of study.

1. *Togo Mizrahi and the Making of Egyptian Cinema,* by Deborah A. Starr

Togo Mizrahi and the Making of Egyptian Cinema

Deborah A. Starr

UNIVERSITY OF CALIFORNIA PRESS

University of California Press
Oakland, California

Suggested citation: Starr, D. A. *Togo Mizrahi and the Making of Egyptian Cinema.* Oakland: University of California Press, 2020. DOI: https://doi.org/10.1525/luminos.91

Library of Congress Cataloging-in-Publication Data

Names: Starr, Deborah A., 1968- author.
Title: Togo Mizrahi and the making of Egyptian cinema / Deborah A. Starr.
Description: Oakland, California : University of California Press, [2020] |
    Includes bibliographical references and index.
Identifiers: LCCN 2020004086 | ISBN 9780520366206 (paperback) |
    ISBN 9780520976122 (ebook)
Subjects: LCSH: Mizrāḥī, Tūjū, 1905–1986—Criticism and
    interpretation. | Motion picture producers and directors—Egypt
    Motion pictures—Egypt—20th century
Classification: LCC PN1998.3.M585 S73 2020 | DDC 791.430/33092—dc23
LC record available at https://lccn.loc.gov/2020004086

Manufactured in the United States of America

29 28 27 26 25 24 23 22 21 20
10 9 8 7 6 5 4 3 2 1

To Elliot, Hannah, and Dina.

CONTENTS

LIST OF FIGURES AND TABLES

FIGURES

TABLES

ACKNOWLEDGMENTS

Putting words on a page is a solo act. Writing a book is not an act but a process, and it involves not one person but many people. I am very grateful for all the support and encouragement I have received from colleagues, friends, and family over the course of researching and writing this book.

I am especially grateful to those who closely read and provided comments on the entire manuscript: Walter Armbrust, Orit Bashkin, Joel Gordon, Elliot Shapiro, and an anonymous reader. Your insights have enriched this book.

I would also like to thank the many people who helped me by reading drafts, discussing ideas, parsing words, and assisting my research in a variety of ways. Thank you to Rama Alhabian, Anindita Banerjee, Nancy Berg, Ahmad al-Bindari, Henriette Bornkamm, Ross Brann, Rebecca Bryant, Andrew Campagna, Yomna Chami, Julia Chang, Ziad Fahmy, Ibrahim Gemeah, Shai Ginsburg, Sabine Haenni, Hanan Hammad, Liat Kozma, Or Pitsui, Gabriel Rosenbaum, Eyal Sagui-Bizawi, Ariel Sheetrit, Yaron Shemer, Salma Shitia, Louis Wasser, Seçil Yilmaz, and Munther Younes. Any mistakes in these pages are my own.

As I wrote this book, I found myself frequently engaging in imagined conversation with two mentors who, sadly, passed away before this book was completed. Sasson Somekh not only taught me about Arabic literature and the cultural expression of Jews from Arabic-speaking countries; he also served as a role model of mentorship. Ibrahim Hamid shared with me his love of Egyptian music, and taught me about composers, performers, poets, and the language of Arabic song.

Jacques Mizart has been incredibly generous with his time and in sharing his family archive. His stories have helped me understand who Togo Mizrahi was as a person, and not only as a public figure. I am also grateful to Maureen McManamny for speaking to her mother, Nancy Angel McManamny, on my behalf, and for sharing stories, photos, and press clippings of her grandparents Leon and Esther Angel, who graced the Egyptian screen in the 1930s as Chalom and ʿAdalat.

I am especially grateful to the librarians and archivists who have helped me along the way: Ali Houissa, Ola Seif, and Robin Dougherty. Thank you to the staff at Cornell's CTI (formerly the Academic Technology Center) and DCAPS for helping me capture screenshots.

Over the years, I have presented excerpts from this project as a work in progress. I would like to express my appreciation to organizers of some particularly generative workshops. Thank you to Moshe Behar, Zvi Ben-Dor Benite, and Yoram Meital for inviting me to participate in the Symposium on Jewish Thought in Arab Societies, 1880–1960 at Ben Gurion University (2014); and to Hannan Hammad and Sami Everett for including me in the Workshop on Minorities in Popular Culture in the Modern Middle East, hosted by SOAS and the Woolf Institute (2015). I am also grateful for the feedback I received at symposia held at the Frankel Center for Jewish Studies at the University of Michigan (2015) and at the Katz Center for Advanced Judaic Studies at the University of Pennsylvania (2018).

I appreciate the support I have received from the Department of Near Eastern Studies and the Jewish Studies program at Cornell University, as well as the other funding sources that supported my research and writing. I launched my research on early Egyptian cinema with a CASA III fellowship in Spring 2009. ʿArab Lotfi, Muhammad al-Rubi, and Abeer Heidar taught me an enormous amount about Egyptian cinema history and criticism, and the language of cinema. I am also grateful for the support of the Cornell Diversity Fellowship Seminar in 2013–14, and for the insightful comments of my fellow participants. My research was supported by a National Endowment for the Humanities Summer Stipend in 2015. I spent spring 2016 as a fellow of the Mandel School for Advanced Study in the Humanities at Hebrew University in Jerusalem. I was a recipient of the Cornell Society for the Humanities Monograph Writing Group stipend in 2018–19. I am grateful to the Cornell College of Arts and Sciences and the Near Eastern Studies Department for providing the funding for a book workshop in April 2019. This book was published with the generous support of the Cornell University Jewish Studies Program, the Hull Memorial Publication Fund of Cornell University, the Robert and Meryl Selig Endowment Fund in Film Studies of the University of California Press Foundation, and the TOME Initiative.

Thank you to David Myers and Todd Presner for selecting this book to launch the Jewish Histories and Cultures series. Thank you to Eric Schmidt, Austin Lim, and Francisco Reinking at University of California Press for their guidance through the publishing process, and to Carl Walesa for his attentive copy editing.

I am grateful every day for the love and support of my family. Thank you to my parents for always believing in me. Elliot, this book could not have happened without you. You are my best friend. You are also my audience and my interlocutor. You listen to my ideas and you provide invaluable comments. You have also made it possible for me to devote the long hours it has taken to research and write this book. Hannah and Dina, thank you for your love, good humor, and patience. Elliot, Hannah, and Dina, this book is for you.

NOTES ON TRANSLATION AND TRANSLITERATION

I have opted for readability over full transliteration of Arabic. I have adopted a simplified version of the IJMES transliteration system. I use the 'ayin (') and the hamza ('), but I have omitted other diacritical marks. I rely on spellings in the *Oxford English Dictionary* for words that have entered the English language, such as *tarboosh* and *galabiya*.

Proper names present a particular challenge. When referring to individuals whose names were not originally Arabic, I have favored the foreign spelling rather than transliterating from Arabic. For public figures, like Gamal Abdel Nasser, I have adopted the accepted English spellings. For individuals involved in the Egyptian cinema industry, I render Arabic names as they are pronounced in Egyptian Colloquial Arabic. Film dialogue is transliterated according to Egyptian colloquial pronunciation, and published work is transliterated from Modern Standard Arabic. I maintain a consistent orthography for names throughout; I do this even in citing written work published in Arabic; for example, I always use Togo Mizrahi rather than Tuju Mizrahi. All translations, including the English-language titles for Arabic-language films, are my own, except where noted.

Upon first mention in a chapter, I identify films by both their Arabic title and the title translated into English. On subsequent reference, I refer to films exclusively by their title in English.

Some of my discussion of the notion of Levantine cinema (chaps. 1 and 3) first appeared in my essay "Masquerade and the Performance of National Imaginaries: Levantine Ethics, Aesthetics, and Identities in Egyptian Cinema," *Journal of Levantine Studies* 1, no. 2 (Winter 2011): 31–57. Part of chapter 3 was originally published as "Chalom and 'Abdu Get Married: Jewishness and Egyptianness in the Films of Togo Mizrahi," *Jewish Quarterly Review* 107, no. 2 (Spring 2017): 209–30.[1] Chapter 4 was originally published as "In Bed Together: Coexistence in Togo Mizrahi's Alexandria Films," in *Post-Ottoman Coexistence: Sharing Space in the Shadow of Conflict*, ed. Rebecca Bryant (New York: Berghahn Books, 2016), 129–56.

Togo Mizrahi, Agent of Exchange

PREVIEW

We hear a band strike up festive music. We see street vendors selling their wares from carts lining a city street. A man and boy, holding hands, walk past the vendors. As they recede into a distant crowd, a pair of young men, both in Western suits and tarbooshes, stroll into and out of the frame. Two riders—one in a dark galabiya and tarboosh, the other in a light galabiya and turban—swing a gondola high into the air, cutting an arc across the screen. Young children circle by, riding on a carousel. Men push a manually operated fun wheel, as car after car filled with children rise and disappear out of the frame. A vendor tips a large, ornate brass carafe, and a translucent liquid pours out of the long spout in a wide curve, filling a glass. In a park, girls in light-colored dresses play chase. A pair of men in overcoats and tarbooshes walk along a path, followed by a group of boys who pause to peer at the camera (fig. 1). In the background, to the left, a woman in black wearing a face veil also looks in the direction of the camera. Behind them to the right, a man in a white galabiya and turban sits on the grass, deep in conversation. At the beach, a family walks along the shore—the distinctive seaside cabins and corniche of Alexandria visible to the right of the frame. People clustered in small groups picnic on the sand. The skirt hems of women dressed in the latest European fashion flap in the sea breeze along with the awnings of beach umbrellas.

This kinetic, carnivalesque montage appears in a 1937 Egyptian feature film, *Al-'Izz bahdala* (*Mistreated by Affluence*).[1] A title screen identifies the celebration as "*Shamm al-nasim, 'id al-sha'b*"—that is, "Shamm al-nasim, the people's feast." Shamm al-nasim ("Smelling the Breeze")—is a spring festival that shares some characteristics with other seasonal celebrations in the region, like Nowruz. Shamm al-nasim is also a uniquely Egyptian festival, with roots in ancient Egyptian practices. Egyptians take to the streets, parks, beaches, and green spaces.

FIGURE 1. Alexandria residents relaxing in a park. Screenshot from *Mistreated by Affluence* (Togo Mizrahi, 1937).

The footage shows what appear to be Alexandria residents engaging in leisure activities in identifiable locales. None of the credited actors appear in the montage. Children display curiosity about the camera. The viewer is invited to read these images as authentic—even as we recognize the constructedness of the montage. Social codes of dress give the viewer cues to categorizing the individuals included in the footage. Members of the rising middle class—the *effendiyya*—are shown seeking entertainment and diversion alongside members of the popular classes.[2] This carefully edited montage constructs a festival day in which Alexandrians across the socioeconomic spectrum celebrate in public spaces together.

While the celebration of Shamm al-nasim is pegged to the Coptic calendar, falling on the day after Easter, in modern times it has historically been celebrated by Muslim, Christian, and Jewish Egyptians alike. The narrative scenes that bracket the montage highlight this intercommunal aspect of the festival. In the scene preceding the montage, two families—one Muslim and one Jewish—prepare together for the next day's feast. As the two mothers and their adult daughters package up the traditional Egyptian dishes they prepared for the picnic, the daughters' fiancés deliver their contribution: *fisikh*, salted fish consumed on the holiday. In the scene that follows the montage, the two families picnic on the beach—literally breaking bread together. Read in tandem, the montage and the narrative scenes portray Shamm al-nasim as a universal practice of all Egyptians regardless of class or religion.

Mistreated by Affluence was written, directed, and produced by Togo Mizrahi, a Jewish native of Alexandria, and it stars a Jewish actor who performed under the screen name Chalom. Shamm al-nasim holds great appeal for Mizrahi; scenes from the festival feature prominently in three of his films, including *Mistreated by Affluence*.³ The holiday is both distinctly Egyptian, and universally celebrated in Egypt. The communal celebration of the festival enacts a pluralist vision of the Egyptian polity that Mizrahi projects in his films.

Another scene in *Mistreated by Affluence* also explores the intersection between coexistence and class. The protagonists—Chalom, a Jew; and 'Abdu, a Muslim—start out impoverished and rapidly climb the socioeconomic ladder together, only to return to their modest circumstances after a fall. At the start of the film 'Abdu is employed as a butcher's assistant, and Chalom is an itinerant lottery-ticket seller. When the butcher dies, 'Abdu unexpectedly inherits the shop. With this windfall, 'Abdu rents the empty storefront next door for his friend. Chalom hangs a bilingual sign (Arabic and French) on his new shop. In Arabic, the sign reads "Chalom, for the sale and redemption of lottery tickets." During the course of the film, the arabophone Chalom demonstrates at least a passing knowledge of Italian and Greek, but he does not speak French. So, when writing his sign, Chalom adopts an accessible model—the common signs for currency exchange in the port city. In contrast to the idiomatic French that appears alongside Arabic in the credits and intertitles of the film, the broken French in Chalom's handwritten scrawl is difficult to decipher, reading as either "Chalom Agen d'echange" or "Chalom, Agen de Change"—Chalom, agent of exchange.⁴

Like many of Mizrahi's other popular comedies and musical melodramas of the 1930s and 1940s, *Mistreated by Affluence* features a convoluted plot of masquerade, role-play, and mistaken identity. In the film, Chalom exchanges identities as well as lottery tickets. As an "agent of exchange," Chalom acts in ways that also set into motion the changes other characters undergo in the film. Plotted in this way, the film's coexistence narrative serves to expose the nation's "masquerade of unity."⁵ The notion of exchange—from cultural exchange to exchange of identities—is a key element in Mizrahi's films. *Togo Mizrahi and the Making of Egyptian Cinema* teases out the relationship between the notion of exchange and pluralist nationalism in Mizrahi's oeuvre.

The storefront also is the site of an assertion of identity. In an earlier scene in *Mistreated by Affluence*, the camera pans by the vacant storefront next to the butcher shop where 'Abdu is employed. Posters advertising Mizrahi's 1933 film, *Awlad Misr* (*Children of Egypt*) plaster the closed grate of the empty shop.⁶ In the context of the coexistence narrative, the inclusion of the ad functions as a willful assertion of identity. The signs read "Togo Mizrahi presents *Children of Egypt*"— but the word "presents" is written in such small letters in both Arabic and French that it is barely visible. So, in the brief moment when the sign is visible, what catches the eye is "Togo Mizrahi" and "*Children of Egypt*." Mizrahi, the Jewish director, wishes to identify himself, along with the Jewish character, Chalom—whose sign

FIGURE 2. Portrait of Togo Mizrahi by Studio Umberto Dorés. Courtesy of Jacques Mizart.

later graces the same shop—as children of Egypt. This book examines the place of Togo Mizrahi, "child of Egypt," in Egyptian cinema history.

Togo Mizrahi was one of the most prolific filmmakers of his day; over the course of his productive sixteen-year career in the Egyptian film industry—from 1930 to 1946—he directed and produced thirty Arabic-language feature films, most of which he also wrote. In addition to his contributions to Egyptian cinema in Arabic, in his Egyptian studio he also produced four Greek-language films between 1937 and 1943 (fig. 2).

The development of a local cinema industry was a source of national pride for Egyptian filmmakers, critics, and audiences alike in the midst of the anticolonial struggle. Mizrahi saw himself as engaged in this collective effort; and his contemporaries heralded his contributions to building a national film industry.

But Mizrahi, like many other Jews who lived in Egypt, never held Egyptian nationality. How did it come about that Mizrahi did not hold Egyptian nationality, even though his family could trace roots in Egypt back several generations?[7] And how did an individual who did not hold Egyptian nationality come to identify with the Egyptian national struggle? In the section that follows I begin to address these questions by exploring the complex relationships between language, identity, and nationality among Jews in Egypt.

Contemporaneous critics and cinema historians alike have often resorted to ascertaining the nationality of filmmakers and actors as an index for determining whether or not to consider a film as "Egyptian." By this measure, the films written, directed, and produced by Togo Mizrahi—a native of Alexandria who held Italian nationality—would not qualify as Egyptian films. For both historical and theoretical reasons, nationality is a problematic criterion for determining the contours of national cinema—itself a problematic term. In the section below titled "National Cinema without Nationality," I review institutions that shaped the development of the Egyptian film industry in the 1920s and 1930s as an alternative model for defining the boundaries of Egyptian national cinema. Then, I articulate ways cinema was viewed during that period as part of a nationalist project, differentiating between national cinema, patriotic industry boosterism, and nationalist cinema. In the concluding section of this chapter, I introduce Togo Mizrahi as a case study for exploring this alternative model of Egyptian national cinema.

EGYPTIAN JEWS: BETWEEN NATIONALITY AND NATIONALISMS

In the mid–nineteenth century, the population of Jews in Egypt numbered approximately five thousand.[8] At its height in the 1930s and 1940s, the Jewish population grew to between seventy-five and eighty thousand.[9] Following the 1948 Arab-Israeli war, approximately twenty thousand Jews left Egypt—Mizrahi among them.[10] In the aftermath of the 1956 Suez War, the Egyptian Jewish community was reduced to between five and fifteen thousand people.[11] At present, only a handful of Jews remain in Egypt.

Discussions of the Egyptian Jewish experience tend to focus either on the achievements of Jews at the peak of this arc, or on a narrative of decline. Proponents of the former tendency draw attention to indices of Jewish successes—economic, political, cultural, and artistic. But such celebrations of an era of coexistence frequently slide into uncritical nostalgia.[12] By contrast, some historians and members of the Egyptian Jewish diaspora adopt what Marc Cohen has termed a "neo-lachrymose" narrative, which traces an unbroken line of Jewish persecution under Islamic rule from the rise of Islam to the present.[13]

The story of Mizrahi's success and the abrupt end to his career could provide evidence to proponents of both views. But Mizrahi's narrative also opens up an array of nuanced, qualitative questions about the nature of Egyptian Jewish identity and the participation of Jews in Egyptian society. Exploring the films of Togo Mizrahi—a noncitizen who identified as an Egyptian nationalist—provides a means to explore the complicated relationships between identity, nationality, and politics among Jews in Egypt.

Jewish Nationalities in Egypt

Egyptian Jews were linguistically and culturally heterogeneous. Late-nineteenth-century economic growth in Egypt spurred Jewish immigration from around the Mediterranean, particularly from other parts of the Ottoman Empire.[14] The Jewish community that predated the influx of immigrants in the nineteenth century spoke Egyptian Arabic.[15] Immigrants from the Maghreb (North Africa) and the Mashriq (Arab East) spoke a variety of Judeo-Arabic dialects. Sephardi Jews who immigrated from Turkey and Greece spoke Ladino, as well as Turkish or Greek. Some Italian Jews spoke Italian, although not all Jews who claimed or held Italian nationality actually hailed from Italy or spoke Italian.[16] A small community of Ashkenazi immigrants who settled in Egypt spoke Yiddish.[17]

Through the late nineteenth century, Italian was the official language of the Jewish community in Alexandria. By the early twentieth century, French had become the preferred language of the emerging Levantine bourgeoisie in Egypt, including the Jews.[18] Arabic was looked down upon by francophone Egyptian Jews, who associated the language with the poor residents of Cairo's medieval Jewish quarter, Harat al-yahud.[19] Mizrahi, whose family was counted among the Alexandrian cosmopolitan elites, spoke Italian at home and was educated in French schools in Alexandria. However, not only do Mizrahi's films demonstrate his affection for Egyptian colloquial Arabic; they also challenged the Egyptian Jewish bourgeoisie to reconsider their relationship to Arabic and to related notions of Egyptianness.[20]

Jews in Egypt also held a wide array of nationalities. There was often little relationship between a family's place of origin and its nationality. Jacqueline Shohet Kahanoff and André Aciman—two Jewish writers who grew up as noncitizen residents of Egypt—both memorably relate how they were confronted with the disconnect between their self-identification and their nationality. Kahanoff, whose father immigrated to Egypt from Iraq, and whose mother was the daughter of immigrants from Tunisia, did not know how to respond when, as a child, strangers on the beach inquired about her identity. "I knew I was not Egyptian," she writes. "[T]hinking of my grandparents, I replied that I was Jewish and Persian, believing that Baghdad, the city they came from, was the country from which all beautiful rugs came."[21] Raised and educated in francophone environs, André Aciman, who as a child aspired to become a diplomat, assumed he was French. His uncle indelicately informed Aciman that he held Italian nationality but that his family was not from Italy; rather, they had immigrated to Egypt from Turkey.[22]

The disorientation Kahanoff and Aciman articulate is, in part, an outgrowth of their families' emigration to Egypt a generation or two earlier. But migration is only one of the factors that contributed to a particularly complex and unstable construction of nationality in Egypt. Under the Capitulations—a series of treaties between the Ottoman Empire and the European powers—foreign consulates were permitted to grant nationality and protégé status to local residents. Foreign nationality was made particularly desirable by the special privileges granted by the Capitulations to bearers of European nationality. As a result of these factors, an individual's nationality might bear little relationship either to external markers of group identity—such as language—or to his or her self-identification.[23]

The notion of nationality—and its legal codification in terms of citizenship—emerged in the late nineteenth and early twentieth centuries.[24] Egyptian nationality was codified in 1929 with the promulgation of the Egyptian Nationality Law. Building on the precedent of a series of administrative decrees starting in 1892, when Egypt was still nominally a province of the Ottoman Empire, the Egyptian Nationality Law, passed in 1929, extended rights of citizenship to those who had been established in Egypt prior to 1848. This law, however, did not lead to a stable, consistent legal definition of nationality, since these rights were not universally extended to all eligible. Egyptian Jews, in particular, were denied nationality in significant numbers. By the late 1940s, approximately forty thousand Jews who, according to the terms of the law, should have been granted Egyptian nationality were registered as stateless.[25]

Sarah Abrevaya Stein employs the term "extraterritorial Jews" to describe the Jewish migrants within the Ottoman and former Ottoman sphere, as well as Jewish protégés of European powers.[26] In the early twentieth century, the notion of nationality was very much in flux and being defined variously by courts, consular officials, customs agents, and other civil authorities, as Stein and Will Hanley demonstrate.[27] Following Stein and Hanley, I approach nationality in interwar Egypt as a negotiated and contingent status, not a fixed identity.

Jews and Egyptian Nationalism

In this book I contend that Mizrahi's oeuvre should be viewed within the context of the nationalist sentiment prevalent in the Egyptian film industry of his time. Throughout his career, Mizrahi produced commercial comedies and popular musical melodramas. Nevertheless, Mizrahi used his films as a platform for addressing social issues, from income disparity to the changing roles of women in Egyptian society. Mizrahi's films also projected a distinctly inclusive national imaginary. Less than two decades before the dispersion of the Egyptian Jewish community, Mizrahi produced films—some featuring Jewish actors Layla Murad and Leon Angel (Chalom)—that articulated a pluralist Egyptian nationalism.

Togo Mizrahi was not the only Egyptian Jew to articulate his commitment to Egyptian nationalist causes. Jewish involvement in Egyptian politics from the late nineteenth century through the 1940s varied widely, both in level of commitment and in political opinion. Jews were to be found in the royal court, on the rolls of the independence-minded Wafd Party, and in Communist organizations.[28] Members of the Jewish bourgeoisie and elites tended to be motivated by the desire to protect their business interests.[29]

Even among Jews who identified as Egyptian nationalists, one can find a range of inflections and political commitments. In the late nineteenth century, journalist and playwright Ya'qub Sannu' embraced an anticolonial Egyptian nationalism in his popular journal of political satire, Abu nazzara zarqa.[30] In the interwar period, the Qattawi family produced two leaders of the Sephardi community of Cairo. Yusuf Aslan Qattawi Pasha, who led the community from 1924 to 1942, was a supporter of the monarchy who served in parliament and in a number of government posts.[31] He embraced a "socially conservative and business oriented" form of nationalism.[32]

His son, René Qattawi, led the Cairo Sephardi community from 1943 to 1946. Togo Mizrahi and René Qattawi were contemporaries, and both appear to have been influenced by the spirit of the 1919 Revolution. When Egyptians rose up against British colonial rule in 1919, their demands for national self-determination were inflected with a pluralist vision of the nation they aimed to liberate. In 1935, René Qattawi established the Association of Egyptian Jewish Youth to promote Jewish linguistic, cultural, and social integration in Egypt under the slogan "Egypt is our homeland, Arabic is our language."[33]

In his capacity as leader of the Sephardi community of Cairo, René Qattawi "aggressively opposed political Zionism."[34] There were few active Zionist youth movements in Egypt and, prior to 1948, few Jews who left Egypt to settle in Palestine as a fulfillment of Zionist ideology. But, unlike René Qattawi, some saw no conflict between identifying as an Egyptian patriot and supporting Zionist efforts in Palestine. Some elite Egyptian Jewish families who supported the Egyptian national struggle also sent donations to aid Jewish settlement in Palestine.[35]

The prolific writings of essayist and poet Murad Farag reflect the seamless integration of two nationalist affiliations that from a later perspective seem utterly irreconcilable. Farag, a Karaite Jew, wrote about the histories and cultural affinities shared by Arabic-speaking Jews and Muslims. Farag contributed nationalist essays to the influential journal Al-Jarida, edited by Lutfi al-Sayyid.[36] He also published a volume of poetry on Jewish themes with Zionist overtones, Al-Qudsiyyat (Sacred/

Jerusalemite Topics, 1923). According to Sasson Somekh, Farag's Zionist poems reflect his desire to "persuade follow Egyptians that Jewish national aspirations are just and in keeping with Egyptian nationalism."[37]

Egyptian Jews, between Conflicting Nationalisms

Although the political commitments or lack thereof varied among Egyptian Jews, their fates were uniformly determined by the rise of parochial-nationalist ideologies in the first half of the twentieth century. Few Egyptian Jews identified as Zionists; but the establishment of the state of Israel ultimately contributed to the dissolution of the Egyptian Jewish community. In Egypt during the interwar period, new "supra-Egyptian" nationalist movements emerged, including the Pan-Islamic movement the Muslim Brotherhood, founded in 1928, and the ultranationalist Misr al-fatat (Young Egypt), established in 1933. Although these emerging strains of nationalism shared an anticolonial agenda, the supranationalists drew inspiration from Arab-Islamic sources and articulated their political agenda in terms shared by other Arabs and Muslims. The ascendant nationalist strains that privileged religious and ethnonational identity increasingly excluded resident non-Muslim minorities.[38]

The arc of Mizrahi's career maps shifting notions of the Egyptian polity and its relationship to Egyptian cinema. By the 1940s noncitizen residents of Egypt—like Mizrahi—were increasingly marginalized. In 1946 Mizrahi wrapped production on what was to be his final film. Within a few years, Mizrahi, like a significant percentage of the Egyptian Jewish community, had left Egypt.

In his day, Mizrahi was viewed by his peers and by contemporaneous critics as a consummate professional who contributed to the drive to establish a cinema industry in Egypt. But later film critics and historians who embraced the socialist-inflected, pan-Arab, and anticolonial nationalism espoused by Gamal Abdel Nasser did not share this view. From their perspective, Mizrahi had three strikes against him: he was a capitalist; he was a foreigner; and he was a Jew accused of Zionist sympathies.[39]

These terms continue to shape how Mizrahi is remembered in Egypt today. In recent years, there has been a resurgence of interest in Egypt's cosmopolitan past, including the Egyptian Jewish community.[40] There is also a concomitant revival of interest in Mizrahi and his films. But many of these efforts are distorted by the polemics of the Arab–Israeli conflict. The headline of a 2005 retrospective of Mizrahi's career, for example, poses the question of whether he was "a cinema director from Egypt, or a booby-trapped Jewish bomb?"[41] This rhetoric obscures Jewish involvement in a project—Egyptian cinema—that was, in its time, deemed a contribution to the country's struggle for independence. This book aims to recuperate the narrative of Togo Mizrahi as an Egyptian filmmaker by disrupting dominant notions of what constitutes Egyptian national cinema.

WHAT IS EGYPTIAN CINEMA?

A study of early Egyptian cinema production and criticism provides insights into the evolving and contested nature of Egyptian national identity in the 1930s and 1940s. The question "What makes a movie Egyptian?" is closely bound up with the question "Who is Egyptian?" Togo Mizrahi did not hold Egyptian nationality, but did he make Egyptian movies? Both contemporaneous critics and film historians scrutinize the identities of participants—behind and in front of the camera—to determine a film's Egyptian bona fides. An unresolved dispute over which film deserves the title "first Egyptian film" exemplifies this practice. Should it be *Fi bilad Tut 'Ankh Amun* (*In the Land of Tutankhamun*, Victor Rosito, 1923) or *Layla* (Vedat Örfi and Stefan Rosti, 1927)? I present the contours of the debate to analyze the underlying assumptions about the criteria critics use to determine what makes a film "Egyptian."[42]

In the Land of Tutankhamun (1923)

King Tut's tomb was discovered in 1922 during a dig led by British archaeologist Howard Carter. The following year, on 11 July 1923, a film set during the famous expedition, *In the Land of Tutankhamun*, premiered in Cairo. Contemporaneous reports about the film indicate that it was a hybrid of genres: a fictional film set in modern Egypt that also documented "the labor involved in opening the tomb of Tutankhamun."[43] The film was directed by Victor Rosito, a Cairo-based lawyer, who, like Mizrahi, lived in Egypt but held Italian citizenship. Rosito is quoted as saying that he was motivated to write, produce, and direct the film in order to "present a good image of [Egypt] abroad."[44] *In the Land of Tutankhamun* featured five actors: three Italian nationals and two Egyptians, including the popular stage actor Fawzi Munib, who, at the time, led a theater troupe together with his wife, Mary Munib.[45] Alexandria resident Muhammad Bayumi, an Egyptian, operated the camera. Bayumi had studied filmmaking in Europe and went on to direct several films, found a cinema school in Alexandria, and play an important role in establishing the Egyptian film industry.[46]

Contemporaneous sources were split over whether or not to celebrate *In the Land of Tutankhamun* as an Egyptian film. In its coverage of the premiere, the daily *al-Ahram* enthusiastically endorsed the film: "We believe that the distribution of this film in foreign countries would return enormous benefit to Egypt and to Egyptians because it shows them as they really are, not how they appear in some exhibitions in Europe and America."[47] The article implies that *In the Land of Tutankhamun* offsets the prevalent Orientalist cinematic gaze of foreign filmmakers—evident in actualities, documentaries, and feature films like *The Sheik* (George Melford, 1921). In doing so, in the *al-Ahram* critic's view, the film serves an important public-relations function abroad.

By contrast, a critic in the cinema journal *Al-Suwar al-mutaharika* is more circumspect, identifying *In the Land of Tutankhamun* as the first feature film "about

Egypt." While the article thanks Victor Rosito for his "individual efforts," and for his respectful treatment of Egyptian culture, the director's nationality prevents the critic from embracing the film as "Egyptian."[48]

Later critics continue to debate what constitutes Egyptian cinema and when it began. In his 1989 survey of early Egyptian cinema, Ahmad al-Hadari pronounces *In the Land of Tutankhamun* the first Egyptian feature film. Al-Hadari minces no words articulating the importance of this film in the development of Egyptian cinema: "We have before us the first Egyptian feature film.."[49] In al-Hadari's view, since the film was shot in Egypt, with modern Egypt as its subject, and since the production involved Egyptians both on-screen and behind the camera, the film should be considered Egyptian. One historian remarks, "[W]hatever misgivings one might have about his views, at the heart of al-Hadari's argument is a celebration of the multinational nature of Egyptian society."[50]

Before al-Hadari published his seminal chronicle of early cinema in Egypt, there was some uncertainty among historians about the length of Rosito's film, and whether it should be considered a feature or a documentary.[51] But since 1989, any scholar or critic wishing to enter the debate needed to contend with al-Hadari's evidence. Di'ya Mar'i reevaluates al-Hadari's sources, drawing the opposite conclusion about the national character of the film. Taking a narrow view of who is Egyptian, Mar'i characterizes early cinema in Egypt as a near monopoly controlled by foreigners—from production to distribution to cinema ownership. For Mar'i, *In the Land of Tutankhamun* represents "the first breakthrough in the foreign monopoly on cinema production by the pioneering Muhammad Bayumi, who was the first Egyptian to stand behind the camera."[52] However, the nationality of the director, Victor Rosito, along with some of his comments, which in Mar'i's view reflect a folkloric representation of Egypt typical of European Orientalist views, disqualify the film from consideration.[53]

Layla (1927)

Popular consensus holds that *Layla*, released in 1927, was the first Egyptian full-length feature film. As Kay Dickinson asserts, "From the very outset, *Layla* was never going to be received as 'just a film'; it was destined to take on a more iconic status."[54] *Layla*'s mythic appeal is evident. The film was spearheaded and financed by a famed stage actress, 'Aziza Amir, and featured a slate of local talent on-screen. In its announcement about the upcoming premier, *al-Ahram* proclaims, "Appearing in the Egyptian atmosphere are bright, shining stars wishing to serve Egypt and its people, wishing to create wonderful propaganda for Egypt and its people— a propaganda that will provide the greatest service to Egypt and its people. This is cinema—pure, Egyptian national cinema."[55] Referring to *Layla* as "a fetish of Egyptian achievement," Dickinson notes, "The lion's share of critical and historical accounts of the film and its creator are . . . saturated with figural speech and nationalist fervor in both their descriptions and appreciation of the movie."[56]

Within a few years, the mythology surrounding *Layla* had firmly taken root. In a survey of the state of domestic film production published in early 1934, Gama'a al-nuqqad al-sinima'iyyin (the Group of Cinema Critics [G.C.C.]) identifies *Layla* as the first truly Egyptian feature film, despite the fact that Muhammad Bayumi, the cinematographer of *In the Land of Tutankhamun,* was the director of the G.C.C.'s Alexandria branch.[57]

The received narrative of *Layla* as a nationalist triumph has become so entrenched that, having cited evidence to the contrary, a contemporary critic sees no contradiction in asserting that "the film *Layla* by 'Aziza Amir marks the real beginning of the long, silent Egyptian film, because those who participated in it—from acting to production—are Egyptian through and through."[58] The production of *Layla*—not unlike that of *In the Land of Tutankhamun*—could, conversely, be held up as a testament to the diversity of the performing arts in Egypt, and to the foreign and minority involvement in the film industry during this era. Vedat (Wedad) Örfi, a Turkish actor, writer, and cinematographer, was originally contracted to direct the film. Although Amir removed him from his role as director partway through production, Örfi continued to act in the film. One of the other actors in the production, Stefan Rosti, replaced Örfi as director. Rosti's mother was an Egyptian resident with Italian nationality, and his absentee father was Austrian. As Dickinson writes: *Layla* itself, like no film prior to it, "enacted these formations of urban multiculturalism without, however, undermining Egypt."[59] Although Amir's production involved cinema professionals from a range of nationalities, "she managed to forge from their interaction something that fitted snugly into the proud new standards of Egyptianness circulating in the 1920s."[60] Dickinson makes clear that the lines critics have historically used to determine what makes a film "Egyptian" are arbitrarily drawn and unevenly applied.

For both historical and theoretical reasons, the nationality of participants is a problematic criterion for determining the national character of a film. Between 1923 and 1940, a total of one hundred seventeen feature films were produced in Egypt. According to one accounting, only five of those films were produced by a cast and crew comprising exclusively Egyptian nationals, the first of which was the 1933 film *Al-Khatib raqam 13* (*The Thirteenth Fiancé*), directed by Muhammad Bayumi.[61] In other words, strict adherence to the criterion of nationality would produce a truncated and distorted narrative of Egyptian cinema history.

NATIONAL CINEMA WITHOUT NATIONALITY

In my analysis of Egyptian national cinema, I take as my point of departure the assumption that the notions of nation and nationality are themselves unstable constructs. The writings of Ernest Gellner, Benedict Anderson, and Homi Bhabha—and the subsequent contributions of a generation of scholars—have argued for the constructedness and indeterminacy of the nation.[62] Further, as Mette Hjort and Scott MacKenzie assert, films do not "simply represent or express the stable features of a national culture"; rather, films "are themselves one of the loci of debates about a nation's governing principles, goals, heritage and history." Hjort and MacKenzie advocate that critics "be attuned to . . . what these films and their categorization as elements of a national cinema may elide or strategically repress."[63]

There are, needless to say, ways to delineate the boundaries of national cinema that do not rely upon the spurious practice of ascertaining the nationalities of everyone involved in a production. Paul Willemen considers two primary factors in delimiting national cinemas: address, and national specificity.[64] For Willemen, "address" refers to presumed audience, recognizing the ways cinema is transnational both in its influences and in its consumption.[65] National specificity is, in his view, "a territorial-institutional matter" that "designates cultural practices and industries on the terrain governed by the writ of a particular state."[66] In other words: "[T]he boundaries of cultural specificity in cinema are established by governmental actions implemented through institutions"—such as economic barriers and incentives, licensing regulations, and censorship laws.[67]

In what follows I outline some of the institutions that provide the framework within which films were produced in 1930s Egypt. A discussion of these institutions and industry-wide efforts to overcome structural barriers can provide us with an alternative way to think of cinema production in Egypt as a national cinema. Further, during the early years, cinema production in Egypt was seen as contributing to a nationalist agenda. In Egypt, cinema professionals of all nationalities, including Mizrahi, participated in a collective effort to launch an industry they deemed to be of national importance. This patriotic spirit extended to both artistic and commercial aspects of cinema production.

Cinema Practices and National Cinema

Cinema houses were both the locus of "address"—the site where audiences viewed films—and an institution against and through which the Egyptian cinema industry coalesced. The interests of cinema owners often conflicted with those of Egyptian filmmakers and Arabic-speaking audiences in the early years of local cinema production. For example, although the production of the film *Layla* was heralded with much fanfare by the Egyptian press, when producer and star 'Aziza Amir sought a screening venue, she met resistance. The interests of cinema owners were, in the early years, at odds with those of the Arabic-speaking Egyptian cinemagoers, and with those of the founders of the nascent Egyptian cinema industry. Cinema owners, many of whom were noncitizen residents of Egypt, were initially dubious that Egyptian films could meet the profit levels of imported films. In order to strike a deal for a weeklong run at Cinema Metropole, Amir had to agree to turn over 30 percent of the proceeds and guarantee the cinema a minimum profit for the week of 400 Egyptian pounds.[68] *Layla* was ultimately a commercial success. Premiering on 16 November 1927, *Layla* ran for a week, as was common at the time for first-run features. The film earned three times what it cost to produce.[69]

The success of *Layla* in 1927 convinced Egyptian financier Muhammad Tal'at Harb to shift the attention of his film-production outfit, Sharikat Misr li-l-tamthil wa-l-sinima (Misr Company for Acting and Cinema), from newsreels to feature films.[70] In January 1934, the umbrella Misr Group announced its plans to establish a state-of-the-art studio on Pyramids Road in Giza. Studio Misr, as it was called, intended to launch its own productions and accommodate needs of other domestic film producers, from soundstages to lab services.[71] Ground was broken in March 1934, and the studio was inaugurated in October 1935. The Egyptian media eagerly followed developments at Studio Misr. The weekly journal *Al-Ithnayn*, which launched three months after construction was begun on Studio Misr, regularly reported on the studio's activities—from personnel changes to gossip about new productions.

Cinema practices helped to galvanize the industry and shape the rhetoric of filmmakers, producers, and critics in other ways as well. With the advent of sound, foreign-language films presented an even greater barrier to Arabic-speaking Egyptian audiences than silent film had. Cinemas commonly projected Arabic translations onto a second screen. While films projected this way served the interests of Hollywood executives and local distributors,[72] Egyptian viewers, and the local press, began agitating for subtitles to be projected directly on the large screen.[73]

In 1933, the Group of Cinema Critics (G.C.C.) took an activist approach to making cinemas more welcoming to Arabic-speaking Egyptian audiences. They issued a series of directives for cinema owners:

1. The Arabic language should always be part of the introduction—in the program and in the films.
2. Arabic translation should be accurate and in proper style.
3. It is the Egyptians' country; treat them with respect.

And they concluded with the admonishment "Remember this well, Cinema owners. From now on we will not forgive you."[74]

In the fall of 1933, coinciding with the publication of the G.C.C.'s directives to cinema owners, as well as with a student-led movement to boycott foreign-owned cinemas,[75] the American Cosmograph theaters in both Alexandria and Cairo were purchased by an Egyptian company, Egyptian Cinematograph Company, under the direction of 'Abd Allah Abaza. From the beginning, the management signaled its interest in serving an Arabic-speaking audience. The opening party at the Cairo cinema once called American Cosmograph but later renamed Cinema Fu'ad, featured a performance by Umm Kulthum, and the theater sought, unsuccessfully, to book the recently released Egyptian film *Al-Warda al-bayda'* (*The White Rose,* Muhammad Karim, 1933), starring Muhammad 'Abd al-Wahab.[76] The American Cosmograph in Alexandria, however, having been denied screening rights to *The White Rose,* instead paired its screening of a Hollywood feature with a short film by Yusuf Wahbi and a sketch by Badi'a Masabni.[77] The following year, Cinema Fu'ad in Cairo was rented out by Josy Films, a company owned by the Jewish-Egyptian Mosseri brothers that distributed films and operated a number of theaters.[78] Under the management of Josy Films, the Cairo theater reverted to the name American Cosmograph, and the cinemas remained committed to screening locally produced films—both "Egyptian" and "*mutamassir.*"[79] The term *mutamassir* (pl., *mutamassirun*) refers to a subset of the noncitizen residents who, like Mizrahi, integrated into Egyptian society. Throughout his career, most of Mizrahi's films premiered at both American Cosmograph theaters.

Through the 1930s and early 1940s filmmakers and critics—along with the owners of Egyptian-oriented cinemas like Cinema Fu'ad / American Cosmograph— sought to make locally produced cinema available to the urban, Arabic-speaking populace. Further, the Egyptian film industry of this era—production, distribution, and criticism—shared a national spirit, and promoted the view that a robust local cinema industry was in the national interest. This phenomenon was not unique to Egypt. As Andrew Flibbert demonstrates, in emerging film markets outside of the United States and Europe, "[s]ound added a dimension to the medium that nationalist filmmakers could deploy to promote national identities."[80]

Nationalism and National Cinema

Egyptian cinema developed in the context of the Egyptian independence struggle. Although still nominally an Ottoman province, British troops occupied Egypt in 1882, and Egypt remained under British dominance until the middle of the twentieth century. Following World War I, Egyptians took to the streets demanding independence, launching the 1919 Revolution. Egypt was granted limited independence in 1922, but British troops remained in Egypt. The Anglo-Egyptian treaty of 1936 pledged withdrawal of British troops and granted Egypt greater autonomy in the conduct of international affairs. But until the 1952 Free Officers revolt, Egypt remained under British influence, and British troops remained in the Suez Canal zone until 1956.

The 1919 revolution brought about the rise of *adab qawmi* (national literature). Literature and the arts echoed the pervasive national spirit. The emerging cinema industry, too, contributed to this "cultural call for national art and literature."[81] In this vein, in a treatise on cinema published in 1936, filmmaker Ahmad Badr Khan laid out guidelines for cinema practices that reflect "the Egyptian spirit."[82] Egyptian film critics, too, championed the emerging industry as a source of national pride. In 1933, the G.C.C. proclaimed: "We are supporters of Egyptian cinema. Its success is our success. With its rise we raise our heads high."[83] Political figures also endorsed cinema as contributing to the nationalist cause. Upon the release of the musical *The White Rose* (1933), filmmaker Muhammad Karim received notes from political figures active in the Wafd Party congratulating him on contributing the nationalist cause: Safiya Zaghlul called it a "nationalistic and futuristic project," while Mustafa al-Nahhas deemed it a "patriotic film."[84] In the 1930s, the production of local cinema in Egypt was widely embraced as a national cause.

The establishment of Studio Misr in 1934 is widely lauded as "the proper foundation of the Egyptian film industry."[85] Yet, Studio Misr never achieved the desired vertical integration from production to distribution to exhibition that characterized the Hollywood model, even after purchasing a cinema in 1938.[86] Nor did Studio Misr achieve industry dominance in Egypt. Instead, in Viola Shafik's words, it "functioned as a catalyst for the rest of Egyptian cinema, as it set new technical and artistic standards"[87] for the robust growth of the local cinema industry. Nevertheless, the Misr Group, which owned Studio Misr, was adept at securing its wide-ranging business interests in the Egyptian economy. It also promoted its image as a force in the Egyptian struggle for economic and political independence.[88]

Studio Misr was not alone in its promotion of what Ifdal Elsaket calls "economic nationalism."[89] Like other Egyptian capitalists at the time, cinema producers saw the growth of local industry as "protecting Egypt from foreign domination."[90] Echoing the calls in other sectors of the economy for import-substitution industries, critics and cinema producers alike viewed the film industry as contributing to the Egyptian fight for economic independence.[91] Until the mid-1940s, the Egyptian government placed few restrictions on the import of foreign films. Tariffs were relatively low, and there were no screen quotas.[92] Over the course of the 1930s, independent studios—which otherwise saw themselves as competitors— attempted to band together to promote state intervention and economic protection of the fledgling industry.

Beginning in early 1936, there were a series of industry-wide efforts to promote the development of Egyptian cinema. In January 1936, industry professionals and highly respected cultural figures, including 'Aziza Amir and Huda Sha'arawi, gathered to discuss ways to collectively support the production of Egyptian cinema. In the opening remarks to the conference, 'Abd al-Rahman Rida characterized the growth of the Egyptian film industry as "a duty" for the benefit of Egypt and the Arab world. He elaborated:

> We cannot live in a world dependent upon what comes to us from the West. We should not be satisfied with it. Regardless of the quality or beauty of the cinema production of the West, thousands or millions of Egyptians and people in the Arab world cannot benefit from Western films because of the difference in language and our audience's inability to understand the dialogue.[93]

While some speakers extolled the virtues of cinema as an art form, the resolutions passed at the conference focused on cinema as a local industry that required government protection.[94] In particular, the conference sought to exempt local studios from duties on imported cinematic equipment and reduce the amusement tax imposed on locally produced films.[95]

In May 1936, the Union of Egyptian Cinema was formed to promote a platform that echoed the resolutions of the conference, and to elicit guarantees from cinema owners to screen Egyptian films. Ahmad Salim, director of Studio Misr, was elected president, and Togo Mizrahi was elected secretary.[96] In the weeks before the convening of the second cinema conference in January 1937, the union splintered. Salim, immersed in the business of running Studio Misr, failed to defend the work of his colleagues against an attack in the press. In response, independent film producers broke off to form their own organization under the leadership of Isma'il Wahbi, Mahmud Hamdi, and Ahmad Galal.[97] Despite the rift, these cinema producers and directors uniformly viewed themselves as promoting a vital national industry and engaging in a cultural project of national importance.

Held in 1937, the second cinema conference explicitly reflected state interests in the growth of cinema. The formal statement issued by the organizing committee unambiguously adopts nationalist rhetoric: "Our goal is for Egypt to become independent: economically, nationally, and cinematically. We hereby pledge to exert all efforts until the Egypt cinema industry becomes completely independent."[98] The conference focused on three aspects of cinema production: artistry, social impact, and financial concerns. The financial considerations were tied closely to the broader goal of "bolstering the national economy" and "achieving economic independence."[99]

Industry Boosterism versus Nationalism

In the 1930s, Egyptian filmmakers, who saw themselves as engaging in an art and industry of national importance, regularly employed patriotic rhetoric to promote their efforts. The press would sometimes take issue with industry practices and call out empty gestures made in the name of national pride. For example, a 1934 editorial that appeared in *Fann al-sinima*, the organ of the G.C.C., took a dim view of the quality of Egyptian film production, dismissing Egyptian films as underfinanced vanity projects, motivated by petty competition. In the view of the critic, audiences flocked to see these "weak individual efforts" driven by a misguided sense of national pride. The editorial satirically sums up the process of Egyptian film production in the early 1930s as follows: "When someone gathers the resources to produce a film, he forms his own company under his own name, and then seeks a subject, whether it be substantial or weak, and produces a film. . . . The camera rolls, there is acting and shooting, and the whole farce is projected on the silver screen."[100] Consistent with Tal'at Harb's announcement the previous month of the Misr Group's plan to build a state-of-the-art studio, the article concludes that the future of the film industry lay in raising greater capital to produce higher-quality films.[101] As the article makes clear, the empty rhetoric of national pride is not sufficient to fuel a successful industry.

Indeed, marketing films on the basis of patriotic sentiment led to some head-scratching associations. Take, for example, an early effort to dub a film into Arabic: *Beyond Bengal* (1934, Harry Schenck). Dubbing held some promise for making foreign sound films more widely available to the Egyptian viewing public, but it was more expensive than projecting translated titles.

After viewing *Beyond Bengal*, a wildlife film shot on location in the Malay Peninsula, two Egyptian cinema professionals—the actor Sarag Munir and the cinema editor for the daily newspaper *Al-Ahram*, Zakariya Sharbini—decided to underwrite dubbing the film into Arabic. They cited the film's educational value as a motivation for making this "rare glimpse at life in the jungle" widely available to the Egyptian viewing public.[102] Only sixty-five minutes long, the film was shot silent and featured voice-over narration, making it, technically speaking, a good choice to experiment with the dubbing process.[103]

The Arabic version premiered in February 1936 under the title *Sadat al-adghal* (*Masters of the Jungle*). The promotion of *Beyond Bengal / Masters of the Jungle* in Egypt played on familiar nationalist tropes. The release of "the first foreign film made into an Arabic-speaking film," an ad in *Al-Sabah* proclaims, serves "the interest of Egyptianizing cinema"[104] Cinema al-Nahda, an Egyptian-owned cinema, vaunted its identification with the nationalist cause by adopting a tagline that paraphrased a popular slogan of the 1919 Revolution: "Egypt for Egyptians." Cinema al-Nahda advertised itself as projecting "cinema created by Egyptians for Egyptians."[105]

But rather than reflecting the pluralist, anticolonial nationalist spirit of 1919, *Beyond Bengal* draws upon the very racist tropes used to justify European colonialism.[106] The film further offers words of praise for the sultan of Perak, who supported the expedition. The sultan appears briefly on-screen, accompanied by a British officer, Captain Lindsay Vears. At the time, Perak was part of the Federated Malay States, a nominally independent British protectorate, much like Egypt.[107]

The Egyptian advertisement for the dubbed version of *Beyond Bengal / Masters of the Jungle* casts the technical achievement as a nationalist endeavor, evoking a slogan of the 1919 Revolution. Yet this rhetoric is employed in the service of an Orientalist, pro-British, royalist adventure-travel docudrama. How do we square the film's politics with the nationalist, anticolonial rhetoric evoked in the ad? Industry boosterism, even when cloaked in a rhetoric of national pride, is not the same as nationalist cinema.

Despite such examples of overreach, Egyptian filmmakers of the 1930s genuinely saw themselves as engaging in a nationalist endeavor. The content of Egyptian cinema in the 1930s and 1940s was not "nationalist" per se. To be sure, the industry steered clear of direct political interventions and topics that might run afoul of state censors.[108] The late 1930s saw two high-profile projects censored as a result of perceived political content.[109] Some historical films, such as *Shagarat al-Durr* (1935), directed by Ahmad Galal, and *Salah al-Din* (1941), directed by Ibrahim Lama, have been read as political allegory.[110] But the bulk of films produced were musical melodramas or comedies. Some films were set in the "legendary past," and featured lavish sets and costumes.[111] Thus, while some Egyptian films produced in the 1930s—like those of Togo Mizrahi—could be described as socially conscious, as a whole, they were not overtly political.

The anticolonial, nationalist lens that dominates Egyptian cultural criticism following the 1952 Free Officers revolt disparaged early cinema efforts, obscuring the nationalist agenda that filmmakers embraced and that the press and audience recognized and celebrated.[112] According to Walter Armbrust, until the 1990s there was widespread critical consensus that "there is little value in most of the films made [in Egypt] in the three decades before the 1960s."[113] Looking back, later critics criticized what they saw as the Orientalist aesthetic in silent cinema—attributable, in their view, to the role of foreigners in establishing the film industry. Evaluating the commercial genre films of the 1930s and 1940s by content rather than their nationalist promotional rhetoric, critics denigrated them as derivative of Hollywood and reflective of decadent, bourgeois values. During World War II, fewer foreign films were distributed, providing an opening in the market. In the years after the war, local capitalists, enriched by the war effort, began to view cinema as a worthwhile investment.[114] Film production rose substantially.[115] As a result of this dynamic, Egyptian critics and film historians cast aspersions on films produced between 1945 and 1952 as a "cinema of war profiteers."

Post-Nasser nationalist histories of Egyptian cinema find two positive developments in the 1930s that set the stage for the development of "serious" cinema: the establishment of Studio Misr, and the rise of social realism. The narrative of Studio Misr as Egypt's first modern studio has survived in a way that is consistent with the perception of the Misr Group as a whole. As Robert Vitalis demonstrates, the Misr Group achieved economic dominance through a variety of capitalist endeavors in the 1940s in a way that secured its position in postrevolutionary anticolonial Egypt. Yet it also managed to control the public's perception of the company as a supporter of Nasser's anticapitalist etatism.[116]

In the 1950s, the idiom of social realism rose to prominence in Egyptian cinema. The genre of melodrama emerged as the vehicle for narrating the national liberation struggle and articulating the postcolonial national imaginary.[117] Later critics widely lauded the 1939 melodrama *Al-'Azima* (*Determination*, Kamal Salim) as the first "sign of maturity of cinema art in Egypt,"[118] in part because of the way it conforms to the political agenda and generic preferences of Nasser-era filmmaking.[119] In a 1996 survey of Egyptian cinema industry professionals, *Determination* was voted the best film ever produced in Egypt. Not a single other film produced in the 1930s made the top-100 list.[120]

TOGO MIZRAHI: A CASE STUDY OF NATIONAL CINEMA WITHOUT NATIONALITY

This book, *Togo Mizrahi and the Making of Egyptian Cinema*, starts from the position that there is indeed a great deal to be learned from examining Egyptian cinema production of the 1930s and 1940s. I have chosen to focus my analysis on the work of a single director and producer. A close examination of Mizrahi's career serves to complicate the focus on nationality that commonly delimits the boundaries of Egyptian cinema. Like Victor Rosito, the director of *In the Land of Tutankhamun*, Mizrahi was an Italian national. Like Stefan Rosti, the director of *Layla*, Mizrahi was *mutamassir*, an acculturated Egyptian, who contributed to local cultural production. Togo Mizrahi was also a Jew.

Like other Egyptian filmmakers in the 1930s and 1940s, Mizrahi avowedly subscribed to the view that developing a local cinema industry was a nationalist project. In 1929, Mizrahi chose to name his newly founded production company Sharikat al-aflam al-misriyya, the Egyptian Films Company. Promotional materials for Mizrahi's films tapped into the audience's desire to see locally produced cinema. For example, an advertisement touted *Al-Bahhar* (*The Sailor*, 1935) as a film of "the Egyptian popular classes," one that showed "the true face of Egypt."[121] After relocating his studio from Alexandria to Cairo in 1939, Mizrahi often included a logo in his films that prominently featured a crest bearing a crescent and three stars, the symbol of the Kingdom of Egypt. A later modification of the company's logo visually integrated cinema and nationalist sentiment: a length of film spooling out from the words "Sharikat al-aflam al-misriyya," winding three times around the crest (fig. 3).

During his career, Mizrahi actively participated in the collective efforts by industry professionals to agitate for state protection of the Egyptian film industry, serving as secretary of the Union of Egyptian Cinema beginning in 1936.[122] The Alexandria branch of the organization, directed by Edmond Nahas, was located in the offices of Studio Mizrahi.[123] Mizrahi also defended the economic viability of the Egyptian film industry in the press.[124]

In October 1936, Mizrahi threw a party at his Alexandria studio that he billed as a celebration of "the signing of the treaty of Egyptian independence." While Egypt had been granted nominal independence in 1922, Great Britain continued to occupy Egypt. The Anglo-Egyptian treaty, signed in August 1936, laid out the framework for Great Britain to withdraw its troops from Egypt. In attendance were a number of luminaries of the Alexandria cinema industry, including cinema owners, and cinema union director Edmond Nahas.

FIGURE 3. Letterhead for the Egyptian Films Company featuring the company logo. Courtesy of Jacques Mizart.

Mizrahi addressed the crowd, congratulating the Egyptian delegation on its success. He wished Egypt prosperity in the future, and offered his good wishes to the recently installed monarch, King Farouk. Actor Hasan Salih, who was featured in Mizrahi's film *Khafir al-darak* (*The Neighborhood Watchman*), to be released later that month, performed several monologues for the guests, including one written in honor of the treaty.[125]

Contemporaneous critics praised Mizrahi for the quality of his films and his contribution to building the Egyptian cinema industry. One 1937 article proclaimed: "No one can deny Mr. Mizrahi's contributions to the world of cinema, nor the rapid steps he has taken toward the advancement of filmmaking in Egypt. It is not an exaggeration to say that such efforts paved his way to making excellent films that were well received by the audience. This reception is well deserved due to the films' high quality."[126]

By contrast, in the years following the 1952 Free Officers revolt, nationalist critics tended to marginalize Mizrahi's contributions to Egyptian film history. Critics have found ways to acknowledge Mizrahi's contributions to Egyptian cinema, but also to downplay them. In 1967, for example, Samir Farid simultaneously inscribes and erases Mizrahi's contributions to the development of Egyptian cinema. Farid, an influential and prolific film critic, describes the history of Egyptian cinema as reflecting the politics and aesthetics of two distinct schools: "We can divide into two categories the schools of directing in Egyptian cinema: the first is the Alexandria school, of which Togo Mizrahi was one of the founders; and the second is the Cairo School, to which most of the directors belong, like Muhammad Karim and Ahmad Badr Khan, Kamal Salim and Salah Abu Sayf."[127] While he identifies Mizrahi as leading a school of Egyptian cinema production, Farid dismisses Mizrahi's filmmaking as irrelevant to Egyptian film history. Anyone with any familiarity with Egyptian cinema history would understand that for Farid, Mizrahi's Alexandria school represents a dead end—Egyptian cinema issued from what Farid calls "the Cairo School."

In recent years, proponents of "cosmopolitan Alexandria" narratives have attempted to recuperate the contributions of foreign and minority industry professionals like Togo Mizrahi. Film critics and historians have also documented the Alexandrian origins of early cinema in Egypt, providing a significant counternarrative to the Cairo-centric view that locates the *real* start of Egyptian cinema with the establishment of Studio Misr in 1934. For example, in *Madrasat al-Iskandariyya li-l-taswir al-sinima'i* (*The Alexandria Cinematographic School*), Ibrahim Dasuqi and Sami Hilmi revisit Samir Farid's distinction with the intent of restoring the image of "the Alexandria school." They elaborate upon Farid's categorization as follows: "Alexandria: the sea and open vistas; cosmopolitanism. In cinematic language: shot on location; coexistence between the races and religions. Cairo: city surrounded by dusty hills closed in on itself. In cinematic language: shot on sets; an expression, essentially, of the Egyptian middle class."[128]

The Alexandria Cinematographic School was published by the Bibliotheca Alexandrina, as part of an effort to document the city's cinematic history and the "pioneering role that foreigners played."[129] Sahar Hamouda and Muhammad Awad, who edit the Bibliotheca Alexandrina series, write:

> There was a synergy between the open city that encouraged innovation, entrepreneurship and modernism, and its people who were a healthy mix of foreigners recently arrived at the port or who had been in Alexandria for a few generations, and Egyptians arriving from Cairo or who had been in Alexandria for a few generations. Such a synergy—the product of a certain time and place—was the reason why Alexandria was a pioneer in many areas, not just the cinema industry, and it was in inspiration and innovation that Alexandria excelled.[130]

Mizrahi epitomizes the cosmopolitan ethos they map—and he plays a central role in the narrative they reconstruct about the importance of Alexandria in the development of cinema in Egypt. Mizrahi, an Alexandrian Jew, directed and produced popular Arabic movies, as well as the first Greek-language films in Egyptian history.

Togo Mizrahi's oeuvre properly belongs to both narratives of Egyptian cinema—the Cairo-centric nationalist narrative and the Alexandria-centric cosmopolitan narrative. This book analyzes how Mizrahi's films articulate both a pluralist nationalism and a locally situated cosmopolitanism.

Building on critical constructions of the notion of national cinema, I seek to situate Mizrahi's films—with their distinctly pluralist vision—within the arc of Egyptian cinema development in the 1930s and 1940s. As Susan Hayward writes: "A national cinema can problematize a nation by exposing its masquerade of unity."[131] Hayward calls for a framing of national cinemas that "perceives cinema as a practice that should not conceal structures of power and knowledge but which should function as a *mise-en-scène* of scattered and dissembling identities as well as fractured subjectivities and fragmented hegemonies."[132] In *Togo*

Mizrahi and the Making of Egyptian Cinema, I seek to contribute to constructing a narrative of Egyptian cinema history in terms of this flexible notion of "national cinema"—a cinema of "national specificity" (Willemen) that "problematizes the nation" (Hayward).[133] Such a construction of the national stands in opposition to "nationalist cinema" characterized by Willemen as "complicit with nationalism's homogenizing project."[134]

The Egyptian cinema industry of the 1930s—a diverse mix of Egyptians, *mutamassirun,* and foreigners—saw itself contributing to a national project. It should come as no surprise that the Egypt reflected in these films mirrored this flexible, inclusive notion of national belonging. Togo Mizrahi's films are emblematic of this phenomenon, but he is not alone. Other films produced in this era—including some produced by Studio Misr and by Assia Dagher's Lotus Films—also expose, in Hayward's terms, the nation's "masquerade of unity."[135]

In my reading of 1930s Egyptian cinema, I adopt the term "Levantine" to critically engage with this cinematic pluralist nationalism. The term "Levantine" has been used to describe an urban diversity of cultures, like the Egyptian urban society that Mizrahi portrays on-screen, and in which he produced his films. The term also refers to residents of the Levant, particularly in contexts in which an observer cannot readily discern the ethno-national or religious identity of the observed. I employ the notion of the "Levantine" to explore the potential of this indeterminacy, and the inherent performativity of crossing between and among cultures, languages, and communal groups.[136]

The way I am using the term "Levantine" is distinct from the term "cosmopolitan." As I argued in *Remembering Cosmopolitan Egypt,* the notion of the cosmopolitan is inextricable from empire.[137] As a philosophical construct, the cosmopolitan emerges out of imperial contexts.[138] With regard to Egypt, the term "cosmopolitan" is often used to refer to an ethno-religiously diverse class of immigrants, foreigners, and minorities in Egypt during a period not coincidentally coterminous with the European colonial enterprise in Egypt. Further, it is most commonly applied to members of the bourgeoisie who by and large did not hold Egyptian citizenship and did not identify with Egyptian culture: most spoke languages other than Arabic; most saw themselves as European.[139]

By contrast, the Levantines portrayed on-screen in the films discussed in this book (like those involved in their production) represent a variety of religions and nationalities. Most of the Levantine characters in these films speak Egyptian Arabic: they are portrayed as part of the fabric of Egyptian society. The multiculturalism, syncretism, and cultural exchange represented by these Levantine films are most evident among residents of lower-class urban neighborhoods. While the term "cosmopolitan" is elitist and distinctly European, the Levantine is not class-specific and is firmly situated in the region.[140] The term "Levantine" highlights both the diversity of Mizrahi's Egypt and the performativity of identity reflected in his films.

In my readings of 1930s Egyptian cinema, I have identified three common characteristics of what I term a "Levantine cinematic idiom." First, Levantine films reflect and engage with an ethics of coexistence. Second, they utilize cinematic tools to construct a pluralist aesthetic. Finally, in true Levantine fashion, these films foreground the performativity of identity. I am particularly attuned to ways masquerade is employed in these films to subvert hegemonic or homogenizing notions of identity.

In chapter 2, I provide an integrated analysis of Togo Mizrahi's biography and filmography. I examine Mizrahi's personal narrative in the context of modern Egyptian Jewish history. I situate his films and their reception within the context of Egyptian cinema history. Tracing the arc of his career, I outline the development of Mizrahi's commitment to producing socially conscious films, and track issues that recur throughout his oeuvre.

In chapters 3 through 7, I read a selection of Mizrahi's films to unpack the ways they employ this Levantine cinematic idiom to construct a pluralist nationalism and a locally situated cosmopolitanism. Through close analysis of Togo Mizrahi's films, I tease out the cultural and political implications of his oeuvre, with particular attention to the construction of pluralist nationalism, the representation of Jewishness, and the disruptive deployment of unstable gender categories.

Chapter 3, "Crimes of Mistaken Identity," establishes how two of Mizrahi's early films utilize liminal characters (the poor, minorities) to define the boundaries of law and nation. I analyze two comedies of mistaken identity in which Levantine pairs—a Jew and Muslim in *Al-Manduban* (*The Two Delegates*, 1934), and a Nubian and a Lebanese in *Khafir al-darak* (*The Neighborhood Watchman*, 1936)—thwart sinister plots of an international crime syndicate.[141] In these films, Levantines subvert social codes and notions of national belonging, but they are also depicted as civic-minded and law-abiding subjects who work for the common good.

With their focus on the plight of the urban lower classes, Mizrahi's films articulate the form of national belonging popularly known in Egypt as "*ibn al-balad.*" As already noted, Mizrahi titled his first sound film *Awlad Misr* (*Children of Egypt*) to echo the plural form of this expression: *awlad al-balad*. Several of Mizrahi's films, I argue, seek to broaden the category of *ibn al-balad*. The construct is usually applied only to Muslims. In chapter 3, I unpack how in *The Two Delegates* Mizrahi expands the notion of "*ibn al-balad*" to include Jews, as a means of asserting arabophone, Egyptian-Jewish nativeness.

In chapter 4, "Queering the Levantine," I examine Mizrahi's *Al-Duktur Farhat* (*Doctor Farahat*, 1935)[142] and *Mistreated by Affluence* (1937). I argue that these films, through their narratives of mistaken identity, queer both ethno-religious identities and gender. For example, *Mistreated by Affluence* opens with Chalom, a Jew, and 'Abdu, a Muslim, waking up together in a shared bed. Starting with this image, I analyze the interrelationship between an ethics of coexistence and destabilized, performative gender identities.

Building on this discussion of Levantine queerness, chapter 5, "Journeys of Assumed Identity," examines how Levantine mobility of identity and physical mobility inform one another. In this chapter, I unpack the journeys of assumed identity in Mizrahi's *Al-sa'a 7* (*Seven O'Clock*, 1937), featuring 'Ali al-Kassar in his signature role as 'Usman 'Abd al-Basit. These journeys serve to explore the boundaries of both nation and identity. The film's three acts depict three distinct itineraries. In the first movement, circular trajectories encompass Alexandria's diversity, in a Levantine ethics of inclusion. In the second movement, the urban migrant's ambivalent return to his native home, Aswan, serves to mark the boundaries of nation. This itinerary also explores racial and cultural variation within that nation. In the third movement—toward Cairo—'Usman masquerades as a Nubian woman, revisiting the queer Levantine idiom explored in the previous chapter.

In the first thirty years of Egyptian sound film production, more than a third of all films produced were musicals.[143] Mizrahi's films produced between 1930 and 1939 in his Alexandria studio feature episodic plots that often contain a song or two. With the move to Cairo in 1939, Mizrahi expands his cinematic idiom to include musicals. Mizrahi's first film produced in Cairo, *Layla mumtira* (*A Rainy Night*, 1939), featured Egyptian Jewish singer Layla Murad, who had already received critical acclaim for her performance opposite Muhammad 'Abd al-Wahab in *Yahya al-hubb* (*Long Live Love*, Muhammad Karim, 1938). In chapters 6 and 7, I examine how Mizrahi's musical melodramas continue to examine both the boundaries of the nation and the boundaries of gender.

Chapter 6, "Traveling Anxieties," argues that itineraries traveled in Mizrahi's musical melodramas—like in his earlier comedies—explore the limits of the Egyptian nation and national identity. In this chapter I discuss the films *A Rainy Night* (1939) and *Al-Tariq al-mustaqim* (*The Straight Road*, 1943). Although these films do not have any explicitly Jewish content, I argue that that they reflect distinctly Jewish anxieties. The itinerary in *A Rainy Night*, from Milan to Cairo to Omdurman, counterposes rising fascism in Europe with Egypt's Levantine and multiracial society. The itinerary also raises questions about the boundaries of the nation elicited by Egypt's colonial designs on Sudan, even as British troops continue to occupy Egypt. In *The Straight Road*, a character en route from Cairo to Beirut drives his car off a cliff along the Palestinian coast; presumed dead, he loses his identity. I tease out how this itinerary reveals Egyptian Jewish anxieties about the impact of Zionist efforts in Palestine on their future in Egypt.

Chapter 7, "Courtesan and Concubine," analyzes the performance of female sexuality and the sexuality of performance in musical melodramas that feature two of the biggest female stars in 1940s Egypt. *Layla* (1942), an adaptation of Alexander Dumas fils's novel *La dame aux camélias* (1848), stars Layla Murad in the role of a courtesan. *Sallama* (1945), an adaptation of 'Ali Ahmad Ba Kathir's novel *Sallamat al-qass* (1941), stars Umm Kulthum in the role of a *qayna*, a singing slave girl. I analyze these films in the context of contemporaneous transformations of women's roles in Egyptian society and efforts to abolish legal prostitution in Egypt.

In 1946, Togo Mizrahi abruptly withdrew from cinema production. In 1952, he settled permanently in Rome, where he lived until his death in 1986. In the concluding chapter, "Frames of Influence," I assess the lasting impact of Mizrahi's films. Long after Mizrahi's withdrawal from cinema production in 1946, his films continued to be available to the viewing public. Mizrahi's films aired on Egyptian and Israeli television, then screened on satellite networks, and currently stream on YouTube. I identify a series of cinematic moments that serve to articulate Mizrahi's influence in Egyptian cinema and beyond. I also explore how Mizrahi figures in Egyptian-Jewish diaspora culture in both Israel and France.

Togo Mizrahi's films assert his identity as "son of Egypt." Combining film analysis with archival research in contemporaneous journals and newspapers, *Togo Mizrahi and the Making of Egyptian Cinema* situates this Jewish, noncitizen filmmaker within the nationalist project of establishing Egyptian cinema as both a local art form and a vital domestic industry.

2

Togo Mizrahi, Work over Words

To usher in the new year, 1941, an Egyptian weekly magazine published a special issue devoted to the arts featuring interviews with high-profile figures. Togo Mizrahi, the successful and prolific film director, was quoted as saying, "No Egyptian actress is fit to stand before the camera."[1] To stanch the furor over his remarks, Mizrahi penned a lengthy letter to the editor. The filmmaker's response to this embarrassing gaffe provides insights into Mizrahi's character and his place in Egyptian culture.[2]

Togo Mizrahi was known to be media shy—a man who "prefers work over words."[3] He granted few interviews, and had little experience dealing with the press. His response letter is one of the few surviving pieces Mizrahi published in the Egyptian press. While in his letter Mizrahi does not deny making the inflammatory statement, he accuses the journalist of distorting his words and taking them out of context. Mizrahi asserts that he had not intended to disparage any of the actors he had worked with. He claims, instead, that he wished to outline for emerging talent what it takes to launch a successful cinema career.[4] A more media-savvy director would have weighed his words more carefully.

The letter also reveals the two roles Mizrahi played in the Egyptian cinema industry. Mizrahi was one of the pioneers of the industry, founding a studio and a production company in 1929. He was also a prolific director of popular comedies and musicals. In his letter, Mizrahi speaks from his perspective as a director when he addresses his relationship with actors. He describes his pride in eliciting strong performances from actors—and the pride of actors when they see their work in the director's hands. But he also signals the importance of his relationships with actors from his perspective as "the director of a company." Mizrahi identified as both director and producer, artist and businessman.

But what is perhaps most striking about this letter is the way it demonstrates Mizrahi's centrality in the Egyptian film industry. One by one, Mizrahi directly addresses the lead actors who had appeared in his films to extol their virtues: Yusuf

Wahbi, 'Ali al-Kassar, Sulayman Naguib, 'Abd al-Salam al-Nablusi, Amina Rizq, Dawlat Abyad, Layla Murad, Mimi Shakib, Zuzu Shakib, 'Aqila Ratab, and Salwa 'Alam. He also expresses his gratitude to Zakariya Ahmad and Riyad al-Sunbati—two of the most prolific and acclaimed composers of Arabic music in Egypt at that time. The letter reads like a who's who of Egyptian cinema in the 1940s.

Togo Mizrahi played an important role in developing Egyptian cinema in the 1930s and 1940s. He was committed to producing quality, popular, and financially viable films. Beyond his own films, he was also committed to building a vibrant domestic cinema culture in Egypt. This chapter traces the arc of Mizrahi's career. I begin with Mizrahi's background, growing up in an elite Jewish family in Alexandria. I divide his career into two periods. In the first period, from 1930 to 1939, Mizrahi directed and produced films at the studio he founded in Alexandria. In this period, he produced melodramas and comedies that reflect a socially conscious Levantine cinematic idiom. In 1939, Mizrahi moved to Cairo, where he launched the second phase of his career with a big-budget musical.

Fortunately, Mizrahi suffered no significant, long-term consequences of his gaffe in 1941. For another five years, he continued to have a productive and celebrated career directing and producing films. Suddenly, in 1946, Mizrahi withdrew from the film industry. The final section of this chapter explores Mizrahi's departure from Egypt, the sequestration of his studio and production company, and his loss of the rights to his films.

TOGO MIZRAHI, A JEWISH SON OF EGYPT

Joseph Elie Mizrahi was born on 2 June 1901 in Alexandria. His parents, Jacques Mizrahi (1870–1935) and Mathilde Tawil (1875–1935), were Alexandria natives.[5] Joseph was the third of eight children (fig. 4). The aristocratic Mizrahi family had made its fortune in the cotton and textile trade.[6] Jacques worked in the management of the Alexandria Bonded Warehouse Company.[7]

Jacques's mother was a descendant of the influential Sephardi Aghion family that emigrated from what is now Italy to Egypt in the eighteenth century.[8] When Mizrahi was born in 1901, his birth certificate was issued by the Jewish community of Alexandria, Egypt (Comunità israelitica in Alessandria d'Egitto), and certified at the Austro-Hungarian consulate.

Few Jews residing in Egypt in the interwar period held Egyptian nationality. Elite Egyptian Jews, among others, received protection, and in many cases nationality, by foreign consulates under the terms of Ottoman-era capitulations to European powers.[9] Nationality among the elites of Alexandria sometimes bore little relationship to a family's origins or self-identity. As with other Egyptian Jews, the full story of the Mizrahi family's origins and their nationality are somewhat unclear.

In September 1919, the grand rabbinate of Alexandria reissued Joseph Mizrahi's birth certificate to supplant the original, which had borne an Austro-Hungarian consular stamp. In the aftermath of World War I, Sephardi Jews living in the

FIGURE 4. Togo Mizrahi (seated, right) with his brother, Félix, who later performed under the screen name ʿAbd al-ʿAziz al-Mashriqi. Circa 1915. Courtesy of Jacques Mizart.

eastern Mediterranean with a connection to the Italian peninsula were granted limited rights as Italian citizens.[10] Joseph, like his parents, held Italian nationality.

In his youth, Joseph became known by the nickname Togo, a reference to the decorated Japanese admiral Togo Heihachiro. One conjecture holds that Mizrahi's family adopted the name in 1905, following Admiral Heihachiro's great victory over the Russian Navy's Baltic Fleet at the battle of Tsushima.[11] Mizrahi's nephew Jacques Mizart recalls his uncle saying that he personally chose to adopt the name out of admiration for Admiral Heihachiro. One can imagine how a boy who later chose a career that entailed ordering around actors, set designers, and camera operators may have become enamored—or associated by his family—with a decorated military leader. A birth certificate reissued in 1920 lists his name officially as Joseph Elie Togo Mizrahi. From that point on, the name Togo appears on his official documents.[12]

Growing up in the Bulkley district of Alexandria, Mizrahi was educated at the Lycée français, completing his studies in 1919.[13] Between 1920 and 1922 Mizrahi studied at the École des hautes études commerciales in Lyon. He continued his studies in Milan, receiving a diploma in commerce in 1925.[14] During his summer vacations, and then after completing his studies, Mizrahi gained experience working for Jewish-owned businesses in Alexandria: J. Rolo & Co. (1921–25);[15] and Aghion Frères (1925–26).[16]

THE MAKING OF THE "TOGO CINEMA FAMILY": ALEXANDRIA, 1929–1939

During the late 1920s, Togo began to build his skills as a filmmaker. He visited and apprenticed at studios in France and Italy, among them, Gaumont Studios.[17] In Paris, Togo met Abel Gance, who invited him to the set of *La fin du monde* (*The End of the World*, 1931).[18] Mizrahi began by shooting short films, newsreels, and advertisements in Rome and Alexandria.[19] Mizrahi appears to have signed a contract with a distributor for the short films he shot while in Europe.[20]

Togo Mizrahi began his career as a narrative filmmaker by staging scenes featuring members of his family. Togo's youngest brother, Alfred, recalls: "At the beginning, he didn't have a studio. He would make short silent films, shooting them at our home. My sisters would give him jewels and accessories when he needed them."[21]

In 1929, Mizrahi set his sights on establishing a studio in Alexandria to produce feature films. One source suggests that Jacques Mizrahi, who expected his son to enter the world of commerce or finance, objected to Togo's plans to become a filmmaker and refused to support him.[22] Togo's brother Alfred recalls otherwise, stating that Jacques, who died in 1935, was very proud of his son's success as a filmmaker.[23] The Behna family—who had already begun to develop commercial interests in the film industry—provided Togo Mizrahi with a loan.[24] With this assistance, in 1929

Togo Mizrahi converted a cinema on Hajar al-Nuwatiyya Street, in the Bacos neighborhood of Alexandria, into a fully functioning film studio with a stage, editing room, projection room, and laboratory. Mizrahi also founded a production company, Sharikat al-aflam al-misriyya, also known as the Egyptian Films Company.

Even after establishing the studio, Togo continued to cast friends and family members in his films. Togo's brother Félix starred in *Al-Hawiya, al-kukayin* (*The Abyss, or Cocaine*, 1930) and *Awlad Misr* (*Children of Egypt*, 1933) under the screen name 'Abd al-'Aziz al-Mashriqi.[25] Togo took a turn acting under the screen name Ahmad al-Mashriqi, playing supporting roles in *Al-Bahhar* (*The Sailor*, 1935), *Children of Egypt*, and *Al-Duktur Farhat* (*Doctor Farahat*, 1935).[26] Togo's first sound film, *Children of Egypt*, was a true family affair: Togo's brother Félix played the lead role of Ahmad; Celine (Nina) Mizrahi, Togo's sister, appeared as Ahmad's sister; and Togo played the role of Husni, Ahmad's friend. Neither of Togo's siblings had any formal training as actors. When he was not appearing before the camera, Félix worked as a supervisor at the port of Alexandria. The script for *Children of Egypt* called for Félix's character to go crazy. According to family lore, in order to elicit the desired performance, Togo locked his younger brother in a garage for over an hour prior to filming.[27]

Other family members later worked in the production of Mizrahi's films. Togo's youngest brother, Alfred, started working at the studio in 1939, and held a number of positions ranging from accountant to production director. In addition to their long-standing, productive working relationship, Togo and Alfred were particularly close; when their parents, Jacques and Mathilde, died in 1935, Alfred went to live with Togo.[28] Alfred received his first screen credit in 1941 as an assistant on the set of *Al-Fursan al-thalatha* (*The Three Musketeers*). By the time *Layla* was released the following year, Alfred had been promoted to managing director. Two of Togo's brothers-in-law also worked for the Egyptian Films Company. Togo's sister Celine married their first cousin, Clément (Sulayman) Mizrahi, who is credited as the general manager of the company during the production of *Layla mumtira* (*A Rainy Night*, 1939). Togo's sister Leila married Zizo (Isaac) Ben Lassin, who is identified as the studio director in the production of *Layla* (1942).

In 1930, as he was launching the production of his first feature film, Mizrahi sought the expertise of cinematographer Alvise Orfanelli, who had trained in photographic technique in the studio of 'Aziz Bandarli and Umberto Dorés.[29] Orfanelli launched his cinematographic career in 1919 with the silent short *Madame Loretta*, directed by Leonard Laricci and staring Fawzi al-Gazayirli. By the time he signed on to work with Mizrahi on *The Abyss, or Cocaine*, in 1930, Orfanelli had already shot six films, and had established his own lab and studio. The collaboration between Mizrahi and Orfanelli continued over four films between 1930 and 1934.

In 1935, as Mizrahi was preparing to shoot *Doctor Farahat*, he paid Orfanelli a visit to contract his services again. Orfanelli was already committed to a project, however, so Mizrahi asked about the availability of 'Abd al-Halim Nasr, his assistant camera operator. Nasr had recently parted ways with Orfanelli follow-ing a dispute over wages. Orfanelli nevertheless provided Nasr with a certificate attesting to his expertise in the film studio and lab. Outside, Mizrahi ran into Nasr, who described the encounter as follows: "I felt a hand tap me on the shoulder with compassion. I turned around to see Togo Mizrahi. Togo knew me because I had shot one of his films while I was working with Orfanelli."[30] Nasr continues: "I handed him the certificate that Orfanelli had given me. He read it quickly and said to me, 'So we've agreed. I went there to come to an agreement with you about some work. So long as I found you, we have an agreement.' And he put his hand in his pocket and handed me thirty Egyptian pounds as payment. He said it was support for three months."[31] Mizrahi then continued, "After I return from Europe I will call for you, and we will start work right away."[32]

Nasr had reportedly left Orfanelli's studio when he was refused a two-pound raise, from seven to nine Egyptian pounds per month.[33] Mizrahi's initial offer not only put Nasr on retainer for the three months before shooting started, but also exceeded his requested salary increase. The collaboration between 'Abd al-Halim Nasr and Togo Mizrahi was very successful and enduring. 'Abd al-Halim Nasr served as cinematographer on all but two of the films Togo Mizrahi directed from 1935 to 1945.[34] This collaboration launched 'Abd al-Halim's prolific, decades-long career as a respected cinematographer.

'Abd al-Halim's brother Mahmud also came to work in Mizrahi's studio in 1935. In an interview, Mahmud provides insights into the workings of Studio Mizrahi at that time: "They were preparing for a film called *Doctor Farahat* that Togo Mizrahi was directing. He left the filming to 'Abdu ['Abd al-Halim] Nasr, and I worked as his assistant. As an assistant cameraman, I received a salary in the amount of two Egyptian pounds per month, as well as a free pass to ride the tram. . . . In addition, as an assistant for lighting, editing, lab, and display, I was able to see what we had filmed."[35] According to Mahmud Nasr, Mizrahi's production team in the mid-1930s amounted to three people—the brothers 'Abd al-Halim and Mahmud Nasr, and Togo himself—with everyone taking on multiple roles in mounting a production (fig. 5). Mahmud describes the labor of film production in Studio Mizrahi during this period:

> We would undertake, the three of us, all of the work, from sweeping the studio to carpentry and the construction of décor and lighting, and perpetually improve upon it until we began shooting the film under Togo's direction, and with Togo's guidance. After the completion of every reel, my brother 'Abd al-Halim or I would carry it on the Ramleh tram to Studio Alvise [Orfanelli's studio] for developing, printing, and editing.[36]

Togo Mizrahi treated filmmaking like a family affair, forging close professional ties with his creative partners and business associates. Filmmaker Ahmad Kamil Mursi, who got his start at Studio Mizrahi, referred to Mizrahi's production team as "the Togo cinema family."[37] Even as his productions expanded, Mizrahi

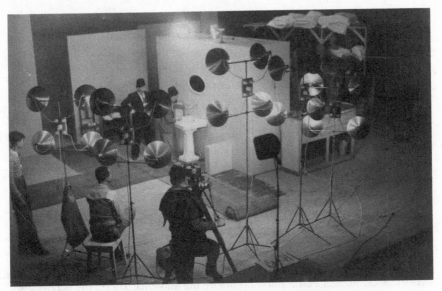

FIGURE 5. Togo Mizrahi (seated) on the set of *The Two Delegates* (1934). Courtesy of Jacques Mizart.

continued to work with the same team, which grew to include set designer 'Abd al-Hamid al-Shakhawi, lab technician Ridwan 'Uthman, production director 'Abd al-Hamid Zaki, and assistant director Ibrahim Hilmi. Ahmad Kamil Mursi, who also cut his teeth at Studio Mizrahi, claims that the group, the "Togo cinema family," was connected by "strong bonds of loyalty, love, and passion for work and life." Mursi elaborates: "Togo always took care to collaborate with a close circle of technicians and artists who worked in most of his films throughout his career and whose names were afterward to be associated with Mizrahi's."[38]

In his Alexandria studio between 1930 and mid-1939, Togo Mizrahi directed seventeen films—two silent films, eleven Arabic sound films, and four sound films in Greek.[39] During those years, Mizrahi's production company, the Egyptian Films Company, produced two additional films that were shot at Studio Mizrahi but that Togo did not direct.

Creation of a Socially Conscious Levantine Idiom

Togo Mizrahi's films produced in his Alexandria studio between 1930 and 1939 represent the struggles of the lower classes. Mizrahi broke onto the cinema scene in Egypt in 1930 with his debut feature, *The Abyss, or Cocaine*. The film delivered a powerful warning about the ill effects of drug addiction, contributing to an ongoing, centralized public-relations and educational effort in Egypt at the time

The trafficking, production, and use of white drugs—cocaine and heroin—rose in Egypt following World War I. By the mid-1920s, Sir Thomas Russell (Russell Pasha), the Cairo chief of police, spearheaded a campaign against white drugs.

On the international front, in 1929 Russell Pasha participated in a delegation to the League of Nations that appealed for the intervention of international law. The same year on the home front, Russell Pasha established the Central Narcotics Intelligence Bureau (CNIB) to combat the drug trade. In addition to the extensive press campaign documented by Liat Kozma,[40] Russell also directly encouraged and supported dramatic representations discouraging drug use.

The Egyptian press avidly covered the production of a film commissioned by the ministry of the interior titled *Al-Mukhadarat (Drugs)*.[41] By early 1930, director Hasan al-Halbawi had brought in sound specialists and modern equipment to record the film as a talkie, and some of the footage was shot on location in the desert. It is unclear if this big-budget, government-funded extravaganza was released in theaters.[42]

On 16 May 1930, after shooting for the ill-fated film *Drugs* had concluded, Russell Pasha attended a performance of an antidrug play titled *Al-Kukayin (Cocaine)* in Cairo. The play, written by Vedat Örfi, was performed by Yusuf Wahbi's troupe at the Ramsis Theater during the 1929–30 season. Following the performance, Russell Pasha stood up before the audience, shook the playwright's hand, and commended him for his great public service. The following day, Russell Pasha published a notice in the press publicly thanking Örfi and the Ramsis troupe for their contribution to the fight against drug use in Egypt.[43]

In February 1931 during Eid al-fitr, the Ramsis troupe reprised their production of Örfi's play *Cocaine* for a matinee performance.[44] The previous evening, Togo Mizrahi's similarly titled feature film, *The Abyss, or Cocaine*, premiered in Cairo at the American Cosmograph Cinema. To confuse matters further, the film shares a title with another play, Muhammad Taymur's *Al-Hawiya (The Abyss)*, written in 1920. Taymur's play *The Abyss* had been revived in the prior season, also by the Ramsis troupe, but publicity for the 1929–30 production of Taymur's play lists it under the title *Al-Mukhadarat (Drugs)*, the same title as the ill-fated film directed by al-Halbawi.[45] All these confusing titles aside, it is safe to say that Togo Mizrahi's premier feature, a drama of "the abyss where so many unfortunate souls drawn to harmful drugs debase themselves," inserted itself into an already dense field of artistic efforts to combat drug use.[46]

In Mizrahi's film *The Abyss, or Cocaine*, Ahmad, a laborer, is married and has a young son. Hasan, a compatriot, falls in love with Ahmad's wife. Hasan tries to get Ahmad out of the way by introducing him to drugs. Ahmad becomes addicted and loses his job. After Ahmad's wife goes to work as a laundress, things deteriorate even further. When she refuses to give Ahmad money she has set aside to buy food, he kills their son. He is arrested, tried, and sentenced to death for his crime. The evil Hasan, too, gets his due: in an obvious parallel to Ahmad's death on the gallows, Hasan falls off a scaffold at a construction site and dies.[47]

The Abyss, or Cocaine is pitched to attract both Egyptian and European audiences. The program praises the performers for their "powerful" and "naturalistic" acting that will "satisfy even the most exacting critic," and hails the film for its universal appeal, calling it "the most powerful film on cocaine use to this day." The cinema program also vaunts the film's local authenticity, inviting viewers to identify familiar urban landscapes depicted in the film:

> Everyone, without exception, must see this impressive drama that destroys an Egyptian family. The life of a worker is picturesquely reproduced in its smallest details with a genuine sincerity and a poignant truth.
>
> In contrast to all other Egyptian films shown to this day, the action of this film does not take place in the countryside, but in the heart of the city, the sites with which we are familiar, making the film the truest, and most successful one that you will ever see. All Egyptians and Europeans alike will appreciate the very real and very powerful value of this good film, with its lifelike portrayal of such a burning issue.[48]

The program stresses the film's authenticity—using no fewer than five synonyms for its depiction of reality. Although there is no pretense that the plot of this social melodrama is based on actual events, the film is billed as truth.

One of Mizrahi's earliest collaborators, Leon Angel, best known by his screen name, Chalom, reportedly drew on his family experience to help develop the scenario for the film.[49] According to colorful family lore, Angel's father had smuggled hashish on the Nile. In 1929 Russell Pasha conceived of the idea of holding a competition for the best screenplay "combatting deadly white drugs," to be underwritten by the Ministry of the Interior.[50] Angel reported that *The Abyss, or Cocaine* won this competition. According to Angel, he and Mizrahi used the prize money to support the production of their next film.[51]

Togo Mizrahi's film *The Abyss, or Cocaine* was moderately successful on the first run,[52] returning for a weeklong second run in Cairo at Cinema al-Ahli in April 1932 during Eid al-Adha.[53] The return of *Cocaine, The Abyss* also coincided with the Cairo premier of Mizrahi's second feature, *05001*, at the Egyptian-owned and -operated Cinema Olympia on 11 April 1932. Holidays were a particularly popular time for both live performances and film releases. Four Egyptian films played at cinemas in Cairo in April 1932 during Eid al-Adha. In addition to Mizrahi's two films, Mario Volpe's *Anshuda al-fu'ad* (*Songs of the Heart*) premiered at Cinema Diana Palace on 14 April,[54] and Muhammad Karim's *Awlad al-zawat* (*Children of the Aristocracy*) returned for a second run, at Cinema Metropole (following a two-week premier showing at Cinema Royal).[55] It is noteworthy that, at the outset of Mizrahi's film career, his first two feature films commanded prime place at two cinemas in Cairo during a major holiday, when the local populace had leisure time to take in a movie.

Little is known about *05001*, and the film is unavailable. Billed as a sports comedy, the film featured Chalom (Leon Angel) and Dawlat Ramzi, along with an actor identified as Hasan Muhammad 'Abdu.[56] Muhammad Awad and Sahar Hamouda offer the following synopsis: "By a stroke of luck Shalom wins lottery ticket number 05001 and becomes rich. Rather than bring him happiness, this wealth causes him trouble. He therefore goes back to his old way of life."[57]

Mizrahi's third film, *Awlad Misr* (*Children of Egypt*), was his first sound film production. *Children of Egypt*, which premiered on 6 April 1933 at Cinema Lido al-Watani in Alexandria, is a social melodrama featuring a love story between a poor student and the daughter of a wealthy man. Ahmad (Félix Mizrahi, credited as 'Abd al-'Aziz al-Mashriqi) strives to overcome class disadvantage through his academic success. Ahmad befriends another engineering student, Husni (Togo Mizrahi, credited as Ahmad al-Mashriqi), who hails from a wealthy family. Ahmad falls in love with Husni's sister Dawlat (Ginan Raf'at). Ibrahim, Dawlat's cousin, who wishes to marry Dalwat himself, conspires to turn her against Ahmad. Following Dawlat's rejection, Ahmad lands in a mental hospital. When Dawlat learns of her cousin's betrayal, she rushes to Ahmad's side. Ahmad recovers and the two wed.[58] Critic Mahmud 'Ali Fahmi identifies in the film a strong undercurrent of sympathy for the Egyptian lower classes: "Togo Mizrahi chose to make the poor boy a genius in his studies. He succeeds on his own merits; he does not make it the way the rich kids do."[59]

Mizrahi's films from the mid to late 1930s continued to direct attention to lower-class concerns. Many of these films are comedies of mistaken identity that also evince a culture of coexistence that cuts across class. Mizrahi's choice of stars for these films reflects an inclusive vision of local subjectivity. Mizrahi made multiple films featuring the same three comic actors, who consistently portrayed lower-class characters: Chalom, who played a Jewish character; 'Ali al-Kassar, who played a Nubian character; and Fawzi al-Gazayirli, who played urban Egyptian characters. Mizrahi's films from this period also regularly feature Greek and *shami* (i.e., Levantine Arab) characters as well as members of the francophone Alexandrian elite. During this period, Mizrahi established a distinctive perspective in his films—what I call a Levantine cinematic idiom. The features of this Levantine idiom, as outlined in the introduction and discussed at greater length in the next three chapters, are an ethics of coexistence, an aesthetic of inclusion, and a construction of identity as fluid and mutable.[60]

Critical Reception of Togo Mizrahi's Films

Over the course of his career, Mizrahi earned the respect of Egyptian film critics and industry professionals. He was widely lauded for his active participation in building an Egyptian national film industry. But in the early years, the Cairo-based national press was somewhat slow to notice the output of Mizrahi's Alexandria studio. As the production in Mizrahi's Alexandria studio increased, his films began to garner the attention of the press. In 1935, a reporter for *Al-Ithnayn* set out from Cairo to interview Togo Mizrahi about his forthcoming release, *Doctor Farahat*:

> Considering the success Togo Mizrahi achieved with his last feature, *The Two Delegates*, when I learned that he would soon release his new feature, I went to the studio in Bacos to obtain an interview for this magazine.

The man met me with his face overflowing with joviality and geniality. Without leaving me time to ask him a question, he rushed to say, "I learned, before all else, that I detest commotion and false advertising. In my view, when film is good and strong, it will definitely capture the audience and compel them to rush in to see it, rather than waiting for the second or third run."

That is the opinion of Ustaz Togo. Following his advice, in promoting the film we will hold fast, and we will not reveal here any details that would give the public any idea about the story of *Doctor Farahat*. The public can judge in favor or against it. The reader may know in advance that the film was produced by Studio Mizrahi in Bacos. The studio is full of technical instruments, and the system and precision of workmanship are pervasive.[61]

Mizrahi's aversion to self-promotion, and his reluctance to court the press, persisted throughout his career. In 1939, a critic for *Al-Ithnayn wa-l-Dunya* observed, "Togo Mizrahi, the director, is a man who works quietly for years without much fanfare, producing film after film with equanimity and mastery."[62]

While Togo Mizrahi preferred to avoid the limelight, he had a reputation in the industry as a "competent and skilled filmmaker."[63] He was known as a consummate professional who worked methodically; one critic noted that he "does not improvise but rather proceeds by taking steps along the correct path."[64] To maintain top performance, Mizrahi did not overtax his production team, filming for around five hours per day.[65] Contemporaneous critics regularly credited Mizrahi with producing well-constructed, high-quality films.[66] Some even hailed Mizrahi as a "genius,"[67] "an amazing director,"[68] and "one of the best cinema producers in Egypt."[69]

Critics at both *Al-Sabah* and *Al-Ithnayn wa-l-Dunya* credit the success of Mizrahi's films to their marriage of artistic merit and "popular spirit."[70] A critic writing in 1936 for *Al-Sabah* elaborates: "Upon watching one of his films, one leaves the cinema hall with a good impression, whether you are a film critic (invested in looking for drawbacks and weaknesses in the film for which you may attack both the film and its maker) or a common spectator looking only for entertainment and recreation. This, in our opinion, is one of the reasons his films are generally successful."[71]

In the 1930s, Mizrahi came to be associated with a particular form of comedy, "punctuated by lots of humorous misunderstandings, as well as clever dialogue and innovative jokes."[72] Critics also noted the social awareness of Mizrahi's comedies, and not just in his early social melodramas. Togo Mizrahi's film *Ana tab'i kidda* (*It's My Nature*, 1938) was, for example, lauded for inaugurating "a new world in local cinema production, the world of sophisticated comedy, which dramatizes the maladies of the society in a humorous manner and in meaningful joking far removed from vulgarities."[73]

While critical reception was generally positive, some complained that Mizrahi's comedies engaged in "excessive exaggeration."[74] Mizrahi's comedies sometimes pushed the boundaries of good taste, and reviewers would call him out when he went too far. For example, in an otherwise positive review, of *100,000 gineh* (*One Hundred Thousand Pounds*, 1936), one critic balks at one scene's overt sexual suggestiveness, advising that Mizrahi use greater restraint and leave more to the viewer's imagination.[75] Notwithstanding these criticisms, throughout Togo Mizrahi's career, his work as both director and producer was generally warmly received by the Egyptian press.

Studio Togo Mizrahi was admired for its state-of-the-art equipment—supplied and updated by Mizrahi during his regular travel to Europe.[76] Critics welcomed the studio's prolific output.[77]

Despite this positive reception and his studio's productivity, through the 1930s Mizrahi's films produced in Alexandria received relatively less media attention than those produced in Cairo by his peers. The press avidly covered every detail of film production at Studio Misr, from the earliest whispers of a new project and contract negotiations with actors to reviews and postrelease coverage of the films' popularity. Likewise, when Assia Dagher's Lotus Films began a new project, notices would appear in the press, accompanied by the occasional tantalizing promotional photograph taken on the set. As the release date approached, the weeklies would publish features about the film, and interviews with Assia Dagher (producer / lead actor), Ahmad Galal (director / lead actor), and Mary Queeny (supporting actor). The press also followed every new development in the career of Cairo-based director Muhammad Karim. Karim was regularly interviewed in the press—not only about his own films, but also about the state of the Egyptian cinema industry in general; during the 1934–35 season, he penned a regular weekly column for *Al-Ithnayn*.

There is no evidence that Mizrahi's nationality or religion had a significant negative impact on the critical reception of his films. Ahmad Kamil Mursi alludes to the circulation of prejudicial gossip about Mizrahi but claims that he was ultimately judged by his peers on the quality of his work: "Due to his religion, people never spared him from gossip. Yet his great work and success would silence his enemies, leaving them no pretext to attack him with slander."[78]

During the period in which the Egyptian film industry was becoming established, Togo Mizrahi was hailed for his contributions to this nationalist endeavor. He produced popular fare for an Egyptian audience. In the Egyptian press throughout the 1930s, Togo Mizrahi was granted the honorific "*ustaz*," thereby implicitly according him insider status; had the press wished to call attention to his religion or foreign nationality, they could have instead employed the honorific "*khawaga*."

By contrast, there had been some debate from the late 1920s through the mid-1930s as to whether the Hollywood-inspired Orientalist fantasy films by the Lama brothers should be considered Egyptian.[79] The Chilean-born Palestinian Ibrahim Lama settled in Egypt, along with his brother Badr (Pedro) Lama, and together they became pioneers of the Egyptian film industry. Ibrahim directed and Badr starred in one of the earliest silent features produced in Egypt, *Qubla fi al-sahra'*

(*A Kiss in the Desert*, 1928). But six years later, a review of their sixth film, *Shabah al-madi* (*Ghost from the Past*, 1934), revisits the debate. Although the review, in effect, puts the question to rest by conclusively determining that the film should be considered Egyptian, the article nevertheless indicates that the debate was still alive.[80] Set in the poorer districts of Alexandria, Togo Mizrahi's 1930s comedies, many of which adapted the personae of popular comic stage actors to the screen, never faced such critical scrutiny in the press.

A number of factors seem to have deterred greater press coverage of Studio Mizrahi and its productions. As already noted, some directors embraced their roles as public figures. Mizrahi preferred to keep a low profile. After Mizrahi demurred to be interviewed by *Al-Ithnayn* in 1935, the magazine ceased prerelease coverage of his films.[81] In addition, other major studios spent more on advertising than Studio Mizrahi: Assia Dagher's Lotus Films took out teaser campaigns, and the Lama brothers' Condor Films often bought multipage spreads in the weeklies to advertise a new release; the independent studios were all surpassed by the splashy advertising campaigns undertaken by Studio Misr. Advertisements for Studio Mizrahi films were, on average, of smaller size and ran for shorter duration than those promoting films by these three other studios. The popular weeklies may well have given greater coverage to the films with larger advertising budgets. Togo Mizrahi's reluctance to be interviewed, his resistance to hype, his studio's location in Alexandria, and his advertising budget all contributed to his relative marginalization by the press in the 1930s, despite his warm critical reception.

"THE DIRECTOR WHO DOES THE EGYPTIAN FILM INDUSTRY PROUD": CAIRO, 1939–1946

Togo Mizrahi's visibility in the press increased significantly following his move to Cairo in 1939. The staff of Mizrahi's Alexandria studio, members of the "Togo cinema family," made the move to Cairo with him.[82] At this time, Mizrahi also reorganized the company. In the early years, Mizrahi benefited from the financial support of business partners. Effective the end of 1939, Mizrahi announced that he had become the sole proprietor of the Egyptian Films Company.[83] Mizrahi leased studio space owned by Isma'il Wahbi, the brother of actor Yusuf Wahbi, on 4 Husni Street in Giza.[84] Over time, as his production needs increased, Mizrahi added a second sound stage to the studio.[85] Mizrahi also reportedly bought land in Giza and built his own studio.[86]

Following the move, the character of Mizrahi's films shifted. Mizrahi began to explore new genres and comedic idioms. In addition to contemporary socially conscious Levantine farces, Mizrahi added bourgeois pastoral comedies, like *Tahiya al-sitat* (*Long Live Women*, 1943). In the 1940s Mizrahi also began to branch out into what could be called costume comedies, like the films starring 'Ali al-Kassar based loosely on narratives from the Thousand and One Nights: *Alf Layla wa-Layla* (*One*

Thousand and One Nights, 1941) and 'Ali Baba wa-l-*arba'in harami* (*Ali Baba and the Forty Thieves*, 1942). Mizrahi also began making big-budget musicals featuring high-profile stars, including Layla Murad and Umm Kulthum. Like his Levantine comedies, his musical melodramas engage with social inequality. Mizrahi's musical films were among many cross-class romances that became popular in the 1940s.[87]

The films Mizrahi directed in the 1940s were the most popular and successful films of his career, receiving high praise from critics and audiences alike (fig. 6). Mizrahi also earned the respect of colleagues in the film industry. Famed musician and film star Muhammad 'Abd al-Wahab and rising filmmaker Ahmad Badr Khan publicly voiced their admiration for Mizrahi's 1941 film *Layla bint madaris* (*Layla the Schoolgirl*).[88] After wrapping production on *Long Live Women* in 1943, actor Muhammad Amin penned a column praising Mizrahi's personal qualities and professional ethic, calling him the consummate artist.[89]

Film critics also held Mizrahi in high regard. In 1942, the Association of Cinema Critics voted Togo Mizrahi the most accomplished filmmaker in Egypt.[90] The association represented critics employed by both daily and weekly Egyptian publications. Muhammad Karim, a highly celebrated director, came in second. By the time this vote was taken, Karim had directed eight features, including five high-grossing films starring singer Muhammad 'Abd al-Wahab. An earlier film by Karim, *Awlad al-zawat* (*Children of the Aristocracy*, 1932), was celebrated as the first Egyptian talkie. Today, Karim is regarded as one of the pioneers of Egyptian cinema; Mizrahi has largely been marginalized. But in 1942, professional cinema critics held Mizrahi in higher regard than Karim. The vote wasn't close. Mizrahi won by a landslide, beating out Karim by a margin of more than two to one.[91]

This admiration is expressed qualitatively as well; in the press, critics often associate Mizrahi with the terms "pride" and "honor." In 1942, a critic for the daily newspaper *Al-Ahram* proclaimed: "Togo Mizrahi's name has become synonymous with excellence—the director who does the Egyptian film industry proud."[92] The following year, *Al-Sabah* devoted a two-page spread to celebrate Mizrahi's innovations, accomplishments, and successes. The article claims that he goes to such extreme efforts as director, producer, and writer not for self-aggrandizing reasons, but rather so that the film industry will take pride in him. Yet even in the limelight, he maintains his characteristic humility: "[N]either in private meetings nor in the promotion of his films will he speak of himself. These are qualities of the consummate artist."[93] Another article echoes these sentiments: "[Mizrahi] has always sought to improve the state of the film industry in Egypt. He was able to achieve that goal, bringing honor to [the industry], as he has brought honor to himself. No director or producer surpasses him."[94]

Audience members also published letters of appreciation. Mizrahi's collaborations with singer Layla Murad, who was also Jewish, were especially warmly received in the Egyptian-Jewish press. Marco Ibrahim Cohen, a reader of the Arabic-language Jewish weekly *Al-Shams*, deemed *Layla the Schoolgirl* "a

FIGURE 6. Togo Mizrahi (center) with the cast and crew on the set of *Layla the Country Girl* (1941). Courtesy of Jacques Mizart.

masterpiece."[95] Another, anonymous reader of the newspaper wrote in as well to congratulate Togo Mizrahi on the film's "dazzling success": "The success of *Layla the Schoolgirl* is attributable both to the mastery of its director, Mr. Mizrahi, as well as to the performance of film and music stars Yusuf Wahbi and Layla Murad.[96] "Mizrahi's films," he concludes, "are epitomes of creativity, and their success is unrivaled."[97]

Not all of his films were hits, of course. Following harsh criticism of the comedy *One Thousand and One Nights*, Mizrahi published a response. Striking a self-deprecating tone, Mizrahi casts aspersions on all of his films, writing, "All of my films are nothing!":

> In my opinion, all the films I have produced are nothing. This is my consistent opinion, as everyone who comes into contact with me knows—workers, employees, and actors, etc. Yes! *Layla the Country Girl*—nothing. *One Thousand and One Nights*—nothing. *Layla*—double nothing. That is my personal view. But does my opinion have any bearing on revenues at the cinema? Absolutely not! Because the audience has the first word and the final say.[98]

Mizrahi continues that what is holding Egyptian filmmakers back from producing films that could rival those made in Europe or Hollywood is not financing per se, but an overreliance on ticket sales. Cinemas' conservative impulses harm the industry by demanding more of the same. He accuses cinemas of having too much control over what gets screened—and what genres, topics, and stars will sell tickets. Adding insult to injury, cinemas take too large a cut of box-office revenue.[99]

Mizrahi, like other directors in Egypt at the time, distrusted and criticized the practices of cinema owners. Even as the domestic industry expanded in the 1940s, cinemas remained reluctant to screen Egyptian films. In spring 1945, cinema producers pressured the government to intervene. Seven major first-run theaters in downtown Cairo were compelled by the Ministry of Social Affairs to screen an Egyptian film one week per year.[100]

Even those cinemas that screened Egyptian films engaged in questionable practices. Take, for example, an incident from 1940. Cinema Cosmo—which was committed to screening Egyptian films—contracted with Assia Dagher to exhibit *Fata mutamarrida* (*Rebellious Girl*, Ahmad Galal, 1940) for five weeks, stipulating that if the film earned enough revenue, the engagement would extend to a sixth week. But in a cynical move Cinema Cosmo, underestimating the demand for *Rebellious Girl*, agreed to premiere Mizrahi's *Qalb imra'a* (*Heart of a Woman*, 1940) in Dagher's sixth week. However, when *Rebellious Girl* turned out to be a success, Mizrahi's film was bumped off the schedule.[101]

Over time, the studios with the greatest output and influence sought to renegotiate their terms with cinema owners, including securing exclusive contracts.[102] Although the distributor of *Heart of a Woman* filed a lawsuit over the lost revenues, it appears that Mizrahi made peace with the owners of Cinema Cosmo. During the 1943–44 season, Studio Mizrahi films virtually monopolized Cinema Cosmo.[103] Following this successful season, Mizrahi convinced Cinema Cosmo to grant him an exclusive contract for the eight films he was projected to direct or produce the coming year. For the entire 1944–45 season, Cinema Cosmo screened only films produced by the Egyptian Films Company.[104]

But even as this arrangement was a marker of Mizrahi's success, it also drew criticism. One somewhat unflattering picture that emerges from press coverage in the 1940s is of Mizrahi as a hoarder of resources. During the final years of World War II, filmmakers were confronted with supply crises. In 1943 a reduction of imports due to the war, coupled with an expanding domestic industry, led to a shortage of film stock. Studio Mizrahi was one of a handful of studios to which the government distributed the scarce resource.[105] When the supply crisis let up the following year, the press reported that filmmakers suffered from a lack of studio space. Mizrahi was criticized for monopolizing two studios.[106]

In time, Mizrahi's frustration with the lack of opportunity to innovate artistically, and his interest in the financial side of filmmaking, translated into an increasing focus on production. The 1945–46 season represented a shift in Mizrahi's career, marking his turn toward producing other directors' films.

FROM DIRECTOR TO PRODUCER: CAIRO, 1944–1946

Anwar Wagdi, an actor who appeared in several of Mizrahi's films before launching his own career as a director, praised Mizrahi's skills as both a director and a producer. Calling Mizrahi "Egypt's number-one director," Anwar Wagdi points to Mizrahi's ability to elicit strong performances from actors who "later failed when they worked with someone else." According to Wagdi, as a prolific producer, Mizrahi wielded significant power to shape the market. However, in Wagdi's view, Mizrahi's creative directorial impulses were in constant conflict with his business interests as a producer.[107]

Beginning in the 1944–45 season, Mizrahi resolved this perceived conflict by turning his attention to film production. As a producer, Mizrahi supported the creative efforts of some of the leading directors in the Egyptian film industry. Mizrahi's Egyptian Films Company produced Yusuf Wahbi's *Ibn al-haddad* (*Son of a Blacksmith*, 1944), *Al-Fanan al-'azim* (*The Great Artist*, 1945), and *Yad Allah* (*Hand of God*, 1946); Niyazi Mustafa's *Shari' Muhammad 'Ali* (*Muhammad 'Ali Street*, 1944); Kamal Salim's *Al-Mazahir* (*Manifestations*, 1945); and Husayn Fawzi's *Aksbris al-hubb* (*Love Express*, 1946). Mizrahi walked a fine line as a producer of other directors' films. Mizrahi maintained that he did not interfere with the creative license of the films' directors.[108] But the press criticized him for abnegating responsibility for the quality of the films that came out of his studio.[109]

Togo Mizrahi's training in business served him well as a producer. In 1942 Mizrahi, writing from his experience in film production, published an article addressing commercial aspects of the industry. The optimistically titled essay, "Egyptian Production Is The Most Complete Production in the World," attempts to debunk claims levied by a critic who, citing limited returns from cinemas, expressed concern about the commercial viability of the Egyptian film industry. Mizrahi counters that film production and box-office receipts were appropriately scaled for the size of the audience and number of cinemas.[110]

Mizrahi's article amounts to a manifesto of sorts, revealing his commitment to the growth and financial health of the Egyptian film industry: "We—people and producers—must all be soldiers in solidarity, standing shoulder to shoulder for the sake of the Egyptian film renaissance so that we can achieve, some day in the future, the perfection sought by the Egyptian people and the brotherly people who also see these films. God alone is the arbiter of success."[111] Mizrahi articulates that his filmmaking efforts are part of a national project, with a Pan-Arab gloss. He grants credit for much of the success of the film industry to the audience for turning out in sufficient numbers to support local production. The essay also gives insights into Togo Mizrahi's self-characterization. He articulates a collaborative spirit and expresses humility. He also, notably, identifies himself, first and foremost, as a producer.

In 1944, director Niyazi Mustafa contracted to direct films to be produced by the Egyptian Films Company. Mustafa, a rising star of the Egyptian cinema industry, had a long-standing and productive relationship with Studio Misr. Mustafa shot his 1944 film *Muhammad 'Ali Street* at Studio Mizrahi, and returned in 1946 to undertake *Malikat al-gamal* (*The Beauty Queen*). In the middle of production, Mustafa walked off the set. Mizrahi stepped in to complete the film, which was released in April 1946 without directorial credit. *The Beauty Queen* was the last film Togo Mizrahi had a hand in directing.[112]

Later that year, Togo Mizrahi reportedly rented out his studio to Hilmi Rafla, who went on to become a prolific director. Rafla had begun his career in the 1930s as a makeup artist for theater and cinema. He worked on six productions that Mizrahi directed, starting with *Layla the Schoolgirl* in 1941. Rafla's directorial debut, *Al-'Aql fi igaza* (*The Mind Is on Vacation*, 1947), was shot in the studio that Togo Mizrahi had built.[113]

THE END OF STUDIO TOGO MIZRAHI

The exact circumstances surrounding Togo Mizrahi's withdrawal from cinema production and his departure from Egypt remain a mystery. Some of the evidence is contradictory; other sources are unreliable. As a result, there has been much speculation and innuendo, leading to the circulation of mistaken information and unsubstantiated rumors. In what follows, I piece together the available evidence about Togo Mizrahi's activities from 1946 to 1952 in an effort to understand his motives for retiring from cinema production at the age of forty-five.

In the 1930s and 1940s, when Mizrahi was actively producing films, the cinema industry, like the local theater scene, scheduled new releases between October and May. This schedule seems to have suited Mizrahi, enabling him to travel to Italy in the summers—as related in 'Abd al-Halim Nasr's story about the filming of *Doctor Farahat*, and as documented in gossip columns from the 1930s.[114] During one of his trips to Europe, Togo met Myriam Donato (1911–2003), a native of Taranto, Italy (fig. 7). They wed on 30 June 1938 at the Egyptian consulate in Rome. Myriam then moved to Egypt with Togo. The couple first resided in an apartment overlooking the Nile in the Doqqi neighborhood in Giza, then settling in a villa near the Pyramids sometime after 1943.[115] The couple remained in Egypt for the duration of World War II, but Myriam did not adapt well to life there.[116] Immediately after Germany's surrender on 8 May 1945, Mizrahi announced that he planned to travel to Italy on "important artistic business."[117]

In the summer of 1946, Togo and Myriam took the first step toward their eventual relocation to Italy. In June 1946, Togo sent a postcard to his brother Alfred in Cairo with the words "my new villa in Rome" scrawled on the back in French.[118] On the front was a photograph of the elegant villa Tre Madonne, where Togo and Myriam occupied a grand garden apartment. The villa was located in Rome's posh Parioli neighborhood, adjacent to the grounds of Villa Borghese. Although Mizrahi may have been based mostly in Italy after purchasing the villa in 1946, reports

FIGURE 7. Togo Mizrahi and Myriam Donato Mizrahi circa 1938. Courtesy of Jacques Mizart.

of his professional activities in the ensuing years suggest that he thought it possible he might return to live and work in Egypt.

In late 1946 news broke in Egypt that an Egyptian studio was providing technical assistance for the production of Zionist films.[119] Further details emerged in the 24 December 1946 issue of the Egyptian newspaper Al-Misbah, in which the Palestine correspondent reported that Togo Mizrahi had agreed to dub the films My Father's House (Herbert Kline, 1947) and Adama (Tomorrow's a Wonderful Day, Helmar Lerski, 1947) into Arabic.[120] Al-Misbah was edited by a Jewish journalist, Albert Mizrahi (no relation), who, in Magdy el-Shammaa's words, engaged in a practice of "dissociation through exposure" of Zionist sympathies or collaboration.[121] The article published in Al-Misbah accuses Togo Mizrahi of participating in the production and dissemination of dangerous Zionist propaganda films in Egypt.[122] The accusations of Zionist sympathies and collaboration on these films could cause damage to Mizrahi's career, whether or not they had any basis in fact.

Both My Father's House and Adama were pro-Zionist films shot in Palestine. It is unlikely that the producers of the films had any intention of releasing Arabic versions of them, as Al-Misbah suggests. My Father's House was an English-language production, but some of the actors were unable to perform in English, and their dialogue required dubbing.[123] Further, according to the Jewish press in Palestine, production was slowed by the lack of local technicians, so it is entirely plausible that they turned to well-established studios in Cairo for technical support.[124]

Studio Mizrahi had experience with dubbing, as did Studios Misr, al-Ahram, and Nahas.[125] Without identifying the accused, the journal *Al-Fanun* urged the Film-maker's Union to put a stop to this activity.[126] There is some suggestion that Miz-rahi was subsequently barred from producing films in Egypt.[127]

There has also been some speculation about the state of Togo Mizrahi's health in the late 1940s. According to one rumor, in 1945, following the release of *Sal-lama*, Mizrahi suffered a nervous breakdown and was admitted to a psychiatric hospital for treatment.[128] In March 1948, a journal published a notice that Mizrahi was being treated in the Hospital for Lung Diseases in Helwan.[129] Mizrahi's family disputes these claims, and denies that health concerns played any role in Mizrahi's withdrawal from the cinema industry.[130]

In a published statement, Togo Mizrahi attributed his withdrawal to economic challenges facing the cinema industry: "From today on, I will be a spectator. I will observe from afar the adversities suffered by Egyptian film. What crises and dif-ficulties production companies will suffer. Some other producer, not me, will bear the responsibility. But I will not personally be the one."[131] He further warned his colleagues: "[T]he producer who presses on alone to stand before this storm risks his production and his money."

Mizrahi, ever the astute businessman, caught the early signs of an industry downturn. During World War II there was a decline in the number of Hollywood films screened in Egypt, reducing the competition for Egyptian films. Rising wages in Egypt also created greater demand for movies: one source estimates that viewer-ship grew 245 percent during the war.[132] As a result, during the war the Egyptian film industry experienced unprecedented growth. Following the war, however, the industry contracted again.[133] In hindsight the industry journal *Al-Istudiyu* praised Mizrahi's intuition and business acumen that led him to withdraw "at the appro-priate moment."[134]

From his residence in Rome, Togo continued to follow developments in the Egyptian cinema industry. He spent three years researching and writing a screen-play for a film about Muhammad 'Ali, who ruled Egypt from 1805 to 1848. Mizrahi hoped to produce and release the film in honor of the centennial of the viceroy's death. But the film was never made.[135]

Although *Al-Sabah* reported a rumor in 1948 that Mizrahi was liquidating his cinema company,[136] a flurry of notes in the gossip columns the following year sug-gested that he was poised for a comeback. In January 1949, *Al-Sabah* reported that Mizrahi had agreed to direct movies produced by Nahas Films.[137] Three months later, in March 1949, Anwar Wagdi was reported to be negotiating with Togo Miz-rahi to direct two films for the following season.[138] In September 1949, *Al-Istudiyu* reported that Mizrahi had hired Ibrahim Hilmi as assistant director on a planned production to be shot in Italy.[139]

Finally, in December 1949 Mizrahi returned to Egypt with plans to resume film production.[140] In an interview with the journal *Al-Istudiyu*, Mizrahi revealed that he was preparing to direct and produce an adaptation of novel *The Count of Monte Cristo* by Alexandre Dumas père. He had shot some footage in Italy and had begun negotiating with actors, but had not yet signed any contracts.[141] However, although a film based on the novel was released the following year, Mizrahi was not involved with the production. Kamal al-Shinawi relates that he was supposed to star in the film with Layla Murad, and that Mizrahi had contracted Behna Films for distribution. Then, Shinawi reports, "[s]uddenly, Togo traveled to Italy and abandoned the idea of the film."[142] In 1950, Assia Dagher's Lotus Films released its adaptation of the novel under the title *Amir al-intiqam* (*Prince of Vengeance*), starring Anwar Wagdi and Samia Gamal, and directed by Henri Barakat. According to Shinawi, who was demoted to a supporting role in the final production, the film became "a source of conflict and an exchange of accusations" between Togo Mizrahi and the Behna brothers on one side, and Lotus Films on the other.[143]

The adaptation of *The Count of Monte Cristo* appears to have been Togo Mizrahi's last attempt at a comeback. Togo's nephew Jacques Mizart relates: "[Togo] saw that the situation had begun to deteriorate for Jews, and since he had developed relations with a number of Italian directors, he decided to go live in Rome, which pleased Myriam."[144] Alfred Mizrahi, Togo's youngest brother, recalls: "He saw Cairo burning in 1952. When ashes reached his balcony [in Giza], he decided to leave Egypt."[145] When it was not safe for Jews in Italy under the Fascist regime, Togo and Myriam made their home in Egypt. When the situation for Jews deteriorated in Egypt following the establishment of Israel, Togo and Myriam found refuge in Italy.

Mizrahi's travel documents concur with Alfred's recollections. On 8 February 1952, the Italian consulate in Egypt issued Mizrahi a passport identifying him as a permanent resident of Egypt (fig. 8). On 5 March 1952, Mizrahi transferred 500 Egyptian pounds from an Egyptian bank to an account in Italy. On 29 March 1952, Mizrahi set sail from Alexandria.[146] In May 1952 Alfred Mizrahi was appointed the administrative director of the Egyptian Films Company, and he was charged with managing Togo and Myriam's private assets in Egypt.[147]

One week prior to his departure, on 21 March 1952, the Egyptian Ministry of the Interior issued Mizrahi a one-year residence permit. This permit represents the last documented evidence of Togo's residence in Egypt in the eyes of the Egyptian authorities.[148] Subsequently, when Mizrahi sought to travel to Egypt—in 1955 and again in 1957—the consulate in Rome issued him short-term visas.[149]

In October 1961, Togo Mizrahi lost the rights to all of the films he produced. All of the assets of the Egyptian Films Company were sequestered, along with the Togo's and Alfred's personal property in Egypt. Stateless, and with no source of income and no assets, Alfred was forced to leave Egypt in 1962 and join his siblings abroad.[150]

On 4 July 1966, the rights to the output of the Egyptian Films Company—thirty-four films in total—were sold to a buyer named Taha Za'afarani Tantawi.

FIGURE 8. Page of the passport issued to Togo Giuseppe Mizrahi by the Italian consulate in Egypt on 8 February 1952. Courtesy of Jacques Mizart.

A letter dated 14 July 1966 from the accountant charged with liquidating the assets of the Egyptian Films Company informs Behna Films, Mizrahi's distributor, of this transfer of property and rights per order 165/65, requesting that they desist from distributing the films.[151]

Mizrahi remained in contact with the George and Michael Behna—and he continued to follow developments in Egyptian cinema. Shortly after the sale of the Egyptian Films Company, Mizrahi wrote to the Behna brothers to request subscriptions to the journals *Al-Mussawar* and *Al-Kawakib*.[152]

Togo Mizrahi continued to appeal to the Egyptian government to recuperate his films. Alfred Mizrahi developed a relationship with Anwar Sadat in the 1960s.[153] In 1970, when Sadat became president of Egypt, Togo Mizrahi was optimistic that he would restore the rights to his films. But Mizrahi's hopes were never realized. The rights to all the films Togo Mizrahi directed and produced were not restored to him during his lifetime.

In Rome, Togo Mizrahi's social circle included prominent members of the film community, including producer Carlo Ponti.[154] Mizrahi continued to work for several years in the Italian cinema industry as a producer and an adviser.[155] His family maintains that Mizrahi stopped directing to pursue his many other interests.[156] Three of Togo's sisters had married French citizens and settled in Paris. Later in life, Togo received a residence permit to live in Paris, but he never settled there permanently.[157] Togo Mizrahi died in Rome on 5 June 1986, forty years after he stopped directing films in Egypt.

After Mizrahi's death, his estate continued to appeal for the restoration of his property. In a letter dated 23 June 1987, the Egyptian cultural attaché in Paris responded to one such request by Togo's sister Camille, stating that the films directed by Togo Mizrahi "are held in the archives of the national library, but are in very poor condition." However, he assures her that "the National Cinema Center indicates that Studio Misr possesses the negatives and could develop them upon your official request, and at your expense," adding that the cost of developing the films could not be estimated in advance.[158]

REEVALUATING TOGO MIZRAHI'S LEGACY

What were Togo Mizrahi's political views? In his few surviving written statements, he projects a fierce patriotism, and a commitment to developing the Egyptian film industry to promote national pride. But Mizrahi left little record of his commitments to the large political issues of the day. What Togo Mizrahi left us are his films.

In this book, I set out to unpack the implied politics of Mizrahi's film oeuvre. Mizrahi's early socially aware melodramas depict the hardships of the lower classes. This interest and awareness of income disparities in Egypt also informs Mizrahi's 1930s comedies of mistaken identity. These films, discussed in the next three chapters, map out Mizrahi's representation of Egyptian heterogeneity. Ahmad Bahjat calls Mizrahi a Zionist;[159] but, as I argue in chapter 6, his film Al-Tariq al-mustaqim (The Straight Road, 1943) can be read as expressing concerns with the effect of Zionism on Jewish diaspora identity. Viola Shafik identifies Mizrahi as a royalist[160]; but, as I argue in chapter 7, his film Layla (1942) critiques the behavior of Egypt's royalty. Togo Mizrahi's legacy has been overdetermined by the assumed politics of his identity as an affluent Jewish noncitizen resident of Egypt. In my analyses that follow, I tease out the cultural and political implications of Mizrahi's films. Togo Mizrahi was a man of "work over words." I seek to let Mizrahi speak through his art.

Crimes of Mistaken Identity

An international crime syndicate that preyed on the unsuspecting residents of Alexandria turned up in Egyptian cinema in the 1930s. Under the cover of a company known as Sharikat naqal al-amwal, the Corporation for the Transport of Capital, thieves printed counterfeit bills, burgled the bourgeoisie, and bilked families out of their savings. The police repeatedly succeeded in breaking up this crime ring thanks to the efforts of infiltrators mistaken for members of the organization's inner circle.

Unlike the protagonists of the film *Raya wa-Sakina* (*Raya and Sakina*, Salah Abu Sayf, 1953), who were based on infamous serial killers targeting bejeweled women on the streets of the Labban neighborhood in Alexandria during the first two decades of the twentieth century, the exploits of the Corporation for the Transport of Capital were not true crime stories. The Corporation for the Transport of Capital is a fictional entity that featured in two comedies directed by Togo Mizrahi and produced in his studio in Alexandria: *Al-Manduban* (*The Two Delegates*, 1934) and *Khafir al-darak* (*The Neighborhood Watchman*, 1936).

The plots of both films revolve around the misguided efforts of lower-class characters to support themselves financially. Through a series of misidentifications, the protagonists are drawn into the criminal exploits of the Corporation for the Transport of Capital. The corporation's illegal money-laundering operations are a sinister distortion of the Levantine "agent of exchange." Eventually the protagonists take advantage of their mistaken identities to assist the police in apprehending the criminals.

The films highlight Alexandria's diversity by pairing protagonists that hail from different religious or ethnonational groups. In *The Two Delegates*, Chalom, a Jew, and 'Abdu, a Muslim, seek to earn enough money to wed. In *The Neighborhood Watchman*, 'Usman, who is Nubian, and 'Azuz, who is Lebanese, try to find a steady source of income after 'Azuz's shop is burgled. In both films, the innocent duo inadvertently stumble into the gangster plot. In this chapter, I argue that *The Two Delegates* and *The Neighborhood Watchman* provide a framework of law and lawlessness through which members of Alexandria's minorities productively participate in Egyptian society. My analyses of the two films unpack the masquerades that unmask the criminals' plots and lead to the restoration of order and justice.

Togo Mizrahi's films privilege fluid notions of collective belonging over legalistic definitions of nationality and citizenship. In their attention to law and lawlessness, *The Two Delegates* and *The Neighborhood Watchman* focus on the actions of the police, who maintain and restore order. Courtroom dramas were not common in 1930s Egyptian cinema, nor did films depict the complicated legal system that adjudicated cases based on the citizenship of the parties involved.[1] The pluralism signified by the characters' friendships in these films derives its authenticity from its homegrown character.

I begin the chapter with a discussion of Levantine farce. I lay out how both farce as a genre and the Levantine cinematic idiom subvert social norms. With their focus on the plight of the urban lower classes, Mizrahi's films articulate a particular form of national belonging—a salt-of-the-earth characterization known as *ibn al-balad*. In the second section below, "Chalom: A Jewish *Ibn al-Balad*," I argue that Mizrahi's films seek to broaden the category of *ibn al-balad*. The construct is usually applied only to Muslims. Mizrahi's films, though, expand the notion to include Jews. In the final two sections of the chapter, "Language of Belonging, Language of Disguise" and "Masquerade and the Levantine Carnivalesque," I argue that *The Two Delegates* and *The Neighborhood Watchman* define and assert local subjecthood in dialogue with evolving discourses of national identity, nationality, and citizenship. In these films, Levantines subvert social codes and notions of national belonging, but they are also depicted as civic-minded and law-abiding subjects who work for the common good.

THE SUBVERSIVE POTENTIAL OF LEVANTINE FARCE

The Two Delegates and *The Neighborhood Watchman* are farces constructed from a series of loosely connected, episodic, character-driven sketches propelled along by misunderstandings and mistaken identities. *The Concise Oxford Companion to the Theater* defines farce as a "form of popular comedy in which laughter is raised by horseplay and bodily assault in contrived and highly improbable situations. . . . It deals with the inherent stupidity of man at odds with his environment."[2] Modern farces are often constructed around "an absurd situation, generally based on extramarital adventures—hence 'bedroom farce.'"[3]

Although farce is a popular form of comedy, critics often disparage the genre. When Togo Mizrahi's farcical films were released, they received mixed reviews in the press. While one critic called Mizrahi's dialogue "clever" and his jokes "innovative,"[4] others complained that his comedies engaged in "excessive exaggeration"[5] and "failed to transcend clowning."[6]

In subsequent decades, Egyptian film historians have tended to side with farce's detractors. For example, in a survey of Egyptian film genres published in 1996, 'Ali Abu Shadi offers a scathing appraisal of Togo Mizrahi's comic films. Abu Shadi was a prominent Egyptian film critic who held a number of influential positions, including director of the National Film Center (2001–8) and state censor (1996–99; 2004–9).[7] In Abu Shadi's assessment, although "Mizrahi's films were very popular and successful at the box office, and they made their stars famous," they featured "contrived and exaggerated" plotlines and lowbrow humor.[8] He continues: "These films are light comedies, there is no character development, no motivation for action, and no subtlety to the words. They seek only to amuse and entertain, and some are farces using mistaken identity and misunderstanding as their primary means of arousing laughs."[9]

Abu Shadi's critique of Togo Mizrahi's farces is consistent with his assessment of genre cinema in general, and of 1930s and 1940s Egyptian comedies in particular. Abu Shadi views genre cinema, including farce, as inherently conservative —expressing "dominant mores and ideology" and affirming "the status quo and its existing values."[10] Abu Shadi contends that Egyptian farces and light comedies of the era, including those by Mizrahi, hewed closely to formulas established by Egyptian comic theater and Hollywood. These comedies, he dismissively notes, "copied, adapted, Egyptianized, and took whole scenes from" Hollywood films.[11]

Although I take a more favorable view of Togo Mizrahi's films than Abu Shadi, I do not dispute some of his basic contentions. Mizrahi's plots of mistaken identity— like all farce—are indeed "contrived and exaggerated." Mizrahi's films also reflect the influence of Hollywood—from content, such as gangster plots, to visual style, such as continuity editing. In *The Two Delegates* and *The Neighborhood Watchman*, Mizrahi integrates elements of the gangster genre with comedy, romance, and musical performance in a manner particularly reminiscent of the Marx Brothers' *Monkey Business* (Norman McLeod, 1931).

I take issue, however, with Abu Shadi's foundational assumption that farce is socially conservative. Farce—"a veritable structure of absurdities," according to critic Eric Bentley—is constructed as an ongoing series of unsettling revelations. Compared with comedies, in which all is revealed in a climactic scene, "in farce, unmasking occurs all along," according to Bentley. This process of unmasking is frequently directed at subverting the tenets of religion, marriage, and moral social codes.[12]

Mikhail Bakhtin also views farce as disruptive. For Bakhtin, farce—like parody and satire—"function[s] as a force for exposing" standards and norms.[13] Bakhtin's writings about the novel have been adapted and widely employed in cinema studies.[14] In particular, film studies scholars have drawn upon Bakhtin's notion of the carnivalesque, with its practice of masquerade and unmasking. Bakhtin derives his notion of the carnivalesque from practices of medieval carnivals that invert power relations and subvert authority. The topsy-turvy nature of the carnivalesque elevates the grotesque and the "lower bodily stratum" over social codes of decorum.[15] Representations of the carnivalesque—like farce—can reproduce these subversive tendencies.

Robert Stam points to a range of ways Bakhtin's carnivalesque is expressed in cinema, including "films that use humor to anarchize institutional hierarchies . . . or direct corrosive laughter at patriarchal authority" and "films that comically privilege, whether visually or verbally, the 'lower bodily stratum.'"[16] Further, the features of farce that appear culturally conservative to Abu Shadi should instead, according to Robert Stam, be read against the grain. As Stam notes: "In a political culture, and a commercial film industry, where radical alternatives have been more or less ruled 'out of bounds' it is not surprising that 'subversion' often takes the apolitical form of comic aggressions that violate respectable decorum and decent standards of bodily behavior."[17] According to Stam, cinematic transgressions of "good manners"—like the humor in Marx Brothers movies—should be analyzed as acts of subversion.

Togo Mizrahi's films deploy the subversive potential of farce to reflect, lampoon, and critique Egyptian culture and society.[18] I argue that the social codes subverted in Togo Mizrahi's comedies include parochial notions of national identity. According to intellectual historians Israel Gershoni and James Jankowski, the 1930s saw the rise of "supra-nationalism" in Egypt—movements that defined Egyptianness in terms of a broader, "supra-national" Arab or Islamic identity.[19] These ascendant nationalist strains increasingly excluded resident non-Muslim minorities, like Togo Mizrahi himself. Further, in the interwar period other exclusionary nationalist discourses such as Greek irredentism, Italian Fascism, and Zionism also circulated among some members of Egypt's resident foreign minority communities, dividing them from one another and from the majority culture.

By contrast, through the 1930s and 1940s Egyptian cinema—including Togo Mizrahi's films—projected a religiously, ethnonationally diverse national imaginary. Egyptian cinema of this era offers an implicit—if not explicit—rejection of "supra-nationalist" perspectives expressed in the press. Cinema resisted deterministic trends by embracing what I call a "Levantine cinematic idiom."

The term "Levantine," as introduced in chapter 1, refers to cultural admixture, and to individuals whose identities transcended sharply drawn ethnonational boundaries and collective identities. The terms "Levant" and "Levantine" are intentionally and necessarily vague. As a geographical term, the boundaries of the Levant are indeterminate, unruly. The term "Levantine" originally referred to residents of the eastern Mediterranean of European origins. Indistinct from the outset, the term "Levantine" evokes the vagueness of its application, and the fluidity and inherent indefinability of the people whom it identifies. As Anat Lapidot-Firilla writes in the inaugural issue of the *Journal of Levantine Studies*, "As it developed alongside colonial practices and Eurocentric attitudes, the term, like other 'culturally impure' terms, acquired derogatory connotations."[20]

I come to the term "Levantine" through the work of Egyptian-Jewish essayist Jacqueline Shohet Kahanoff. Writing in 1950s and 1960s Israel, when fears of cultural admixture espoused by the Ashkenazi Zionist leadership were derogatorily dubbed "Levantinization," Kahanoff embraces and reappropriates the term. Drawing upon her experiences growing up in interwar Egypt, Kahanoff calls for actively adopting the Levantine as a model for constructing Israeli society. Thanks to Kahanoff's writings, the term "Levantine" has evolved into an adjective describing a social formation or cultural force. In Kahanoff's writing, the Levantine becomes an agent of exchange.[21]

By applying the term "Levantine" to cinema, I aim to highlight the transnational nature of filmmaking. While film industries developed along national lines, film is inherently a collaborative medium. It is also a traveling and transnational medium. Further, the term acknowledges the ways many individuals associated with film industries—like Togo Mizrahi—challenge restrictive constructions of national identity.

I employ the term "Levantine" to analyze 1930s and 1940s Egyptian cinema as a locally situated project reflecting a pluralist ideal. I am not suggesting that the term "Levantine" (or its equivalents in Arabic, French, Italian, etc.) would have had currency in 1930s Egyptian film criticism—either among Egyptians or the resident minorities and foreigners.[22] Rather, I have adopted "Levantine" to index the vagueness and porousness of the boundaries of identity that the term evokes.

Levantine films share several characteristics. First, these films' representations of Egyptian pluralism reflect and engage with an ethics of coexistence. To be clear, while Levantine farces represent Egyptian diversity, they do not necessarily feature a plot that promotes a pluralist agenda. For example, Togo Mizrahi's Chalom and 'Abdu films *The Two Delegates* and *Mistreated by Affluence* quite evidently espouse an ethics of coexistence. By contrast, in *The Neighborhood Watchman*, the friendship that develops between Nubian and Lebanese characters appears as an incidental detail within an episodic plot structure.

Second, Levantine films utilize cinematic tools to construct a pluralist aesthetic. Like the carnivalesque Shamm al-nasim montage from *Mistreated by Affluence* discussed in chapter 1, many scenes in Togo Mizrahi's 1930s comedies were shot on location in Alexandria's streets, cafés, beaches, parks—sites where people came in contact with one another. In *The Two Delegates,* Chalom and 'Abdu—a Jew and a Muslim, respectively—stride out of a café together arm in arm (fig. 9). The 1937 film *Al-Saʿa 7 (Seven O'Clock)*, discussed in chapter 5, opens with a lengthy, all-encompassing traveling shot through the busy streets of central Alexandria. In these scenes the camera's inclusive gaze underscores the pluralist ethics of the diegesis.

FIGURE 9. 'Abdu ('Abdu Muharram, left) and Chalom (Leon Angel) leave a café arm in arm. Screenshot from *The Two Delegates* (Togo Mizrahi, 1934).

Third, Levantine films foreground the performativity of identity. Plots of mistaken identity highlight the fluid and mutable character of identity as performance: they do not *merely* arouse laughs, as Abu Shadi contends. My analyses of mistaken identity and masquerade reveal the plot device's subversive potential.

The Levantine cinematic idiom is evident in a range of genres in 1930s and 1940s Egyptian cinema, and in films produced by a number of different studios. In this chapter and the two that follow, I examine Levantine farces written, directed, and produced by Togo Mizrahi.

As already noted, critics like 'Ali Abu Shadi dismiss 1930s and 1940s genre films as decadent and derivative of Hollywood.[23] Nationalist critics of Egyptian film have also favored socialist realism over comedy, viewing melodrama as the vehicle best suited to a cinema of substance. As a genre, melodrama has the capacity to reveal social ills. It was also the genre of choice for depicting the anticolonial struggle. As Joel Gordon demonstrates in *Revolutionary Melodrama*, Egyptian melodramas produced following the 1952 Revolution articulate, enact, and disperse ideologies of the postcolonial Egyptian state.[24] I argue that, in contradistinction to "revolutionary melodrama," Levantine farces articulate, enact, and disperse ideologies of pluralist nationalism.

CHALOM: A JEWISH *IBN AL-BALAD*

In Togo Mizrahi's 1937 film *Mistreated by Affluence,* a boarded-up shop front is plastered with advertisements for his earlier film *Awlad Misr* (*Children of Egypt,* 1933). I argued in chapter 1 that the self-referential (and self-promotional) posters for *Children of Egypt* in a film about friendships between Muslims and Jews asserted an inclusive notion of nativeness. More specifically, the posters served to identify Jews—including Togo Mizrahi and the character Chalom—as children of Egypt.

The film's Arabic title, *Awlad Misr,* evokes an Egyptian colloquial term that is used to describe the urban lower-classes: *awlad al-balad* (pl.; *ibn al-balad,* m. sing.; *bint al-balad,* f. sing.). In popular usage, the term *ibn al-balad* or *bint al-balad* signifies a person of simplicity, goodness, and purity of heart. Plain-speaking *awlad al-balad* prize themselves on their sense of humor. According to Sawsan el-Messiri, the term emerged in the eighteenth century to describe native crafts-people, distinguishing them from Turko-Circassian elites, from Arabic-speaking immigrants from outside of Egypt, and from foreigners.[25] The terms "*ibn al-balad*" and "*bint al-balad*" function as markers of both indigeneity and class.

The notion of *awlad al-balad* possesses a self-reflexive and performative qual-ity; it does not reflect a rigid classification. A subject's *baladi*-ness is enacted via dress, behavior, speech patterns—in other words, through performance. *Baladi*-ness is a status of mutual belonging accorded upon recognition of shared affinities.

While el-Messiri's study of the term's historical evolution passes quickly over the period during which Mizrahi's films were produced, one of her informants, a craftsman self-identified as an *ibn al-balad,* offers some insight into the term's associations in the interwar period. From his vantage point in the late 1960s or early 1970s, when el-Messiri conducted her fieldwork, he notes that *awlad al-balad* of an earlier generation "used to attend the theater, especially the plays of Naguib al-Rihani and ['Ali] al-Kassar."[26] In other words, according to el-Messiri's infor-mant, in the early twentieth century *awlad al-balad* were, in part, defined by their attendance at theatrical performances that shaped and defined their sense of self.

Togo Mizrahi was actively engaged in perpetuating and disseminating this per-formance of identity. 'Ali al-Kassar, a quintessential "*ibn al-balad*" of the stage, worked extensively with Togo Mizrahi. Mizrahi was instrumental in helping al-Kassar bring to the screen his popular stage persona: 'Usman 'Abd al-Basit, a down-on-his-luck Nubian.[27] Between 1936 and 1944, al-Kassar starred in nine films directed by Mizrahi, including *The Neighborhood Watchman.*

Although Mizrahi and al-Rihani never made a film together, al-Rihani's long-time writing partner, Badi' Khayri, collaborated with Mizrahi on several films, including writing the lyrics to the songs featured in *The Two Delegates.* Naguib al-Rihani had a long stage career leading a popular theater troupe, and a success-ful star turn on the silver screen.[28] Naguib al-Rihani's most famous character, Kish

Kish Bey, is a mayor of a fictional village called "Kafr al-Balas." Despite his association with this lower-class notion of collective belonging, both al-Rihani's onstage *Franco-Arab Revue* and the film projects with which he was associated represent Egyptian diversity across classes.[29]

Togo Mizrahi's socially conscious films produced in his Alexandria studio between 1930 and 1939 feature two other comic stars who also portray lower-class characters: Fawzi al-Gazayirli and Chalom, who appear together in the film *The Two Delegates*. Fawzi al-Gazayirli frequently played a shop owner named Bahbah, and other simple characters of limited means. In addition to his featured role as Amina's father in *The Two Delegates*, al-Gazayirli appeared in *Al-Bahhar* (*The Sailor*, 1935) and starred in *Al-Duktur Farhat* (*Doctor Farahat*, 1935), discussed in the next chapter. After a five-year hiatus, in which he appeared in several films written and directed by his son Fu'ad, Fawzi al-Gazayirli returned to Studio Mizrahi to appear in two comedies directed by Togo Mizrahi: *Al-Bashmaqawil* (*The Chief Contractor*, 1940) and *Al-Fursan al-thalatha* (*The Three Musketeers*, 1940).[30]

Chalom was the screen name and on-screen persona of Leon Angel, an Alexandrian Jew of Greek nationality. Unlike other film comics of his era, most of whom started their careers in comedy troupes, Leon Angel had no experience onstage.[31] Angel developed the character "Chalom" for the screen. He starred in three films directed by Togo Mizrahi: *05001* (silent, 1931), *The Two Delegates*, and *Mistreated by Affluence*. Angel is credited as assistant director of *The Two Delegates*. Angel went on to direct two additional films in which he also starred. In 1935, Angel forged out on his own to direct and star in *Chalom al-turgaman* (*Chalom the Dragoman*), which was shot at Studio Alvise Orfanelli.[32] His second film, *Al-Riyadi* (*The Athlete*, 1937), was shot at Studio Mizrahi and produced by the Egyptian Films Company. Angel pseudonymously codirected *The Athlete* with Clément Mizrahi, Togo's first cousin and brother-in-law.[33]

In *The Two Delegates*, Chalom sells lottery tickets in the streets and cafés. His sidekick, 'Abdu ('Abdu Muharram), is a butcher's assistant who suffers at the hands of his employer. Angel's character, Chalom, challenges commonly held assumptions about both nativeness and Jewishness in 1930s Egypt. The terms "*ibn al-balad*" and "*bint al-balad*" have generally applied only to the Muslim majority. I argue that Togo Mizrahi's Chalom and 'Abdu films expand the notion of *awlad al-balad* to include lower-class, Arabic-speaking Jews.

In addition to broadening the notion of nativeness held by the populace at large, the character Chalom also unsettles perceptions of arabophone lower-class Jews held by the francophone Jewish bourgeoisie. In dress and speech Chalom shares traits common among the Jews from the popular districts in Cairo and Alexandria. Members of the Jewish bourgeoisie, and those with upwardly mobile bourgeois aspirations, spoke French and dressed in Western fashion. The Egyptian Jewish bourgeoisie looked down upon the poverty and traditional religious values characteristic of the residents of Harat al-yahud, Cairo's medieval Jewish quarter.

Many also spurned the use of Arabic.[34] They never saw themselves as embracing the identity of the *ibn al-balad* that Chalom represents.[35]

A response to Chalom's on-screen persona that appeared in the Jewish press illustrates and complicates this class and cultural divide. Following the release of the second Chalom and 'Abdu film, *Mistreated by Affluence*, in 1937, Raphael Mosseri, a reader of the Arabic-language Egyptian-Jewish newspaper *Al-Shams*, wrote a letter to the editor complaining that the film debases Jews. While he appreciated the portrayal of amity between "two Egyptian families living in Egypt—one Jewish and the other Muslim," Mosseri found Chalom's behavior a disgrace to the community. Chalom steals meat from the butcher shop where 'Abdu works. At moments in the film, his character comes across as petulant, selfish, and stingy. Mosseri implores Mizrahi to use his great talent to avoid depicting Jewish characters with such shortcomings. Mosseri writes: "It is incumbent upon [Mizrahi] as a Jew to show the virtues of his fellow Jews, ennobling their appearance on the silver screen."[36] Mosseri, an arabophone Jew engaged in the public sphere of the Arabic-Jewish press, published his views in a journal that advocated for the integration of Jews into Egyptian culture. Yet Mosseri rejects Chalom. The Jewish *ibn al-balad* is not the role model he wishes to see on-screen.

Mosseri, however, misses the point. Chalom was not a figure for emulation. Like Charlie Chaplin's tramp, Chalom holds a mirror up to society. Chalom, the *ibn al-balad*, reflects Togo Mizrahi and Leon Angel's desire to articulate a particular vision of Jewish belonging within the Egyptian polity. The character Chalom boldly inserts lower-class, arabophone Egyptian-Jewish nativeness into the cultural imaginary.

LANGUAGE OF BELONGING, LANGUAGE OF DISGUISE: *THE TWO DELEGATES* (1934)

Togo Mizrahi's *The Two Delegates* illustrates these distinctions between arabophone Jewish *awlad al-balad* and the local francophone foreign-minority residents. The film, I argue, depicts both of these groups as part of the cultural fabric of the city, in contradistinction to incomprehensible "foreigners." The film also portrays a locally situated, Alexandrian culture of coexistence. I argue that the film foregrounds cultural practices shared by Jews and Muslims. In particular, the representations of Chalom's and 'Abdu's weddings highlight these shared rituals and downplay differences of religious rite.

Chalom, a Jewish peddler of lottery tickets, wishes to marry Esther (Esther Angel, credited as 'Adalat);[37] and 'Abdu, a Muslim butcher's assistant, seeks to wed Amina (Siham). Both women are products of middle-class families with bourgeois aspirations.[38] When Chalom and 'Abdu extend proposals of marriage, they are rejected by the brides' mothers on class grounds (fig. 10). Independently, both prospective mothers-in-law identify the suitors' native garb—the galabiya—as a

FIGURE 10. Chalom (Leon Angel, center) comes to ask Solomon (Muhammad al-Salamuni, left) to marry his daughter, Esther (Esther Angel, credited as 'Adalat). Screenshot from *The Two Delegates* (Togo Mizrahi, 1934).

sign of poverty and backwardness. The protagonists' adventures throughout *The Two Delegates* are motivated by their desire to marry.

This narrative of becoming an effendi—a term that, according to Lucie Ryzova, reflects education, dress, and, to a certain extent, class—was playing out in Egyptian spaces both domestic and public, as well as on the Egyptian screen.[39] Chalom and 'Abdu strive to meet the middle-class expectations of their future in-laws. The two dejected friends set out to purchase a suit and tie to replace the scorned galabiya. By changing their appearance, Chalom and 'Abdu are engaging in a form of masquerade. The scene in the tailor's shop where they buy the suits highlights the disjuncture between their sense of self and their appearance; the sight of 'Abdu trying on a top hat sends the two friends into a fit of laughter. Dressed in a Western suit and tarboosh, Chalom and 'Abdu can pass as members of the *effendiyya*.

The change in costume also sets the two friends up for the case of mistaken identity that renders the film a Levantine farce. After purchasing the suits, Chalom and 'Abdu slip into a barbershop for a shave. When they leave the barbershop, they mistakenly don the wrong suit jackets—ones bearing lapel pins that identify them as members of an international organized-crime outfit (fig. 11). A local band of

FIGURE 11. Chalom (Leon Angel, left) and 'Abdu ('Abdu Muharram) notice the insignia on their lapels. Screenshot from *The Two Delegates* (Togo Mizrahi, 1934).

thieves, under the cover of the Corporation for the Transport of Capital, is antici-pating the arrival of two delegates from abroad. World-renowned safecrackers, the international representatives have been brought in to review the corporate books (!) and to oversee a covert operation. Chalom and 'Abdu are mistaken for the visiting delegates and gain access to the organization's secret lair.

The Two Delegates is the earliest surviving film directed by Togo Mizrahi. He had made the transition from silent to sound in *Children of Egypt,* his feature released the previous year. *The Two Delegates* retains a heavy reliance on the physical com-edy of the silent era. They key moments in Chalom's and 'Abdu's transformation and their mistaken identification as the delegates all take place without words. The scenes are shot silent and played with accompanying nondiegetic music. The bar-bershop scene where Chalom and 'Abdu put on the wrong jackets is accompanied by a rousing instrumental rendition of "Puttin' on the Ritz." The scene cuts to a female representative of the organization awaiting the arrival of the two delegates on a street corner in al-Manshiyya, the commercial center of Alexandria. She flir-tatiously flashes the organization's secret gesture. Chalom, flirting back, mimics the gesture. She beckons, and the two men follow. The interaction on the street, conducted without words, is accompanied by instrumental Arabic music.

Miscommunication like the misinterpretation of nonverbal symbols—the pin and the gesture—sets up comic misunderstandings that serve to highlight particular characteristics of the film's construction of native Egyptianness. Mizrahi also explores failures of communication: the alienation of confronting foreign languages. These miscommunications serve to underscore the identity of the protagonists as plain-speaking, lower-class residents of popular quarters—*awlad al-balad*—who, in the popular imagination, represent authentic Egyptianness. By reviewing these comic miscommunications, I would like to draw attention to the distinction between speakers of foreign languages and (presumed) foreigners. I argue that *The Two Delegates* establishes two discourses of otherness. The first, defined by class and language difference, is locally situated, familiar, and culturally comprehensible even in its unfamiliarity. The characters who speak French are portrayed as local residents who expect their address to be received and understood. The second form of otherness, by contrast, is enacted by gibberish-speaking locals pretending to be foreigners. The imaginary "foreigner" they represent is one of radical otherness.

In *The Two Delegates,* language—both the language and idiom spoken and the mode of address—also signals communal identification. In *The Two Delegates,* when Chalom first enters the apartment of Esther's parents, he greets them with the Hebrew phrase "Shalom 'Alekhem"—also a play on his name. Chalom, Esther, and most of Mizrahi's other Jewish characters speak the same urban Egyptian Arabic dialect that their Muslim counterparts do. The character Vittoria (Vittoria Farhi), Esther's mother, employs a number of expressions that linguist Gabriel Rosenbaum has identified as distinct to Egyptian Jews.[40] Jewish audiences were attentive to Vittoria's dialogue, although they were not necessarily supportive of Mizrahi's portrayal of a Jew as speaking differently from their neighbors. In the letter to the editor of *al-Shams* discussed above, Raphael Mosseri complained that Vittoria's manner of speaking was an exaggerated affectation.[41]

A lengthy massage-parlor scene in *The Two Delegates* illustrates the first form of miscommunication—between Arabic-speaking and French-speaking locals. Chalom and 'Abdu repeatedly demonstrate that they don't speak or understand European languages commonly heard on the streets of Alexandria. In the course of a chase scene in which they are trying to escape from one of the criminal thugs, Chalom and 'Abdu seek refuge in a posh massage parlor. The receptionists, manager, and clientele all speak French, while the massage therapists are a linguistically mixed lot. The accented French of one of the clients and the massage therapist, Marie, for example, suggests that they are Alexandrian Greeks.[42] Misunderstandings abound. 'Abdu is taken for a job applicant. Chalom is presumed to be a client.

At first glance, it would be easy to dismiss this comic interlude as sensationalism, an excuse to show some skin. Nearly twelve minutes long, this scene features no less than three women in various states of undress. Further, this lengthy excursus has little direct bearing on either the romantic plot or the gangster narrative.

However, I would like to suggest that this scene serves to establish the nexus between language and class, illustrating the valences attached to Arabic and French in this film. The series of miscommunications in this scene between the protagonists' Arabic and their interlocutors' French serves to draw attention to particular characteristics that define their nativeness. Poor and uneducated, but bearing the street smarts, charm, and good humor of *awlad al-balad*, Chalom and 'Abdu speak exclusively Egyptian Arabic. French is a language associated with the bourgeoisie. It is also the common language among noncitizen local residents, including the foreign minorities.

The film verbally indexes the miscommunication that plays out throughout the scene. When the manager ushers the new hire, 'Abdu, into a treatment room, he provides instruction in French. Then he turns to 'Abdu, rhetorically inquiring, "*Compris?*"—that is, "Understood?" He leaves without receiving a response. 'Abdu shrugs and mutters to himself in Arabic, "*Ana ma fahimtish wa-la haga*" ("I didn't understand a thing")—a sentiment he repeats several times throughout the scene. The manager incorrectly assumes the addressee to be a French speaker who would understand the plain meaning of his spoken utterances, as well as an experienced massage therapist who would possess the appropriate lexicon to assimilate his specific technical instructions.

This scene places Arabic-speaking protagonists from humble origins in contact with local residents who belong to, aspire to, or provide services for the francophone bourgeoisie, to whom the massage parlor caters. The protagonists eventually manage to overcome linguistic barriers with the francophone women in the treatment rooms and the mixed, unfamiliar social codes of physical contact between sexes.[43] With the gestural guidance of his client, 'Abdu manages to learn some massage technique on the spot. The scene ends when the spa director, in a trilingual tirade ["à la porte"; "*fayn al-flus?*"; "door"], throws Chalom out when he can't pay for his massage.

The second form of miscommunication—an utterance intended to confuse or deceive—is, by contrast, intentionally insurmountable. In *The Two Delegates* this incomprehensible address takes place during the first encounter between the protagonists and the band of thieves. Seated at the head of a conference table, surrounded by his underlings and across from the visiting delegates, the local crime boss—in a nod to Hollywood gangster films—reports (in Arabic) on recent activities, summarizes the annual take, and pays tribute to their members who were killed. He notes to his members that the visiting delegates do not understand Arabic, so they must communicate with signs. During the course of this meeting the crime boss invites 'Abdu to address the local membership in his own language, "Globes-talk." 'Abdu obliges by animatedly launching into a gibberish monologue.[44]

In *The Two Delegates*, Jewish and Muslim characters are depicted as Egyptian-Arabic-speaking local subjects. Chalom and 'Abdu, in particular, share many of the qualities associated with *awlad al-balad*. The experiences of lower-class Egyptian Muslims and Jews are one and the same. The locally situatedness of these characters is further cemented by the presence of two forms of otherness: the francophone cosmopolitan bourgeoisie; and foreigners (as enacted by gibberish-speaking locals masquerading as foreigners).

The francophone cosmopolitan bourgeoisie, while lacking the native authenticity of the arabophone Levantines—Muslims and Jews alike—nevertheless constitute part of the local landscape. Foreigners, as imagined—and mimicked—by the locals, are portrayed as uncomprehending and incomprehensible intruders into the local social fabric. In Mizrahi's films, Jews are not portrayed as part of either of these categories. *The Two Delegates* vaunts a native authenticity derived from a relationship to language (Arabic) and place (Alexandria). The film articulates a locally situated pluralism that minimizes markers of difference.

The friendship and collaboration between Chalom and 'Abdu—Jew and Muslim—also contributes to the restoration of order and justice. At the end of the film, Chalom and 'Abdu return to the headquarters of the Corporation for the Transportation of Capital and fight two of the criminals. When the crime boss hears the commotion, he and his lackeys go to investigate, giving an undercover police officer the opportunity to call for backup. The police arrive, and the criminals are apprehended. Back at the station, the police chief thanks Chalom and 'Abdu for helping to capture this dangerous band of criminals. He presents them with a cash reward for their efforts. The windfall—coupled with their earlier wardrobe upgrade—makes it possible for Chalom and 'Abdu to wed Esther and Amina.

Despite its episodic digressions, the plot of *The Two Delegates* builds toward the dramatic conclusion of the dual weddings. After Chalom's and 'Abdu's proposals are turned down, two mysterious, wealthy-looking suitors extend proposals of marriage to Esther and Amina. The suitors woo the future mothers-in-law with the promise of financial security. The "suitors" are actually members of the Corporation for the Transport of Capital. They con the families into turning over their savings. Only after a visit by a police investigator do the families learn of the deception and the loss of their money.

Chalom and 'Abdu's reward—equivalent to the amount Esther's and Amina's families squandered on the fake suitors—prompts the families to accept their proposals of marriage. Despite their windfall and their new wardrobe, Chalom and 'Abdu are no more financially secure than they were at the beginning of the film. They have not secured civil-service jobs that would ensure their place among the rising middle class, the *effendiyya*.[45] *The Two Delegates* offers an early cinematic representation of the process Lucie Ryzova calls "becoming efendi," which includes, but is not limited to, dressing the part.[46] The mere appearance of Chalom and 'Abdu's class mobility—their performance of identity—meets the families' equally hollow class aspirations. Chalom and Esther, and 'Abdu and Amina, wed in the final scene of the film.

The wedding scene is shot to visually emphasize the close friendships between the film's Jewish and Muslim characters. The narrative of coexistence is mirrored in the Levantine aesthetic of the wedding montage. In the film's final scene, the nuptials occupy one minute of screen time, and are presented entirely without dialogue. The wedding scene begins with the sound of ululation that signals the families' acceptance of the marriage proposals and carries over to a shot of festive decorations outside the house. The scene cuts to Amina in her wedding gown as we begin to hear the sound of the *zaffa*, the wedding procession, accompanied by a brass ensemble known as a Hasaballah band.[47] The music plays in a continuous, unbroken stream over a montage of wedding images featuring both couples.

In this scene, Togo Mizrahi depicts only shared idioms of celebration. It is perhaps not surprising that Mizrahi chooses weddings to represent shared cultural practices. In a study on Middle Eastern popular culture, Sami Zubaida offers wedding ceremonies as an example of the confluence of popular religious practice that cuts across confessional groups.[48] The scene in *The Two Delegates* reflects wedding celebrations as practiced in Egypt's cities, including both traditional elements and Western attire that reflects bourgeois class aspiration.[49]

The Two Delegates does not, however, depict religious elements of the wedding ceremonies. A similar absence is particularly apparent in the longer, more extensive montage of Chalom's and 'Abdu's nuptial festivities that appears in *Mistreated by Affluence*, including a celebration welcoming the delivery of furniture to the future home of the bride and groom; a henna ceremony; communal preparation of food for the wedding feast; seating of the bride and groom facing the guests at the wedding party; and a processional, led by musicians and a dancer, escorting the newlyweds out of the party toward their new home. Yet, there is no huppah and breaking of a glass; no handshake accompanied by the recitation of the Fatiha.[50] The absence of wedding ceremonies in Mizrahi's films is entirely in keeping with the common practice in Egyptian cinema of that era. Couples announced their plans to wed, and films featured wedding parties. Yet in the context of Mizrahi's lengthy, detailed representation of other traditions that are also not generally depicted on-screen, the absence of wedding ceremonies is striking.

Both *The Two Delegates* and *Mistreated by Affluence* rapidly intercut between the two celebrations in honor of Chalom and Esther and of 'Abdu and Amina. This technique serves to blur distinctions between the Jewish and Muslim weddings. By representing the celebrations in this way, the nuptials serve to underscore the films' ethics of coexistence—their representation of deeply intertwined communities of Jews and Muslims coexisting as equals.[51]

MASQUERADE AND THE LEVANTINE CARNIVALESQUE: *THE NEIGHBORHOOD WATCHMAN* (1936)

In *The Neighborhood Watchman*, 'Ali al-Kassar plays his signature role, 'Usman 'Abd al-Basit, a poor Nubian immigrant to the city.[52] 'Usman is a simple, good-hearted, and honest—but luckless—character. Despite his best efforts, 'Usman can't hold a job. At the beginning of *The Neighborhood Watchman*, 'Usman is employed as domestic servant for a member of the foreign-minority elites. Preparing for a banquet, 'Usman is charged with transporting a large tray of food to a bakery for baking in its large oven. En route, hungry birds descend upon the tray, making off with some of the food. When Usman returns to the home of his employer, he is berated, beaten, and kicked out. The episodic plot of the film follows this formula: 'Usman pursues increasingly contrived—and humorous—employment opportunities; and each failure is met with verbal lashings or physical beatings. Yet when confronted with an opportunity to earn money through illicit means, 'Usman refuses.

Over the course of the film, 'Usman is regularly mistaken for someone else. The title of the film is derived from a series of nested masquerades in which 'Usman is mistakenly hired to serve as a neighborhood watchman. The film then takes a carnivalesque turn as 'Usman and his sidekicks try their hand at popular forms of entertainment. The film ends with a body-double plot as 'Usman is mistaken for the crime boss of the Corporation for the Transport of Capital. The subversive potential of *The Neighborhood Watchman* lies in its Bakhtinian, carnivalesque inversions of power and authority.

In *The Neighborhood Watchman*, the police serve as the figures of authority, charged with protecting the populace. But over the course of the film, 'Usman's actions erode this authority. At the beginning of the film, when birds steal food from 'Usman's tray, he humorously tries to report the "theft" to the police. But the officer he contacts berates 'Usman and tosses him out of the station for making a mockery of justice.

'Usman's employment as a night watchman—the title role of the film—is the result of a double case of mistaken identity: he is first given someone else's job, then sent on assignment under another's name. 'Usman's nagging and abusive wife, Umm Ibrahim (Zakiya Ibrahim), reports him to the police commissioner, accusing him of negligence. 'Usman is hauled into the station. 'Usman does not know the reason for the summons, and concludes he must be under investigation for stealing meat from his former employer. While he is awaiting his fate, 'Usman bends the ear of Ba'za'(Ahmad al-Haddad), who has come seeking employment as a night watchman.[53] Ba'za' has handed over his letter of introduction and is waiting to be interviewed. In the first mix-up, 'Usman is invited into the police chief's office and is offered the job, while Ba'za' is called into the assistant's office and given a stern warning. When Ba'za' emerges, confused, his wife intercedes, and the police chief eventually offers him a job, too.

The second mix-up occurs after 'Usman and Ba'za' show up together for training as night watchmen. 'Usman and Ba'za' are called in for a medical exam. The doctor's assistant inquires about their identity and seems confused when their names do not correspond to the names on his sheet: Muhammad 'Issa and 'Ali Abu Zayd. When the assistant steps out, 'Usman and Ba'za' poke around the exam room. Ignoring the poison sign on the medicine cabinet, they sniff an open bottle and then steal fistfuls of something that looks like candy. When the assistant returns, their mouths are full and they can only grunt when he inquires again about their identity. Thinking they are Muhammad 'Issa and 'Ali Abu Zayd, he dismisses them for assignment.

'Usman's masquerade as a guard causes a breakdown of the public trust when a crime occurs on his watch. 'Usman and Ba'za' are stationed in the vicinity of a store owned by 'Azuz (Hasan Salih), a *shami* (Levantine Arab) merchant. The thieves, members of the Corporation for the Transport of Capital, implement a diversionary tactic. A female member of their organization, dressed in traditional attire, approaches 'Usman and Ba'za' in distress. She eventually manages to convey that her husband has disappeared and implores them to help her locate him. While they attend to the distressed woman, the thieves are left free to rob 'Azuz's store without arousing suspicion.

At precisely this juncture, when 'Usman's masquerade as a watchman is poised to erode the authority of the police, the film takes an explicitly carnivalesque turn. The film does not depict the thieves at work, nor does it show the efforts of 'Usman and Ba'za' to assist the woman in distress. Instead, the scene cuts to a second encounter, disrupting the narrative flow between depiction of the watchmen's ineptitude and their dismissal from their jobs. This carnivalesque scene is inserted without context, and without any clear motivation within the diegesis.

A clock strikes two; then the scene fades to a doorway from which masquerading revelers are slowly—and noisily—emerging. Two tall figures in full head masks appear (fig. 12). Meanwhile, 'Usman and Ba'za' cower on a bench, trying to convince one another that they are not afraid of the dark. The costumed revelers spot the anxious guards and decide to give them a fright. Standing partially in shadow, the pranksters remove their masks. As their heads are obscured by black cloth, from the perspective of the frightened guards it looks like the figures have removed their heads. Ba'za' exhorts 'Usman to "be a man." Unconvincingly bragging of his own bravery, Ba'za' is rendered speechless by the approaching headless apparitions. The revelers then silently trade "heads" and then rest them on a bench. As the frightened guards grasp on to one another and shuffle away, the camera zooms in on two wet spots on the bench and the visible urine stains on their backsides.

Mizrahi's comedies do not shy away from lowbrow antics. Scatological humor sold tickets (and still does). 'Ali Abu Shadi specifically cites Mizrahi's willingness to include such scenes as evidence that Mizrahi was a commercial filmmaker who produced entertainment devoid of social value.[54] However, by contrast, I read this scene as an articulation of the destabilizing potential of the carnivalesque. Mikhail Bakhtin asserts that "downward movement is inherent in all forms of popular festive merriment." "The mighty thrust downward" of the carnivalesque draws our attention to "the material bodily lower stratum."[55] Bakhtin writes: "Down, inside

FIGURE 12. Revelers leave a costume ball. Screenshot from *The Neighborhood Watchman* (Togo Mizrahi, 1936).

out, vice versa, upside down, such is the direction of all of these movements. All of them thrust down, turn over, push headfirst, transfer top to bottom and bottom to top, both in the literal sense of space and in the metaphorical meaning of the image."[56] The conclusion of the masquerade scene may cross the boundaries of good taste. But, following Bakhtin, we can read this elevation of the vulgar and debasement of the cinema as an embrace of the subversiveness of carnivalesque farce.

The prank is also transformed into a self-referential joke when it is revealed that one of the masked revelers is Togo Mizrahi himself. The pranksters briefly remove their masks in the street, and their discussion about spooking the guards takes place with their faces exposed. Thus, Togo Mizrahi's cameo in this scene in particular—his identity revealed by removing a mask—indexes the Levantine idiom of masquerade and the subversive threat posed by Levantine performativity of identity.

The prank scene also functions as a narrative hinge; up until this point, the Egyptian Ba'za' was 'Usman's sidekick, but following the theft, 'Usman's fate instead gets tied up with that of the robbed *shami* shop owner, 'Azuz. After the theft, 'Azuz and his Egyptian wife (Zuzu Labib), a singer, lose their apartment. 'Usman's wife also kicks him out after he loses his job. Together, the Nubian former watchman, the *shami* former shop owner, and the Egyptian singer find two rooms in a shared

FIGURE 13. 'Azuz (Hasan Salih, left) and 'Usman ('Ali al-Kassar, center) work as magician's assistants. Screenshot from *The Neighborhood Watchman* (Togo Mizrahi, 1936).

hovel. This way, too, the prank scene signals the transgressive intersection of the carnivalesque and the Levantine.

The carnivalesque atmosphere persists as 'Usman and 'Azuz seek employment. 'Azuz's wife returns to the stage to help support her family. A magician performing in the same variety show hires 'Azuz and 'Usman as his assistants (fig. 13). 'Usman appears onstage in a clownish pointed hat and an oversized fake moustache. Although 'Usman tries to play it straight, the audience laughs and jeers at his antics. Ever the fool, 'Usman bungles the first trick by unwittingly revealing the magician's secret to the audience. 'Usman and 'Azuz are then summarily dismissed. Meanwhile, Ba'za' tries his luck performing in the streets with a dancing monkey. These carnivalesque performances, while not themselves subversive, index the subversive potential of the performance of Levantine identities elsewhere in the film, including the film's concluding episode, which involves inverted identities.

Eventually, 'Usman and 'Azuz are drawn into a con by the same band of thieves who had robbed the shop. A representative of the Corporation for the Transport of Capital offers 'Usman and 'Azuz a job. They share the information with their struggling friend Ba'za'. The three men are provided with large banknotes, and asked to fan out over the city to make change. The innocent job seekers do not

FIGURE 14. 'Ali al-Kassar in his double role as the crime boss. Screenshot from *The Neighborhood Watchman* (Togo Mizrahi, 1936).

comprehend that they are helping to circulate counterfeit bills printed by the gangsters. They are unwitting agents of exchange.

This false currency exchange is then mirrored in the final act of mistaken identity. It turns out that 'Usman resembles the crime boss (also played by al-Kassar; fig. 14). When the members of the Corporation for the Transport of Capital see 'Usman, they take him for their ruthless leader, treating him with respect and deference. Strange women vie for 'Usman's attention, thinking he is the crime boss. The plot of mistaken identity leads to a series of humorous interactions and mistaken romantic liaisons before it dawns on 'Usman that they think he is someone else.

Reading people's reactions, 'Usman comes to realize his resemblance to the boss. He also figures out that the money they were asked to change is counterfeit. He calls the police chief from the thieves' lair and reports the crime. When the police eventually arrive at the scene, the crime boss assumes 'Usman's identity to elude capture. 'Usman's wife, Umm Ibrahim, arrives, but she cannot initially distinguish between the two men: she mistakenly unleashes her wrath on the crime boss instead of her husband (fig. 15).

Umm Ibrahim devises a plan to reveal the men's true identity. She demands a moment in private with each man. She then positively identifies her husband.

FIGURE 15. Umm Ibrahim (Zakiya Ibrahim, center) cannot distinguish between the crime boss and her husband, 'Usman ('Ali al-Kassar, left). Screenshot from *The Neighborhood Watchman* (Togo Mizrahi, 1936).

The crime boss is apprehended. 'Usman and Umm Ibrahim are reconciled. And, thanks to his role in assisting the arrest, 'Usman is reinstated in his former job as a night watchman.

The ethical behavior (and cunning) of the Levantine characters working together thwarts lawlessness. In *The Neighborhood Watchman*, disruptions presented by the Levantine idiom are unmasked as harmless—mere pranks or apparitions that may seem threatening but pose no real danger. The film instead vaunts the power of coexistence, of Levantine ethics, to combat crime that threatens the livelihoods of hardworking Alexandrians of all classes and backgrounds.

CODA: LEVANTINE MASQUERADE AND SUBVERSIVE SEXUALITY

Togo Mizrahi was not the only filmmaker producing Levantine films in Egypt. Nor are *The Two Delegates* and *The Neighborhood Watchman* the only films produced in 1930s Egypt that explore the subversive potential of Levantine masquerade through the unmasking of criminal activity. Take, for example, in the 1936 film *Zawja bi-l-niyaba* (*Wife by Proxy*, Ahmad Galal), in which a violent crime sets

FIGURE 16. Nahid (Assia Dagher) watches Amina (also Assia Dagher) put on jewelry. Screenshot from *Wife by Proxy* (Ahmad Galal, 1936).

into motion an extended masquerade. In *Wife by Proxy*, Nahid (Assia Dagher), a Lebanese country girl fleeing an arranged marriage, stows away on an Alexandria-bound passenger ship anchored in Beirut's harbor. The wealthy Egyptian Amina Hanim (also Assia Dagher) is returning home from a vacation in Istanbul. Nahid and Amina, both played by Assia Dagher, of course resemble one another (fig. 16). A Jewish jewel merchant named Cohen shows his wares to Amina Hanim and permits her to take some pieces back to her cabin to try on. Meanwhile, skirting away from a suspicious crew member, the stowaway, Nahid, takes refuge in Amina's cabin. There, she witnesses Amina's murder at the hands of a jewel thief. Recognizing her resemblance to the deceased, Nahid does the only sensible thing under the circumstances: she dons Amira's gown and strides into the ballroom, assuming her identity. On the boat, Nahid confronts the thief and insists that he return the jewels to Cohen. After disembarking, the thief, who has recognized Nahid, tries to blackmail her with threats to reveal her true identity. Nahid eventually metes out justice, shooting the jewel thief just as he had shot Amina.

Wife by Proxy was a production of Assia Dagher's company Lotus Films. Dagher, born in Lebanon to a Maronite Christian family, moved to Cairo in the

1920s in pursuit of an acting career. Dagher was a pioneer of the Egyptian film industry and remained an important film producer through the 1960s. Like her many other successful films of the 1930s, *Wife by Proxy* was a family affair. The film featured Dagher's niece Mary Queeny and Mary's husband, Ahmad Galal, who also directed the film.

The Levantine masquerade in *Wife by Proxy* integrates the *shami* immigrant into both an Egyptian body and the Egyptian body politic. The poor Lebanese migrant fleeing from an arranged marriage finds herself assuming the identity of a wealthy, married Egyptian woman. Nahid continues the masquerade with Amina's husband, providing the opportunity for a series of comic deferrals of the couple's amorous reunion. When all is revealed, Amina's husband decides to stay together with his deceased wife's double, and the couple continue the masquerade of marriage together. Like *The Two Delegates* and *The Neighborhood Watchman*, this film explores both the subversiveness and crime-fighting power of fluid Levantine identities. But *Wife by Proxy* adds another twist—sexualities that disrupt the conventions of marriage. In the next chapter, I explore at greater length subversive sexualities in two of Togo Mizrahi's Levantine bedroom farces: *Doctor Farahat* and *Mistreated by Affluence.*

4

Queering the Levantine

IN BED TOGETHER

In the opening shot of Togo Mizrahi's 1937 film *Al-'Izz bahdala* (*Mistreated by Affluence*), the camera pans across the rooftops of a popular district of Alexandria. The image cuts to chickens feeding on one of the rooftops, then fades to the interior of the adjacent one-room apartment. An alarm clock rings, waking Chalom (Leon Angel), a Jewish seller of lottery tickets. He quiets the alarm, leans over, and wakens his bedmate, 'Abdu (Ahmad al-Haddad), a Muslim butcher's assistant (fig. 17).

This image of a Jew and a Muslim in bed together functions as a point of departure for this chapter's analysis of the construction of coexistence in Togo Mizrahi's films produced in his studio in Alexandria. I approach the phrase "in bed together" as not just a metaphor of coexistence, but as a key to unlocking Mizrahi's projection of sameness and difference, self and other, in 1930s Alexandria.

From the outset I should note that the sight of these two impoverished characters sharing a bed need not—and indeed should not—be understood as signaling sexual desire or a romantic affiliation between them. They share a bed because they are poor, not because they are homosexual. However, in this chapter I argue that Togo Mizrahi's Alexandria comedies do queer gender identity in a variety of ways, and that we can't dismiss out of hand the gender and sexuality implications of this opening scene. My contention here is not unlike that made by Steven Cohan about the 1940s Bob Hope and Bing Crosby "*Road to*" movies. Cohan asserts that "the comedic framework of the series plays upon intimations of homoeroticism, and . . . the queer shading of their buddy relation must be taken into account."[1]

In this chapter, I argue that Togo Mizrahi's films *Al-Duktur Farhat* (*Doctor Farahat*, 1935) and *Mistreated by Affluence* queer both gender and ethnoreligious identities. *Doctor Farahat* overtly troubles assumptions about gender and sexuality. *Mistreated by Affluence* foregrounds coexistence. By reading these films together,

FIGURE 17. Chalom (Leon Angel, left) and ʿAbdu (Ahmad al-Haddad) wake up in bed together. Screenshot from *Mistreated by Affluence* (Togo Mizrahi, 1937).

I aim to demonstrate how these two articulations of the performativity of identity—gender and the Levantine—inform one another in Mizrahi's work.

QUEERNESS AND THE LEVANTINE

My characterization of the performativity of identities—Levantine on the one hand, and gender and sexuality on the other—is indebted to Judith Butler's influential work *Gender Trouble*.[2] Since her debunking of the myth of compulsory heterosexuality and stable categories of gender, the epistemological questions about identity that Butler raises burst open interrogation of other forms of identity formation. Richard Thompson Ford, for example, models his own critique of racial identity politics on Butler's critique of gender: "Queer theory's anti-identitarianism is the key to its portability. . . . The queer critique of (nominally) gay identity politics would seem to apply to identity politics in general."[3] In labeling Mizrahi's Levantine film idiom "queer," I am referring both to the particularities of the performativity of gender and sexuality, and to its broader destabilizing potential, as explored by Ford, for "identity politics in general."[4]

In the introduction to *Outtakes*, a volume of essays on queer theory and film, Ellis Hanson takes a similarly broad view of the term's significance. He defines the term "queer" as

a rejection of the compulsory heterosexual code of masculine men desiring feminine women, and it declares that the vast range of stigmatized sexualities and gender identifications, far from being marginal, are central to the construction of modern subjectivity; but it is also, as Michael Warner has pointed out, a resistance to normalization as conceived more generally as a sort of divide-and-conquer mentality by which cultural difference—racial, ethnic, sexual, socioeconomic—is pathologized and atomized as disparate forms of deviance.[5]

Hanson acknowledges the broad significance of the term "queer" in destabilizing received categories including but not limited to gender and sexuality. In the second half of the quote, he asserts the power of queer theory to expose the dynamics of other forms of social marginalization.

Mizrahi's Alexandrian bedroom farces destabilize prevailing gender categories in 1930s Egypt. The films poke fun at emerging middle-class assumptions about modernity and the nation. Wilson Jacob has mapped what he terms "effendi masculinity"—a subject position reflecting middle-class aspirations toward and performance of modernity that began emerging in the last decades of the nineteenth century. This "effendi masculinity" was commonly recognizable by the 1930s. Jacob reads as performance these new forms of gendered, national subjectivity that emerged in British colonial Egypt.[6]

Mizrahi's 1930s comedies feature lower-class characters ill at ease with middle-class expectations. The bumbling characters portrayed by Chalom, 'Ali al-Kassar, and Fawzi al-Gazayirli simultaneously confront modernity and emerging gender norms to which they do not conform. Class mobility is linked in these films with the performance of normativized gender expectations that look a lot like the "effendi masculinity" Jacob identifies. The lens provided by Jacob permits us to see the ways in which, by extension, Mizrahi's films reflect upon and subtly critique emerging normativizing discourses and Egyptian articulations of modernity.[7]

According to Israel Gershoni and James Jankowski, the new *effendiyya* were also the driving force behind a shift in the conception of the nation that Egypt underwent in the 1930s—a shift that ran counter to Mizrahi's Levantine construction of identity and threatened the coexistence of Jews and Muslims portrayed in his films. As articulations of a queer Levantine urban localism, Mizrahi's farces—including *Doctor Farahat* and *Mistreated by Affluence*—offer an alternative to parochial, homosocial, and heteronormative national imaginaries.[8]

SUITORS IN SWIMSUITS: *DOCTOR FARAHAT* (1935)

Like Mizrahi's other films from this era, *Doctor Farahat* is fundamentally a comedy of assumed identity. Hilmy, a successful surgeon who has been living in England for fifteen years, returns to his native Alexandria to get married. In addition to his wealth, he is considered a minor celebrity for his medical discoveries. A match has been arranged to Nona (Amina Muhammad), a woman he has not yet met. Concerned that she is a gold digger, he seeks an opportunity to court her without her knowing his identity. So he arranges to meet her twice, once in disguise as the stuffy, bearded and bespectacled Doctor Hilmy (fig. 18), and once looking and acting naturally, but under the assumed name Mustafa.

FIGURE 18. Hilmy in disguise as Doctor Hilmy. Screenshot from *Doctor Farahat* (Togo Mizrahi, 1935).

To add to the confusion, upon Hilmy's arrival, he dodges reporters by ask-ing an employee of the hotel, Farahat (Fawzi al-Gazayirli), to assume his identity. The impoverished and uneducated Farahat has been employed as a translator by the hotel under false (and humorous) pretenses. Nevertheless, the ruse succeeds: the reporters snap Farahat's picture, convinced they have taken the photo of Hilmy, setting in motion this additional plotline of mistaken identity.

Nona's family, eager to meet the young suitor, sends for Hilmy but instead gets his geriatric pretender, Farahat. As the title suggests, it is Farahat's humorous mis-adventures as "Dr. Hilmy" that dominate the plot. Farahat and his sidekick 'Ali (Ahmad al-Haddad), in the role of the doctor's secretary, pay a visit to Nona's house. Nona and her friend Tahiya (Tahiya Carioca) privately mock the suitor, and set out to humiliate him in the hopes of calling off the engagement.

It is within this multilayered charade of mistaken identity that one encounters gender play. In what follows, I unpack two articulations of the queering of gender identity in *Doctor Farahat*. First, I examine instances when same-sex pairs share the same bed. Then I discuss moments in the film that individually and collectively can be read as highlighting a performative construction of gender identity.

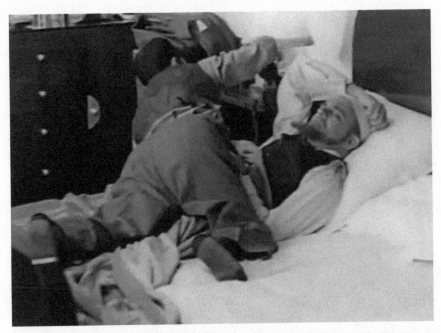

FIGURE 19. 'Ali (Ahmad al-Haddad) climbs over Farahat (Fawzi al-Gazayirli) to answer the telephone. Screenshot from *Doctor Farahat* (Togo Mizrahi, 1935).

Much of the plot of *Doctor Farahat* revolves around Nona's efforts to exhaust "Dr. Hilmy" (Farahat) and drive him away. The women first keep the men walking until midnight along the Corniche, the promenade along the seawall over-looking the Mediterranean; then Nona calls at five o'clock the following morning to invite them for a swim. Nona has also arranged for notable doctors to attend a lecture later the same morning to be given by "Dr. Hilmy," and in the afternoon she entices "Dr. Hilmy" and 'Ali to join her for a party on a boat that lasts until late in the evening.

On four occasions, during the brief intervals between these engagements, Fara-hat and 'Ali flop onto the plush double bed in their shared hotel room. These comic scenes are rife with sight gags and tame verbal innuendo. On the first occasion, 'Ali removes his jacket on Farahat's side of the bed and starts to climb over Farahat. Farahat exclaims, "Hey, brother, why not enter from the door of your house?" 'Ali responds, "But it's a long way from here. Let me pass through your roof." The root of the verb *kharama*, here used in its form that signifies "pass through" or "take a shortcut," can also signify "pierce"—adding to the suggestive double entendre of the exchange. Later in the scene, when the phone rings, 'Ali, in his role as the esteemed doctor's secretary, again climbs over Farahat, this time to answer the call (fig. 19).

FIGURE 20. Farahat (Fawzi al-Gazayirli) and Umm Ahmad (Ihsan al-Gazayirli) in bed. Screenshot from *Doctor Farahat* (Togo Mizrahi, 1935).

Although the men remain fully clothed, physical contact between them in bed—like the sight of 'Ali climbing over Farahat—elicits laughs.[9] By contrast with this scene, while the opening sequence of *Mistreated by Affluence* leaves no question that we are viewing a comedy, the *fact* that the two men share a bed is not played for laughs. Farahat and 'Ali would, like their counterparts in that film, think nothing of sharing a bed with a male friend in their own cramped domestic quarters. The luxurious bed in the hotel is large and inviting, and despite the presence of a couch in the suite, neither character seems to question that they would share the bed. Farahat objects to the way 'Ali enters the bed, but not to his presence.

The scenes with Farahat and 'Ali confirm heteronormative sexuality within homosocial Egyptian norms. Any ambiguity of these bedroom scenes is resolved in the final iteration of this repeating pattern (fig. 20). Throughout the film, Umm Ahmad (Ihsan al-Gazayirli), Farahat's wife, chases after him. After failing in her attempt to follow him to the party on the boat, she lies in wait. After the party, Farahat falls drunk into bed and starts to brag about kissing Nona. Umm Ahmad indignantly reveals herself and demands an explanation. We are restored to the standard heteronormative extramarital love triangle of the bedroom farce.[10]

Just prior to the first scene of Farahat and 'Ali in bed together, Nona and Tahiya are also shown sharing a bed. After the long walk on the Corniche, Nona sits on the bed in a negligee, stretches, proclaims that she is tired, and then lies down

FIGURE 21. Nona (Amina Muhammad, left) and Tahiya (Tahiya Carioca) in bed. Screenshot from *Doctor Farahat* (Togo Mizrahi, 1935).

under the covers. Tahiya, sitting on the edge of the bed undressing, concurs, adding, "If you think you're tired, what about them?" This scene reads as a (male) voyeuristic view into the women's boudoir.

Later, at the conclusion of the party scene, Nona and Hilmy, as "Mustafa," embrace in the moonlight. The scene cuts abruptly to Nona's bedroom—the second scene showing the women in bed together. In this short scene, Nona lies awake repeating Mustafa's proclamation of love to her, while Tahiya drifts off to sleep beside her (fig. 21). The film then cuts to Umm Ahmad hiding under the covers awaiting Farahat's return from the party. As with the scene between Farahat and Umm Ahmad that follows, Nona's wakeful reflection appears to restore heteronormative desire. But Nona muses on Mustafa's words—"I love you, Nona"—rather than giving voice to her own emotions. Unlike the conclusion of the scene between Farahat and Umm Ahmad, the self-reflexivity of Nona's utterance simultaneously troubles the predominant narrative axis of heterosexual desire that it appears to assert. The ambivalence of Nona's assertion also fails to completely displace the titillating queerness of two scantily clad women in bed together.

As my reading of these bedroom scenes implies, Nona's role as an object of desire and as a desiring subject bears closer examination. Nona believes she has three male suitors in the film: Farahat, in the guise of "Dr. Hilmy"; Hilmy acting

the part of the stuffy Doctor Hilmy; and Mustafa, who is really Hilmy acting naturally but using a pseudonym. Male desire is focalized through the main character, Farahat. Viewers recognize that Farahat is a buffoon. His age and his coarse,
uneducated, lower-class manner make him appear an inappropriate suitor for
the wealthy, modern, Westernized Nona. We also know that Farahat is already
married.[11] While he inadvertently falls into the role of suitor, he persists in the
charade for the promise of access to Nona's body. Each time Farahat considers
walking away, Nona draws him back in, first by feigning affection and then, after
the appearance of Mustafa, by fomenting jealousy.

Nona embraces her performance of femininity to deceive Farahat. Take, for
example, the early-morning swim. In the cabana with 'Ali, Farahat decides that it
is too cold to swim. He steps outside to inform Nona. Borrowing a visual idiom
already established by Hollywood cinema, the camera reproduces Farahat's
desirous gaze of Nona's body by tilting from toe to head. The sight of Nona in her
bathing costume changes Farahat's mind.

But the bathing scene that follows troubles these very same gendered assumptions about agency and desire. As she is changing into her bathing suit, an exasperated Nona proclaims that perhaps the women should "drown [the men] and be
done with them." Tahiya, it appears, takes Nona's suggestion seriously. A lengthy
silent montage (accompanied by upbeat music) intercuts Tahiya wrestling with
'Ali, and Nona attempting to coax Farahat into the water. As the scene progresses,
Tahiya's malicious intent becomes more apparent with each subsequent dunking. What is striking about this scene is its violence—violence perpetrated by the
female characters.[12] Tahiya's physical contact with 'Ali in the water is simultaneously ludic and menacing, playful dunking that verges on attempted drowning. In
the final image of the scene, Nona is shown dragging Farahat screaming into the
cold water. This is torture, not play. Thanatos, not Eros.

In the swimming scene the male characters are emasculated by an aggressive,
predatory, violent femininity. And over the course of the film, Nona's cruel tricks
become increasingly more emasculating. The final indignity involves Nona pilot-
ing a small plane with Farahat as a passenger. Nona's aerial acrobatics frighten
Farahat, causing him first to wet his pants and then pass out. As in *The Neighborhood Watchman* (discussed in chap. 3), the use of scatological humor suggests
inversion of power. Everything is topsy-turvy. In the airplane scene in *Dr. Farahat*,
the act of flying upside down catalyzes the final (corrective) inversion of high and
low. It is worth recalling that this violence and cruelty is committed in the service
of repelling a prospective suitor, deferring marriage.

Tahiya encourages Nona in her sadistic yo-yo of attraction and repulsion
toward Farahat. Her motives begin to emerge in the cabana as the two women
change into their swim suits. As Nona begins to unbutton her shirt, Tahiya casts
her own desirous gaze at her friend's body (fig. 22). Farahat, it seems, is not the
only one to leer at Nona's body. Not only is Nona the object of the male gaze within

FIGURE 22. Tahiya (Tahiya Carioca) watches Nona (Amina Muhammad) undress. Screenshot from *Doctor Farahat* (Togo Mizrahi, 1935).

the film (and for that matter, the object of the masculine gaze of the audience); she is also the object of a desirous female gaze.[13] Tahiya's desire for Nona poses a complication for (but not a replacement of) the heteronormative reading of the women's bedroom scenes.

Nona appears oblivious to Tahiya's affections. And, as the plots of mistaken identity unravel, we encounter a final (but not complete) restoration of heteronormativity. After Farahat passes out on the plane, the real Dr. Hilmy revives him. Hilmy and Farahat reveal their true identities. Hilmy requests Nona's hand in marriage from her puzzled parents. Nona's parents agree, although they admit they don't understand what has happened. When Tahiya bows out, she, too, expresses her confusion. After dodging marriage for the whole film, Nona agrees to wed. Nona and Hilmy embrace, as do the happily reunited Farahat and Umm Ahmad. Tahiya, however, is not paired off at the end of the film, despite the presence of a suitable male mate—a friend of Hilmy's who appears in several scenes. Tahiya's designs on Nona are thwarted; however, her same-sex desire is not normativized.

Though I grant that even for a farce this film narrates an unusually convoluted plot, it is unusual for the characters in Mizrahi's films to remain confused once all has been revealed. The boundaries of identity—and gender—have been troubled.

FIGURE 23. Nona (Amina Muhammad) and Hilmy (Togo Mizrahi credited as ʿAbd al-ʿAziz al-Mashriqi). Screenshot from *Doctor Farahat* (Togo Mizrahi, 1935).

The characters' confusion at the end of the film reflects the residue of the disturbances wrought by masquerade. We may end up with two male–female pairs, but the film does not conclusively or universally restore heteronormativity.

So far, I have focused my attention on masquerade as an articulation of gender instability in *Doctor Farahat*. I would also like to point to the way this film also marks fluidity of identity as Levantine. Hilmy first appears on-screen in a disguise, insisting on embracing the fluid possibilities afforded by Levantine subjectivity. He counts on names as a signifier of an ethnoreligious affiliation just as he relies upon the physical (and linguistic) undifferentiability of Levantines.

Hilmy makes his first appearance as "Dr. Hilmy" as he enters the hotel. In the first words he utters, "Dr. Hilmy" confirms with his secretary, ʿAli, that a room has been booked. He continues: "Under what name?"

"'Doctor Hilmy,'" replies ʿAli.
"You idiot," exclaims "Dr. Hilmy," "Didn't we agree that you shouldn't register under the name 'Doctor Hilmy'?"
"What should I have written?" retorts ʿAli.
"Write any name you want. Write 'Boutros.' Write 'Mikhaʾil.'"

In this originary moment—this masquerade that sets into motion the multiple layers of role play in the film—lies the (nominally) Muslim character's desire to hide behind a Christian name.

There is yet another layer to this Levantine passing. The credits identify the actor playing Hilmy as 'Abd al-'Aziz al-Mashriqi. This is a pseudonym. The actor playing Hilmy is none other than Togo Mizrahi (fig. 23). In other words, a Jewish actor performing under a pseudonym plays a Muslim character who seeks cover under a Christian name. Like in the films discussed in the previous chapter, Hilmy's masquerade represents the subversive potential of the Levantine.

A PARTING KISS: *MISTREATED BY AFFLUENCE* (1937)

In *Doctor Farahat* the Levantine idiom is articulated primarily through gender play as masquerade, with limited, but notable, articulations of an ethics of coexistence. *Mistreated by Affluence* inverts this formula, emphasizing coexistence over masquerade. As noted earlier, at the start of *Mistreated by Affluence*, the protagonists, Chalom and 'Abdu, live together in a cramped room on the roof of an apartment building.[14] The families of their respective fiancées, Esther (Esther Angel, credited as 'Adalat) and Amina (Amina Fardus), reside side by side in modest middle-class apartments on the floor below. Although the families sleep in their separate quarters, they are frequently shown socializing in one another's apartments. This construction of domestic space, and the characters' actual or virtual cohabitation, serve as a microcosm for coexistence in the society at large.

Mistreated by Affluence is not *about* coexistence, though. The film neither interrogates nor problematizes difference. Nor does *Mistreated by Affluence* rely upon ethnoreligious stereotypes as a source of comedy.[15] The narrative takes for granted that Jews and Muslims could be long-standing friends and neighbors in 1930s Egypt. This domiciled, or perhaps domesticated, coexistence serves as the solid foundation against which the film's contrived, farcical plot unfurls. Uncertainty lies beyond the confines of the domestic space and the quarter.

Buffeted along by chance, Chalom and 'Abdu bumble into (comical) situations beyond their control. 'Abdu is mistrusted, berated, and beaten by Hasan, the butcher for whom he works. But when Hasan dies, he bequeaths the shop to his assistant. 'Abdu shares his newfound wealth with Chalom, enabling his friend to open a small shop from which to sell lottery tickets and exchange currency. The money also enables the men to get married after lengthy engagements. Following the weddings, Chalom purchases a bundle of paper on behalf of his friend to use for wrapping meat. He discovers that what he thought was scrap paper is instead a bundle of stock certificates worth over 650,000 Egyptian pounds. Chalom insists on splitting the newfound wealth evenly with 'Abdu. They decide to purchase a bank, and settle into neighboring villas with their wives and in-laws. But money sows discord, and the friends have an altercation. In the end, chance again prevails: the bank fails, and Chalom and 'Abdu lose their wealth. Chalom and 'Abdu reconcile, and they rejoice along with their families in the return to their homely coexistence.

The sharing of food and a shared food culture underpin the film's construction of coexistence between Jews and Muslims. The representation of meals as an example of commensality, according to Rebecca Bryant, points to their exceptionality, and to the preexistence of notions of difference overcome by the shared practice.[16] In *Mistreated by Affluence*, the families are regularly depicted eating together in a series of scenes that intertwine the film's Levantine ethics and aesthetics.

As described in chapter 1, near the beginning of *Mistreated by Affluence*, the two families prepare a picnic for Shamm al-nasim—the popular spring festival that is celebrated by Egyptians of all religious affiliations. The day of the festival is heralded by the lively montage of documentary footage of Alexandria. Following the montage, the scene cuts to a long shot in which we see the Jewish and Muslim families crowded around covered crates, picnicking together in front of a bank of cabanas.

The picnic scene is shot to give the impression of a busy beach during a popular festival. The wide-angle establishing shot of the group picnic offers an inclusive vision of cosmopolitan Alexandria, like the montage that precedes it. Several figures from a range of classes cross between the seated picnickers and the camera: a male bather; a police officer; a woman in bourgeois, Western attire holding a parasol; a fisherman carrying his gear. Two barefoot children sit cross-legged in the foreground, eating, and in the background another man in a bathing suit engages in calisthenics. Even as the camera zooms in to a tighter group shot of the picnic, the scene retains its inclusiveness as the camera pans to show all eight characters eating and conversing.

This vision of coexistence is disrupted only when Vittoria (Vittoria Farhi) verbally abuses Chalom, her future son-in-law. The continuous take is broken by a cut to a close-up of Chalom asking about a dish not included in the feast. Vittoria berates him for having spoiled the dish by clumsily knocking it over. Chalom, chastened, gathers up loaves of bread, excuses himself, and prepares to retreat, inviting Esther to join him. But even in this moment of familial discord, a Levantine aesthetic persists. The camera pans from Chalom to Vittoria and back. Rather than shooting the argument in a shot-reverse-shot sequence of the two characters, the interaction is shot panning from one character to the other, with other members of the group in view. This continuous, inclusive camerawork mirrors the content of this scene, in which Jews and Muslims break bread together in celebration of a shared festival.[17]

Vittoria's condemnation of Chalom turns to praise after the families relocate to posh estates. The Jewish and Muslim families remain neighbors, residing in adjacent villas. The families continue to gather in their new homes and take meals together. But the pleasures of eating are denied to them just as they can finally afford expensive delicacies. In a comic subplot, two nurses, pretending to be doctors, insinuate themselves into the families. They diagnose imaginary diseases so they can be paid for providing ongoing care. In the meantime, they sidle up to

FIGURE 24. Chalom (Leon Angel, left) and 'Abdu (Ahmad al-Haddad), in their roles as bank executives, dress as members of the *effendiyya*. Pressbook for *Mistreated by Affluence* (Togo Mizrahi, 1937). Courtesy of the Rare Books and Special Collections Library, The American University in Cairo.

the young brides, hoping to woo them away from their husbands. Their "medical advice" consists primarily of manipulating access to food.

In one scene, when Chalom and 'Abdu are delayed at the bank, the families begin dining in their absence under the doctors' vigilant eyes. The older generation is ordered to abstain from anything but milk and boiled vegetables. The young women, by contrast, are plied with wine and rich foods. Like the picnic, the scene opens with a long establishing shot showing the families gathered around a formal dining table. A servant enters carrying food to the table. But the camerawork then mirrors the rupture between this dining experience and the former communal preparation and consumption of food: the dining-room scene is constructed with a discontinuous series of two-shots rather than the inclusive zoom and pan of the picnic scene.

In *Mistreated by Affluence* the masquerade is one of passing, involving Chalom and 'Abdu's (failed) efforts to act like members of the elite following their chance windfall (fig. 24). Their behavior is a comic exaggeration of the boorishness and ostentation of the nouveau riche. When they host a cocktail party for business associates, Chalom and 'Abdu wear engraved name badges on their lapels listing their titles. A bank manager charged with introducing the guests to the receiving line disdainfully flicks Chalom's pin and asks in a scornful voice, "What are you wearing? What is that? Take that thing off!" Chalom, puzzled, responds, "Why? Shouldn't people know that I am the director of the bank?" Gesturing toward 'Abdu, he adds, "And him too?" The exasperated manager exclaims, "Director of the bank? Take it off! That is something janitors wear!" This misjudgment reflects the myriad missed codes and social cues of their adopted titles and assumed identities.

Chalom and 'Abdu take advantage of their newfound wealth and position of power to chase women. In the dalliance that renders *Mistreated by Affluence* a bedroom farce, Chalom and 'Abdu pursue the affections of a singer, Zuzu (Zuzu Labib), and a dancer, Ruhiya (Ruhiya Fawzi), respectively. In contrast to *Doctor Farahat*, the heterosexual love triangle itself is the site of gender instability in *Mistreated by Affluence*.

Following their introduction at the nightclub where the women perform, Chalom and 'Abdu agree to a date at the women's apartment. Chalom and 'Abdu are cowed by the women's overt sexuality and forwardness. The viewer understands that these "artists [*artistat*]" are to be understood as loose women, if not downright prostitutes.[18] Ruhiya beckons 'Abdu to enter her dressing room as she disrobes behind a shoulder-high barrier. While in this state of undress, she beckons 'Abdu to give her a kiss. Meanwhile, Chalom is instructed to enter the adjoining room, where he finds Zuzu soaking in a tub. Covering his eyes as he approaches, Chalom hands Zuzu a bouquet of flowers. He crouches next to the tub and presents her with a bracelet, which he accidentally drops in the water. He pushes up his sleeve and reaches into the tub. Realizing what he has done, he runs out of the room, only to find that 'Abdu has also retreated. Chalom is rendered speechless, and resorts to gesturing and whistling to describe his interaction with Zuzu.[19] The women's overt expression of sexual desire and, as in *Doctor Farahat*, predatory female sexuality poses an affront to the men's masculinity.

Chalom and 'Abdu regroup, and resolve to reassert their masculinity. 'Abdu steels himself to return to Ruhiya, saying: "Listen, Chalom, *we need to be men* [my emphasis]. Ruhiya! I must speak to her. I must tell her that I love her. I must hold her. I must kill her with my kisses. Yes, I must!" Pushing Chalom out of the way, 'Abdu warns, "Watch out!" and marches back toward Ruhiya's door. Thumping his chest, Chalom concurs, "Yes! Men!" He attempts to repeat 'Abdu's rousing speech, but gives up when he can't remember the exact words. Instead, Chalom tips his tarboosh forward, puffs up his chest, and, as he dramatically prepares to march himself toward Zuzu's quarters, says, "Men! I will go! Watch out!"

The men, however, remain passive recipients of the women's affections. When Chalom enters Zuzu's boudoir, she is toweling her thighs, wearing only a bathrobe. She invites a nervous Chalom to kiss her, and he hesitantly responds with a chaste kiss on the top of her head. With further prompting, he kisses her on the cheek. Zuzu finally takes charge, throws herself into Chalom's arms, and passionately embraces him. Likewise, after his second encounter with Ruhiya, a grinning 'Abdu is shown with lipstick marks all over his face—but not on his lips. Although the camera does not follow this encounter, the visible evidence also places him in a passive role.

Zuzu's and Ruhiya's emasculating rhetoric sets into motion a sequence of events that devolve into a fight between Chalom and ʿAbdu as they seek to reassert their masculinity. In the climactic party scene, Chalom and ʿAbdu hide behind a curtain, planning to surprise Zuzu and Ruhiya with bouquets of flowers. Instead, they overhear the women disparaging them. Ruhiya calls ʿAbdu an oaf, but admits she likes the contents of his wallet. Zuzu casts aspersions on Chalom's virility, calling him a grasshopper, and likening his floppy mustache to a shrimp. She concludes with the kicker "That half-pint [nus al-rubʿ da], you call that a man?"

From their hiding place, Chalom and ʿAbdu also overhear the nurses professing their love to Esther and Amina. Impotent to respond to the women's insults on their own, Chalom and ʿAbdu call for their in-laws to intervene. Following a chaotic shouting match, the nurses are escorted out of the party, but the protagonists are still smarting from the insults and spoiling for a fight. When Chalom overhears a guest claiming that he would be nothing without ʿAbdu, it is the last straw. Chalom pours out his wrath upon ʿAbdu, and his friend reciprocates. In the heat of the argument, each claims to have made "a man" out of the other. Destabilized gender identity threatens to upset the narrative of coexistence. Esther's and Amina's families appeal to Chalom and ʿAbdu to reconcile, urging the men not to let their fight undermine a thirty-year friendship between the families.

The emasculation of the bourgeois lifestyle and the threats it poses to coexistence are reversed only after Chalom and ʿAbdu lose their wealth and the characters all return to their old residences. Likewise, at the end of the film, the equal access to communal food—along with the inclusive Levantine aesthetic—is restored. In the penultimate scene, the Jewish and Muslim families once again crowd around a table to share their favorite foods. As with the picnic, this scene comprises a single shot that includes all of the characters in the frame. The closing shot of the film also serves to reassert Chalom's virility. Chalom is shown returning to the street in the old neighborhood, hawking lottery tickets—but this time he is carrying infant twins.

By way of conclusion, I would like return to a brief scene that depicts the intersection of the two idioms of Levantine fluidity I have traced: communal or ethnoreligious identity on one hand; gender and sexuality on the other. On their way to their first encounter with their prospective mistresses, Chalom assuages ʿAbdu's performance anxiety by offering him a tutorial on kissing. Holding up a bouquet of flowers, Chalom advises: "Say to her, 'Take this present.' Say to her also, 'Come here, my love.'"[20] And just like in the movies . . ." Chalom then leans over and plants a kiss on ʿAbdu's lips (fig. 25).

For Mizrahi, it was not sufficient to draw laughs by depicting the two men kissing. The camera cuts to a second angle showing the driver observing the embrace in the rearview mirror and then turning his gaze to the back seat (fig. 26). The presence of a witness, an audience, signals the film's self-awareness of the act as a performance. The narratives of coexistence and the queering of identity evidenced in Mizrahi's films meet with the touch of Chalom and ʿAbdu's lips.

FIGURE 25. Chalom (Leon Angel, left) and ʿAbdu (Ahmad al-Haddad) kiss. Screenshot from *Mistreated by Affluence* (Togo Mizrahi, 1937).

FIGURE 26. A driver watches Chalom (Leon Angel, left) and ʿAbdu (Ahmad al-Haddad) kiss. Screenshot from *Mistreated by Affluence* (Togo Mizrahi, 1937).

CODA: "THE STORY OF A WOMAN WHO WAS TRANSFORMED INTO A MAN"

In early 1938, the same team that produced *Wife by Proxy* (discussed in chap. 3) released another queer Levantine comedy of mistaken identity, *Bint al-basha*

FIGURE 27. Hikmat (Assia Dagher), disguised as a man, sits on a bed beside her love interest, Tawfiq (Ahmad Galal). Screenshot from *The Pasha Director's Daughter* (Ahmad Galal, 1938).

al-mudir (*The Pasha Director's Daughter*, Ahmad Galal).[21] An educated young man who had fallen on hard times is hired as a live-in tutor for a wealthy family in the countryside. When he is seriously injured in a car accident, his sister, Hikmat (Assia Dagher), takes the post in his name. Her dislocation, as well as her journey from woman to man, set the stage for a queer love triangle. As a teaser ad for the film proclaims:

> Who is Hikmat Effendi? Is that shadowy figure wrapped in secrets a man or a woman? By day he is a man who enthralls women, and by night he is a woman who enthralls men. He descended upon the al-Qubrusli estate and spread his enormous charm. Badriya, the pasha's daughter, sees him and falls madly in love with him, and wishes with all her might that she will succeed in marrying him. Tawfiq, the Pasha's son, sees an enchanting woman and falls madly in love with her, and wishes with all his might that he will succeed in marrying her. But Hikmat Effendi is also Mademoiselle Hikmat.[22]

Living as a man, Hikmat is privy to the men's world. But she still seeks the company of women. At a wedding, Hikmat dresses as a woman and joins the celebrations of the bride. Tawfiq (Ahmad Galal) and Hikmat meet, and it's love at first sight. Meanwhile, Badriya (Mary Queeny) falls in love with the tutor—Hikmat in her male guise. Hikmat toggles between these identities until the masquerade inevitably catches up with her. The head of the household gets wind of his daughter's budding romance and betroths her to the tutor. Hikmat prepares to flee.

Like in Mizrahi's films *Doctor Farahat* and *Mistreated by Affluence,* two apparently same-sex characters wind up in bed together. The night before the wedding, Tawfiq pays a late-night visit to Hikmat's room (fig. 27). Tawfiq implores Hikmat to change into pajamas and join him in bed for a late-night heart-to-heart. As the two lie side by side, Tawfiq admits that he is hopelessly in love with the mystery woman. Little does he know that she is lying next to him in bed, disguised as a man. Even as all is revealed in the end and two heteronormative couples wed, *The Pasha Director's Daughter* explores Levantine fluidity of gender identities. Hikmat's physical mobility parallels her gender fluidity. Hikmat's displacement facilitates her masquerade and the ensuing misunderstandings. The next chapter unpacks significance of the trope of mobility in a queer Levantine film of masquerade and coexistence, Togo Mizrahi's *Al-Sa'a 7* (*Seven O'Clock,* 1937).

Journeys of Assumed Identity

Seven O'Clock (1937)

Togo Mizrahi's film *Al-Sa'a 7* (*Seven O'Clock,* 1937) opens with a traveling shot as the credits roll. The camera travels four blocks along Sharif Street, passing through Manshiya Square, the heart of Alexandria's commercial business district. It then takes a right turn on al-Saba' Banat Street, passing the French Gardens. The shot ends as the camera approaches the seawall overlooking the Mediterranean.

In this footage, in addition to the mobility of the camera, the viewer witnesses a city in motion: pedestrians, horse-drawn carriages, cars, a bus, and a tram traverse the city streets. The footage reflects the spontaneity of an actuality: a youthful pass-erby leaps joyfully into the frame, mugging for the camera (fig. 28). Yet the camera manages to capture a cross section of Alexandrian society. Men and women in Western dress walk alongside laborers in galabiyas carrying sacks and rolling large spindles. The camera also records police officers, carriage drivers, construction workers, and a Sufi cleric.

On the right side, as the camera approaches the seawall, we see a monumen-tal structure under construction. The visible semicircular colonnade would soon house a statue of Khedive Isma'il, Egypt's ruler from 1863 to 1879. Isma'il is known as the builder of the Suez Canal and modern Cairo, as well as the architect of Egypt's late-nineteenth-century debt crisis. In 1938, one year after the film was shot, the monument, a gift from Italy, would be ceremonially unveiled by the Ital-ian community of Alexandria. Both the colonnade and the statue were positioned to face the Mediterranean, symbolizing "Egypt turned toward the West."[1]

By contrast to the symbolic positioning of the monument, the visual narrative of the film does not continue in a straight line northward from the port of Alexandria to the northern shore of the Mediterranean. In *Seven O'Clock,* the seawall serves as a barrier. The traveling shot ends. The film cuts to footage shot from a fixed camera positioned at the seawall, pivoting to display—and mimic—the curved coastline of

FIGURE 28. Manshiyya Square, Alexandria. Screenshot from *Seven O'Clock* (Togo Mizrahi, 1937).

Alexandria's eastern harbor. At the end of the shot, the camera has turned around, orienting itself inward toward Egypt, *ad Aegyptum*. In the diegesis, too, circular urban trajectories give way to a journey along a linear axis. From its position on the Alexandria seaside promenade, the camera points southward, establishing the trajectory of the narrative.

Seven O'Clock was the first of three Egyptian comedies to appear in close succession that explore the relationship between travel and fluid Levantine identities. These three films were produced by different studios, were directed by different filmmakers, and starred different comic actors. Mizrahi's *Seven O'Clock*, starring 'Ali al-Kassar, was released in October 1937. Studio Misr's *Salama fi khayr* (*Salama Is Fine*), directed by Niyazi Mustafa, followed a month later. In *Salama Is Fine*, Prince Kandahar (Husayn Riyad), from the fictional country of Bloudestan, arrives in Egypt seeking romance. Tired of being pursued by women who are after his money, he hatches a plan to find true love. In a nod to *The Prince and the Pauper*,[2] Kandahar hires a poor Egyptian named Salama (Naguib al-Rihani) to take his place. Salama, a lowly farrash—a gofer—knows nothing of state etiquette, setting in motion this comedy full of misunderstandings, role play, and plot reversals. Opening in January 1938, Lotus Films' *The Pasha Director's Daughter* (described in chap. 4) features Assia Dagher playing a character who takes refuge in an assumed identity on a boat sailing from Beirut to Alexandria. In all three films physical displacement sets in motion an exploration of mobile identities.

In this chapter I analyze the journey of mistaken identity in Mizrahi's film *Seven O'Clock*, with reference to Mustafa's *Salama Is Fine*. In *Seven O'Clock*, 'Ali al-Kassar plays 'Usman 'Abd al-Basit, a courier for a bank in Alexandria who delivers cash to local businesses. 'Usman's journey consists of three itineraries: circular movement within Alexandria; travel from Alexandria to Aswan; and travel from Aswan to Cairo. The first movement, following 'Usman's daily deliveries, maps a series of circular trajectories that encompass the city's cosmopolitan, ethnonational diversity. The second movement begins when 'Usman falls asleep and dreams that he is accused of stealing the bank's money. He takes flight, setting in motion a journey that speeds along the rails from Alexandria to Aswan, tracking a spectrum of racial-national identities. The third movement, from Aswan to Cairo, where 'Usman finds employment as a domestic servant, maps a queer Levantine journey of mistaken identity. 'Usman's trajectories, I argue, serve to map the limits of the nation, exploring ethnic and racial diversity within its boundaries.

MOVEMENT I: CYCLING IN ALEXANDRIA

Films featuring 'Ali al-Kassar's tend to be episodic—and *Seven O'Clock* is no exception. Viola Shafik refers to this structure as "anecdotal narration," and identifies this narrative form with a long-standing popular theater practice in Egypt called *fasl mudhik* (comic sketches).[3] As Shafik reads the film, the thrust of the narrative begins when 'Usman falls asleep and is resolved at the end of the film, when he wakes up and realizes it was all a dream. For Shafik, then, the circularity of the first movement, including 'Usman's search for his bicycle, "decompos[es] the whole, rather simple and point-oriented, narration."[4] Shafik elaborates: "Although these events are supposed to prepare the ground for 'Usman's dream of the burglars' break-in, the context is almost totally subverted because of the internal dynamics of the scene."[5] Shafik reads *Seven O'Clock* as a narrative driving toward a single point, traveling along a single trajectory. I argue, by contrast, that the film, rather, explores the notion of mobility itself. While some of the trajectories are linear, the film loops through multiple journeys rather than driving toward a single destination.

Shafik notes that the opening scenes involve characters from Alexandria's resident foreign-minority communities: the thief who steals 'Usman's bike wears European dress; and 'Usman's drinking partner, George, is Greek. Each of these characters propels 'Usman's movements. I argue that the circular motion involving these "European" characters serves to draw lines encircling an Alexandrian ethnonational diversity that also encompasses a range of socioeconomic classes. I take these two examples in turn to unpack their significance.

In *Seven O'Clock*, 'Usman delivers cash for payroll—a cyclically recurring event. His regular visits are underscored by his friendly banter with the clients. The points on his trajectory within Alexandria are fixed: the bank, the clients' offices, his home, and the café. He travels within a closed circuit.

'Usman sets out on his bike to his first client of the day, parks his trusty vehicle in front of the client's building, and walks away. In his absence, the bike is stolen. The bicycle thief is represented as a member of one of Alexandria's resident foreign minorities. He wears trousers, a threadbare wool blazer, and a newsboy cap.

After a lengthy search, 'Usman gives up and proceeds on foot. However, later in the day 'Usman emerges from another client's office to find his bike unexpectedly parked outside. A police officer sees 'Usman mount the bike, recognizes that he is not the rider who had dismounted, and accuses him of attempted theft. The honest, hardworking, good-hearted 'Usman in his Nubian dress stands accused, while the thief, in his Western clothes, is mistaken for the rightful owner.

The thief is addressed as "*khawaga*." Egyptian Arabic speakers use this word as a term of address or salutation for resident foreign minorities, as well as for foreigners in general. In contradistinction to the salt-of-the-earth nativeness of law-abiding *awlad al-balad*, as discussed in chapter 3, "*khawaga*" connotes outsider status. Presumably Italian or Greek, the thief reflects a socioeconomic diversity among the foreign populations in Alexandria that is often left out of the nostalgic portrayals of cosmopolitan Alexandria.[6] When the *khawaga* returns, he denies his ownership of the bike and slips away from the scene. 'Usman's ownership of the bike is validated and he rides off, continuing along his trajectory.

The first movement of *Seven O'Clock* metatextually doubles this sense of circularity by including two instances of self-referentiality. At the opening of the clip, when 'Usman looks for his bike in a nearby stand, he is positioned before an advertisement featuring 'Ali al-Kassar (fig. 29). Later, he follows a cyclist carrying a second bike on his shoulder. The cyclist parks both bikes and enters Studio Mizrahi. Just as the character 'Usman is searching for his bike, one is delivered to the studio. Are we to understand that this bike will be used as a prop in filming? Or is it destined for the studio's own courier, who will extradiegetically travel the same streets as the fictional 'Usman? 'Usman throws up his arms and walks past, and then the camera cuts to a scene shot on the soundstage just inside that door.

Magdy el-Shammaa has pointed out that Mizrahi was an innovator in this sort of filmic self-promotion.[7] As previously discussed, in *Mistreated by Affluence*, an ad for Mizrahi's film *Children of Egypt* (1933) appears pasted on the doors of a closed shop. In *Seven O'Clock*, the self-referentiality, with a nod and a wink to the viewer, mimics 'Usman's own circular motion in the film's first movement.

A brief discussion of the competing film *Salama Is Fine* throws a few elements of my analysis into relief. As already noted, *Salama Is Fine* was released a month after *Seven O'Clock*. Salama, too, carries a large sum of money from his employer to deposit at Bank Misr. In the course of the plot, Salama is also accused of stealing

FIGURE 29. ʿUsman (ʿAli al-Kassar) searches for his missing bicycle. Screenshot from *Seven O'Clock* (Togo Mizrahi, 1937).

the money he is charged with protecting. Both films are Levantine comedies of assumed identity: Salama is invited to play a prince; ʿUsman later disguises himself as a woman. Like *Seven O'Clock, Salama Is Fine* engages in a form of self-promotion: Studio Misr, where the film was produced, and Bank Misr, which appears in the film, are part of the same corporate group founded by the Egyptian financier Muhammad Talʿat Harb. Finally, and most importantly for our purposes here, in both films, bicycles are associated with theft.[8]

Like ʿUsman, Salama physically travels through a limited geographic area, moving in tight circles within Cairo's central commercial district: department store; bank; upscale hotel. Seeing a purse snatcher escape by bicycle, Salama views bikes as a threat. He tries to avoid bicycles as he picks his way through the crowded city streets, only to find himself standing in the middle of the street as competitors in a bike race rush toward him. Salama takes flight, trying to run ahead of the pack of bicycles. The camera is fairly mobile in this scene, but in a way that preserves a sense of stasis: at one point the dolly tracks to maintain a fixed distance between the camera and Salama, giving the impression that he is running in place. For Salama, bicycles block his progress, hindering his ability to get from the store to the bank. By contrast, for ʿUsman, whose moving image travels across the frame of a fixed camera, the bicycle is a means of transportation—and its theft is a hindrance to his mobility. The loss of his bike does not ground him; 'Usman proceeds along his circular trajectory more slowly on foot.

The second instance of circular motion in the first movement of *Seven O'Clock* involves George ('Ali 'Abd al-'Al), a Greek neighbor. After a fight with his mother-in-law, 'Usman repairs to a local watering hole, where he finds George. Having imbibed a bit too much, 'Usman and George get confused about their destination and end up in one another's apartments. George is confronted by 'Usman's mother-in-law. When 'Usman hears the shouting, he goes to investigate. The stunt ends with the two men safely installed in their own beds. Although the apartments—George's bachelor pad and 'Usman's marital home—are distinct, there is a sense of equivalence or parity. Like 'Usman's regular rounds and his search for his bicycle, this shared circular trajectory of the Nubian urban migrant and the Greek resident maps a route of Alexandrian coexistence.

MOVEMENT II: NUBIAN WHITEFACE AND BORSCHT BELT MINSTRELSY

Words uttered by 'Usman's shrewish mother-in-law, Saniya (Zakiya Ibrahim), set into motion the events that propel 'Usman out of the confines of his cyclical mobility and launch his movement along a linear trajectory. In the course of their argument, Saniya repeatedly insults 'Usman by calling him *"Ya, aswad al-wish* [you blackface]" (fig. 30).

In response to her insults, 'Usman goes to the café, where he drinks too much beer (and may have consumed some drugged dragées). Once the confusion over the apartments is resolved, 'Usman falls asleep in his own bed. In a drunken stupor, 'Usman dreams that two thieves, wearing the same costume as the bicycle thief, enter the apartment and steal the bank's money. His dream continues: The following day he goes to his employer to explain the theft, and overhears that the police consider him the prime suspect. Fleeing the police, he boards a train in Alexandria to his ancestral home, Aswan, reversing the trajectory of his migration. In Aswan, he pays a visit to his wealthy uncle and requests a loan to repay the bank.

To viewers not steeped in the conventions of Egyptian theater and cinema, Saniya's racial slur appears misplaced. 'Ali al-Kassar had a successful stage career stretching back twenty-one years prior to the release of *Seven O'Clock*. Since 1916 al-Kassar had headlined a Cairo-based traveling troupe that performed comic musical reviews. Al-Kassar regularly appeared onstage as the character 'Usman Abd al-Basit, a good-hearted, uneducated Nubian; in the early plays in which he appeared, he was, he insisted, "half-Nubian, half-Sudanese, and all Egyptian."[9] Al-Kassar performed 'Usman onstage in blackface. In the early plays, both British and Egyptian authorities regularly uttered racial slurs at 'Usman—particularly the same words Saniya uses in the film: *"Ya, aswad al-wish."*

FIGURE 30. Saniya (Zakiya Ibrahim, center) berates 'Usman ('Ali al-Kassar), calling him "you blackface," as his wife, Bahiga (Bahiga al-Mahdi), looks on. Screenshot from *Seven O'Clock* (Togo Mizrahi, 1937).

Eve Troutt Powell argues that in these plays, 'Usman's Nubian identity "becomes a conduit through which Egyptians could express anger at British racism" and "serves as a criticism of indigenous racial attitudes."[10] The character embodied an Egyptian nationalism "that reinforced the idea of unity of the Nile Valley."[11] Powell reads al-Kassar's appropriation of Sudanese identity as an appropriation of territory. She also sees the character 'Usman denouncing both "English racial discrimination" and "the hypocritical and self-hating mannerisms of wealthy Egyptians."[12] Powell concludes that one must read Egyptian blackface as a site of ambivalence: "Perhaps what 'Usman really does is wipe away all racial difference, rendering it a distraction from true Egyptian national identity. Whether he succeeded in this depends, I think, on who his audience was, and what color they chose to be. I have come to consider the character of Osman the embodiment of a double colonialism, a perspective of both colonizer and the colonized."[13] There is a lot in al-Kassar's act to make a culturally sensitive critic uncomfortable: he is called "barbarian"; he dons blackface; his scripts portray blackness as demeaning. Powell both provides historical context for the development of this discourse in al-Kassar's performance, and unpacks its inherent dualities: colonizer/colonized; demeaning/empowering; racism / critique of racism.

From its founding in June 1934, the weekly magazine *Al-Ithnayn* closely followed—and promoted—the careers of the two popular, rival comic actors: 'Ali al-Kassar and Naguib al-Rihani. Early in its publication, the magazine placed a caricature of al-Kassar in blackface inside the front cover with the caption "'Ali al Kassar—I chose the role of the barbarian because we are in a time that blackens the face" (fig. 31). This statement confirms that al-Kassar's practice of donning blackface continued to function as a form of protest against British control in Egypt into the 1930s. In al-Kassar's rhetoric, blackface functions as a metaphor of colonial subject-hood—a visual sign of how colonial rule demeans subject peoples.

Al-Kassar billed his character 'Usman as "*al-barbari al-misri al-wahid* [the only Egyptian barbarian]." Another comic actor, Fawzi Munib, who, incidentally, appeared in the 1923 film *In the Land of Tutankhamun* (discussed in chap. 1), billed himself as "*al-barbari al-'asri* [the modern barbarian]." Munib flaunted his "barbarian" credentials in the ads for a film called *Al-Abyad wa-l-aswad* (*The White and the Black*, Fu'ad al-Gazayirli), released New Year's Eve 1937.[14]

'Ali al-Kassar ushered in the year 1937 differently. The same week that Munib's film *The White and The Black* was released, al-Kassar debuted a new character onstage, appearing without his usual blackface makeup.[15] In response, *Al-Ithnayn* staged a satirical debate in its pages between the black al-Kassar and the white al-Kassar.[16] Calling the newcomer a thief, the black al-Kassar claims authenticity, originality, and a popularity that confirms the territorial integrity of the Nile Valley: "[M]y light eclipses the stars—from here all the way to Khartoum." The white al-Kassar prefers the shape-shifting potential of a blank (racially unmarked) slate, arguing: "One day I can be a sheik, one day a pasha, and one day an effendi, or any character. But you are a barbarian and nothing else." Each character brags and boasts and hurls insults in colloquial rhymed prose.

Al-Ithnayn's lighthearted response treats al-Kassar's decision as purely artistic—a decision that liberated an actor from his signature character, giving him freedom to explore new roles. But I would also like to suggest that, just as al-Kassar's donning of blackface holds political significance, so does its removal. On 22 December 1936, the Anglo-Egyptian treaty was ratified. The following week, al-Kassar appeared onstage without his blackface makeup. The Anglo-Egyptian treaty redefined the relationship between the two parties, diplomatically ending the occupation, and limiting the number of British troops on Egyptian soil during peacetime. Extraterritorial rights for British citizens were eliminated, and the treaty stipulated that the countries would work to abolish both the Capitulations and the Mixed Courts. The terms for dismantling the Mixed Courts, which had adjudicated civil and commercial disputes between foreigners and locals, and between foreigners of different nationalities, were laid out by the Montreux Convention, signed a few months later, in May 1937. As the loopholes for sustained British influence and the return of British troops became apparent over time, Egyptian opposition to the terms of the treaty grew. However, in 1936 the Wafd Party, the liberal nationalist political party, hailed the treaty as a major step

FIGURE 31. Caricature of 'Ali al-Kassar in blackface. The caption reads: "'Ali al-Kassar—I chose the role of the barbarian because we are in a time that blackens the face." *Al-Ithnayn*, 13 August 1934.

toward Egyptian independence. Negotiations concluded in August 1936, four months before ratification, so the terms of the treaty were discussed and debated in the press.[17] In October 1936, less than two weeks before the release of al-Kassar's film *The Neighborhood Watchman*, Togo Mizrahi hosted a party celebrating "the signature of the treaty of Egyptian independence." In this celebratory atmosphere, al-Kassar appears to have decided that with the end of the British occupation, the times no longer blackened the faces of Egyptians.[18]

Al-Kassar did not abandon his creation 'Usman 'Abd al-Basit. The beloved character remained relevant, and continued to entertain Egyptian audiences from the stage and screen. The film *Seven O'Clock* premiered in October 1937— al-Kassar's first film since *Al-Ithnayn* announced his removal of blackface onstage. 'Usman 'Abd al-Basit is the same good-natured character—and subject to the same racial insults he always incurred—even without the blackface makeup. In other words, Saniya's words are not as misplaced as they first appeared: the journey of racial exploration is not a journey of mistaken identity. That is yet to come. In the discussion that follows, I unpack the signification of the white-faced al-Kassar's performance of a Nubian character under a pretense of implied or vestigial blackface.

The traveling scene to Aswan opens to the nondiegetic sound of drumming. 'Usman boards a train in Alexandria, and as the engine speeds along the track, the musical rhythms stand in for the sounds of a train in motion. 'Usman alights from the train and walks through the dusty streets. The scene cuts to a wedding celebration, the source of the music. As a vocal track enters the rhythmic drumming, the camera shows an official registering the marriage. Only then does the camera pan the room, showing celebrants clapping and swaying to the music and, finally, the band accompanying two male dancers, each wearing a *manjur*.[19] This music is kinetic. The swaying of the dancers' hips produces the rhythm (fig. 32).

This "Nubian" wedding scene carries 'Usman's performance of virtual racial marking over to the entire wedding party. In contrast to the "Africanness" of the performers and their performance, the majority of the wedding guests— 'Usman's cousins and the groom's family—are fair skinned. In the room where the female guests are gathered, a few African-looking guests in traditional Nubian dress ring the room, but their presence only highlights racial, cultural, and class distinction: the women belonging to this affluent family are fair skinned and wear Western dress.

The musical performance parallels 'Usman's whitewashed appropriation of Nubian identity and culture: the music performed in this scene is not exactly Nubian, but neither is it wedding music. This type of ensemble, known as *fann al-tanbura*, typically performs this sort of music at a *zar*, a ritual to exorcise spirit possession. The *zar*, thus performed, is a tradition that originated in the Horn of Africa and spread to Sudan and the Arabian Peninsula.[20] Its inclusion in this film is a form of exoticization that fails to recognize Saharan and sub-Saharan cultural specificity: Nubians? Sudanese? They're all the same. Wedding? Exorcism? What difference does it make?

To be clear, no one expects realism from 1930s comedies either from Hollywood or from Egypt. I concede that since the character of 'Usman refers to his earlier,

FIGURE 32. Performers at a wedding celebration in Aswan. Screenshot from *Seven O'Clock* (Togo Mizrahi, 1937).

blackface stage persona, he may here, too, implicitly lay claim to Sudanese ancestry. But we also can't ignore the way this footage exoticizes Nubia for the urban Lower Egyptian viewer, and fails to distinguish between distinct Afro-Muslim cultures.

In keeping with Powell's reading of al-Kassar's blackface, I view this musical scene as a site of ambivalence: cultural appropriation on the one hand, and inclusion on the other. The only black characters in other Egyptian films of this era were servants.[21] Despite its problematic portrayal of Nubian culture, I maintain that this scene represents an effort by the writer, 'Ali al-Kassar, and director, Togo Mizrahi, toward inclusion, toward an expansive view of the Egyptian nation. For al-Kassar, as Eve Troutt Powell writes, 'Usman "taught his audiences an important geographic lesson, in which the Sudan and Nubia must always be considered part and parcel of the Egyptian nation."[22] For Mizrahi, the inclusion of Nubian characters is an articulation of a pluralist vision of Egyptianness. This scene is shot on a soundstage in Alexandria featuring Saharan musicians who are part of the cultural fabric of the city.

But I would like to complicate this picture a bit more. As I have already noted, Egyptian nationalist film critics dismiss 1930s Egyptian cinema as derivative of Hollywood. The most apparent Hollywood intertexts for Mizrahi's oeuvre are films featuring Jewish vaudevillians. Drawing from the work of Michael Rogin, I would like to sketch out an additional aspect of how al-Kassar's vestigial blackface performance of the "Nubian" 'Usman participates in a wider cinematic project of normativizing liminal characters and projecting a pluralist vision of Egypt.

In his book *Blackface, White Noise*, Rogin argues that minstrel acts in which Jewish vaudevillians performed in blackface contributed to the process of Jewish immigrants integrating into America, and of Jews becoming white.[23] Mizrahi makes several clear nods in his work to the Marx Brothers, as noted in chapter 3. I also see the influence of Eddie Cantor, who was enormously popular among critics and moviegoers in 1930s Egypt. In December 1933 an ad for *Palmy Days* (Edward Sutherland, 1931) appeared in a short-lived but high-minded journal, *Fann al-sinima*, published by the Cinema Critic's Association; the journal also ran a translation of an interview with Cantor, who starred in the film, and featured the film as pick of the week. In 1936 the premier cinema in Cairo, Cinema Royal, kicked off its season with *Strike Me Pink* (Norman Taurog, 1936), starring Cantor and Ethel Merman.

The influence of Eddie Cantor—who included a blackface minstrel number in each film—is perhaps most evident in Mizrahi's collaborations with 'Ali al-Kassar. Many of Cantor's films involve journeys of mistaken identity, like *The Kid from Spain* (Leo McCarey, 1932) and *Ali Baba Goes to Town* (David Butler, 1937), an Orientalist fantasy coincidentally released the same week as *Seven O'Clock*. The journey in *Roman Scandals* (Frank Tuttle, 1933)[24] turns out to be a dream sequence, like the framing device of *Seven O'Clock*.

Mizrahi's films utilize liminal characters, like al-Kassar's 'Usman, to define the boundaries of the nation racially, culturally, and geographically. Read against the Hollywood intertexts, *Seven O'Clock* reflects a complicated construction of nativeness—one that projects to its audiences images of al-Kassar's trans–Nile Valley native authenticity while simultaneously echoing the same Jewish minstrel acts that, Michael Rogin argues, were performing whiteness and American national belonging by donning blackface.

MOVEMENT III: QUEER LEVANTINE MOBILITY

The third journey 'Usman undertakes in *Seven O'Clock* enacts a different sort of masquerade—the performance of gender. Just as 'Usman's first journey shared some affinities with *Salama Is Fine*, his third journey similarly parallels Hikmat's experiences trying to pass as a man in *The Pasha Director's Daughter*. In *Seven O'Clock* the Aswan police, in pursuit of 'Usman, search his uncle's home. 'Usman takes refuge in the bridal chamber. When the police come knocking, 'Usman is dressed as the bride. The uncle sends 'Usman away, and he takes flight dressed as a woman. Aboard a Cairo-bound train, 'Usman introduces himself to fellow passengers as "Farida." In my discussion of this final movement of the film, I examine the intersection of this journey of assumed identity and the notion of the "queer Levantine" explored in the previous chapter.

FIGURE 33. On the train, a male passenger (Hasan Rashid) buys "Farida" ('Ali al-Kassar) a drink. Screenshot from *Seven O'Clock* (Togo Mizrahi, 1937).

This is not al-Kassar's first role in a dress, nor, for that matter, is it his first appearance cross-dressing on film. 'Ali al-Kassar made his first foray from stage to screen in 1920, with a silent short called *Al-Khala al-amrikiyya* (*The American Aunt*, Bonvilli). The film was an adaptation of a popular British farce, Brandon Thomas's *Charley's Aunt* (1892). In the play, when Charley's aunt is delayed, his friend dresses in drag and assumes her identity. Little is known about al-Kassar's film adaptation, now lost, except that he plays the title role in drag.[25]

In *Seven O'Clock*, from the outset 'Usman intends to change out of his costume on the train. But his plans are thwarted when a pair of chic young women join him in the cabin. The scenes in the train car are intercut with footage of a train steaming along the tracks. With each cut, as the train charges toward Cairo, 'Usman becomes more deeply committed to continuing the masquerade. His first innocent foray into the women's realm permits him to witness the young ladies adjusting their belts and stockings. When the women alight, 'Usman, as "Farida," is joined in the cabin by a widower (Hasan Rashid), who buys her (as I will refer to "Farida") a cold drink and offers her cigarettes (fig. 33). By the final cut, "Farida" has agreed to go home with the widower and serve as part of his domestic staff—committed to perpetuating the masquerade until she has saved up enough money to repay the bank.

The widower's interest in "Farida" is sexualized from the outset. When she leans out the window to purchase a cold drink from a vendor at the station, he leers at her backside. In case we missed his expression on the first occasion, he does it a second time. When he strikes up a conversation with her, the first question regards her marital status. She obligingly responds that she is a widow.

In addition to cross-dressing, in becoming "Farida," 'Usman also undergoes a class shift. As 'Usman he was a trusted (if low-level) employee of the bank; as "Farida," he has been demoted to domestic labor. By entering the home of a single man, even one with an adult daughter at home, "Farida" exposes herself to abuse. If this were a post-1950s melodrama, we would expect the lonely widower to attempt to seduce her.[26] Instead, since this is a 1930s comedy, once in the domestic space, the widower vows to marry "Farida."

Nevertheless, "Farida"'s queer body is subject to physical abuse from other quarters. A male servant (Ibrahim 'Arafa) in the widower's home is mute; he communicates through gesture and nonsense sounds. He made an appearance earlier in the film as an acquaintance of 'Usman's and a customer of the bank. He recognizes "Farida"'s resemblance to 'Usman. In a violent gesture, to ascertain the new domestic's identity, he cops a feel of her breast. She beats him back, but in the scuffle he notices not only that is she wearing pants under her dress, but that 'Usman's signature keychain dangles from her belt.

Once he establishes 'Usman's identity and gender, the fellow servant becomes his ally. He tries to help 'Usman escape and restore his gender identity (even if it would not solve the underlying financial and legal problems). "Farida" starts to transition back to 'Usman—wearing 'Usman's headgear and "Farida"'s clothes, she/he looks in the mirror and proclaims, "I am 'Usman on top, and Farida on the bottom." 'Usman's performance as "Farida" is restored when the two realize that there is a police officer stationed by the door. 'Usman is believed to be an outlaw, while the Levantine, shape-shifting, queer "Farida" can avert capture through her continued masquerade.

Farida's queer body is subject to further violence at the climax of the film. The widower's daughter invites her seamstresses, Saniya and Bahiga (Bahiga al-Mahdi)—'Usman's mother-in-law and wife, respectively—to make a dress for Farida. They immediately notice the striking resemblance between their client and their missing son-in-law and husband. Saniya reaches around Farida's torso to measure her and ends up unraveling the stockings stuffing her bra. The queer body of 'Usman/Farida is chased, beaten, and stripped by the angry throng. Her dress is ripped off, revealing the male body beneath.

The police are called. The ringing of the doorbell merges with 'Usman's seven o'clock alarm. 'Usman wakes up in his bedroom in his apartment in Alexandria. He is once again dressed as a man. The money is in the drawer where he left it, and he realizes it was all just a dream. 'Usman's name and identity are restored, as is his reputation as an honest, hardworking, law-abiding man.

With hindsight, the viewer can enumerate how as the plot's plausibility declines, the evidence that it was a dream increases. For example, on the northbound train from Aswan, Farida repeatedly tells her travel companions that she is headed to "*Misr*"—that is, Cairo. But characters from Alexandria keep showing up in the widower's apartment—a clue to the viewer that something is amiss.

At the end of the film, 'Usman's wife, Bahiga, comes to wake him up so he can prepare for another day at work. We have returned to the circular narrative of the first movement. But just as 'Usman is shaken by the dream, the residue of the linear narratives to Aswan, Cairo, and back continues to shake the foundations of identity. The film concludes with a heteronormative embrace, but the queer Levantine narrative that precedes it has served to trouble the lines of identity.

CODA: JOURNEY OF THE LIVING DEAD

For his last film of the 1937–38 season, Togo Mizrahi produced and directed another comedy of mistaken identity that revisits the travel motif. In *Ana tab'i kidda* (*It's My Nature*, 1938), Ahmad al-Kabriti (Fu'ad Shafiq) informs his wife (Zuzu Shakib) and his colleagues that he is leaving Cairo for a business trip to Sudan. But his true intended destination is a guesthouse in Alexandria. He returns to this pension each year to resume a romance with the proprietor, Bahiga (Bahiga al-Mahdi). When he arrives, he discovers that Bahiga has married a doctor, and they have turned the welcoming guesthouse into an austere sanitarium.[27] Ahmad, trapped as a patient in the clinic, fears that the sadistic and jealous doctor will learn of his relationship with Bahiga.

Not only does the film defamiliarize the destination—a pension turned into a sanitarium; it also defamiliarizes home: when Ahmad returns to Cairo, he finds that his power-hungry assistant (Stefan Rosti) has feigned his death. The train aboard which Ahmad was supposedly traveling to Khartoum had derailed. Instead of revealing the truth of Ahmad's whereabouts, the assistant spreads the word that his boss perished in the fiery crash. When Ahmad confronts his assistant, he maliciously retorts: "In the eyes of the law and the people you are no longer among the living." In an inversion of the masquerade plot, Ahmad must convince his bereaved wife that he is still alive.

It's My Nature presages some coming transitions in Togo Mizrahi's productions. In Mizrahi's previous films, Alexandria was the primary setting or the point of departure. By contrast, in *It's My Nature*, Ahmad's home is in Cairo. Although Ahmad's destination is located in Alexandria, the camera, like the protagonist, gets stuck behind the walls of the sanitarium. Unlike the opening traveling shot in *Seven O'Clock*, or the Shamm al-nasim montage from *Mistreated by Affluence*, *It's My Nature* features no footage identifiably shot on location in Alexandria. Togo Mizrahi, too, was beginning to turn his sights to the capital city, which had, since the founding of Studio Misr in 1934, become the center of the Egyptian cinema industry. After producing films in Alexandria for almost a decade, within six months of wrapping production on *It's My Nature*, Togo Mizrahi began producing films in Cairo.

Also, although *It's My Nature* is a comedy, the darker plot anticipates Mizrahi's turn toward melodrama in his Cairo productions. In the following chapter, I analyze the trope of travel in two of Togo Mizrahi's musical melodramas produced in Cairo. While al-Kassar's character claims Nubian and Sudanese origins, and *It's My Nature* feigns a trip to Omdurman, Mizrahi's next film, *Layla mumtira* (*A Rainy Night*, 1939) takes the viewer across the border into colonial Sudan. My analyses of *A Rainy Night* and *Al-Tariq al-mustaqim* (*The Straight Road*, 1943), a film that that traverses the Levant, examine the ethnonational and geographic boundaries of Egyptian national identity.

6

Traveling Anxieties

A graduate of the University of Paris with an advanced degree in hydroelectric engineering from Rome held a position as chief engineer for Azienda Electra in Milan. Sometime between the fall of 1938 and the spring of 1939, the engineer was dismissed from his job. In presenting his credentials to a prospective employer in Cairo, the multilingual, out-of-work engineer, speaking in Arabic, described his experience in Italy as follows: "One day, a law was passed that prohibited foreigners from working in the professions. They began to eliminate all non-Italian employees in manufacturing and commerce. Of course, the law pertained to me, like everyone else."

The events that I mention above are from neither a memoir nor an oral history. Nor, despite the conclusions one might credibly draw, is the engineer a Jew. The protagonist is, rather, an Egyptian Muslim named Ahmad Khalid, a fictional character in a feature film, *Layla mumtira* (*A Rainy Night*), first screened in at the Cinema Cosmograph in Alexandria on March 9, 1939.[1] Indeed, there are no Jewish characters in the film. However, the character Ahmad and the scenario described are the product of the imagination the Egyptian Jewish filmmaker Togo Mizrahi.[2] The film features a rising musical star, Layla Murad, also an Egyptian Jew, in her second role on-screen.

Yusuf Wahbi, an actor and theatrical impresario, played the role of Ahmad in the film.[3] In the 1930s Wahbi, already the director of the Ramsis theater troupe, expanded into cinema—as an actor, director, producer, and screenwriter. In 1936 Yusuf Wahbi, in collaboration with his brother Isma'il, a lawyer by training, opened a studio in Giza.[4] In 1939, when Togo Mizrahi decided to relocate his operations to the capitol, he rented out Studio Wahbi. Mizrahi produced two films in which the studio is identified as Studio Wahbi: *A Rainy Night*; and the comedy *Salafini 3 gineh* (*Lend Me Three Pounds*, 1939). Mizrahi continued operating out of the location in Giza as Studio Mizrahi.[5]

Yusuf Wahbi and Togo Mizrahi did not know one another before working together on *A Rainy Night*. In the program for the film, Yusuf Wahbi relates that he was initially reluctant to work with Togo Mizrahi because he had a reputation as a stubborn perfectionist. But their collaboration changed Wahbi's mind about Mizrahi, whom he calls a "first-class gentleman." Wahbi praises Togo Mizrahi for his clarity of vision and the strength of his perception. Wahbi also describes the strong bonds of friendship he forged with Mizrahi over the course of filming, and expresses his hopes that they will work together again. Mizrahi returned the compliments, calling Wahbi, "the greatest actor I have worked with in the cinema."[6]

Yusuf Wahbi and Togo Mizrahi collaborated on three more films over the following four years. Wahbi played opposite Layla Murad in two additional musical melodramas, both released in 1941: *Layla bint al-rif* (*Layla the Country Girl*) and *Layla bint madaris* (*Layla the Schoolgirl*.)

The pair's fourth collaboration, *Al-Tariq al-mustaqim* (*The Straight Road*, 1943), featured a script by Wahbi based on Mizrahi's scenario. But when Mizrahi was preparing to start shooting, Wahbi was under contract with Nahas Films. The competing studio was still upset that Mizrahi had previously refused to loan them Layla Murad for a picture. So Nahas Films initially refused to grant Wahbi permission to appear in *The Straight Road*.[7] The drama over Wahbi's participation in the film fueled the gossip columns for months. Mizrahi contracted with Mahmud Dhu al-Faqar to play the lead, and then broke the contract when Nahas Films relented.[8] Ultimately, Wahbi starred in the film. Dhu al-Faqar sued Mizrahi for breach of contract and won the case.[9]

In the musical melodrama *The Straight Road*, Wahbi plays a bank executive, Yusuf Fahmi. Fahmi falls in love with a singer who bilks him out of his wealth. In the film's climax, Yusuf, en route from Cairo to Beirut, drives his car off a cliff along the Palestinian coast; presumed dead, he loses his identity.

Although *A Rainy Night* and *The Straight Road* lack explicitly Jewish content, in this chapter I tease out how they reflect distinctly Jewish anxieties of belonging in Egypt. In *A Rainy Night*, an itinerary from Milan to Cairo to Omdurman both counterposes rising fascism in Europe with Egypt's Levantine and multiracial society, and serves to unsettle the boundaries of the nation in light of Egypt's colonial designs on Sudan, even as British troops continued to occupy Egypt. *The Straight Road*, I argue, reveals Egyptian Jewish anxieties about the impact of Zionist efforts in British Mandatory Palestine on the Jewish future in Egypt.

Following the call of Moshe Behar and Zvi Ben-Dor Benite in their article "The Possibility of Modern Middle Eastern Jewish Thought," I seek to unpack ways Togo Mizrahi's films position themselves within a distinctly Middle Eastern cultural milieu while also engaging in dialogue with European political and cultural developments.[10] My analysis focuses on the ways Togo Mizrahi's films represent a particularly Egyptian idiom inflected with Jewish concerns.

Both *A Rainy Night* and *The Straight Road* send Egyptians beyond the borders, into other Arabic-speaking countries. However, rather than seeking an extraterritorial Pan-Arabism, these itineraries, I argue, serve as a way of testing the boundaries of the nation. Due to censorship regulations, Togo Mizrahi could not take a stand on British colonialism in Egypt. However, as I demonstrate, these two films explore the ambivalences of Egyptian-Jewish identity within and through colonial institutions. My discussion of the films proceeds along three itineraries: Egypt–Italy and Egypt–Sudan in *A Rainy Night*; and Egypt–Palestine–Lebanon in *The Straight Road*. Through my analysis, I examine the films' articulation of Egyptian-Jewish anxieties—anxieties about the place of Jews within the Egyptian nation.

ITINERARY I, EGYPT–ITALY: A *RAINY NIGHT* (1939)

The salacious plot of *A Rainy Night* nearly prevented the film from being released at all. Government censors ultimately relented, following extensive pressure from the local press.[11] In the opening scenes of *A Rainy Night*, Saniya (Layla Murad), a young woman from a wealthy family, falls for a crook, 'Ali (Stephan Rosti), whose primary interest lies in extorting her father's wealth. 'Ali flees the country when the police close in on him, leaving a pregnant, unwed Saniya in a difficult position. Saniya's servant finds a suitable match for her with Ahmad (Yusuf Wahbi), the only son of an ailing mother and deceased father. Ahmad's family, once wealthy, has fallen on hard times. Ahmad trained in Europe as a hydroelectric engineer, but can find no work in Egypt. When he discovers that his mother needs an operation he cannot afford, Ahmad agrees to marry Saniya.[12] Saniya's father prohibits Ahmad from seeking employment, but Ahmad eventually rejects his father-in-law's patronage and finds work as an engineer. When Saniya's pregnancy becomes public knowledge, Ahmad asks for immediate transfer to a project in Sudan. After Saniya gives birth to a baby boy, Ahmad is called back to Cairo for business. He discovers that 'Ali has also returned and is trying to blackmail Saniya. Ahmad confronts 'Ali. The police arrive to arrest 'Ali, and he is killed in the scuffle. Back at home, Ahmad overhears Saniya expressing her love and respect for him, and he reveals his feelings for her. At the end of the film, Ahmad and Saniya can begin their life together.[13]

My analysis of *A Rainy Night* focuses on the portrayal of Ahmad as a means of accessing the films' construction of Egyptian subjecthood. Ahmad's physical mobility from Milan to Cairo to Omdurman indexes a mobility of identity, and its attendant anxieties—here termed "traveling anxieties." I argue that the various forms of mobility in *A Rainy Night*—and the anxieties they provoke—reflect a particularly Levantine-Jewish sensibility. Through my analysis of the character Ahmad, I aim to access the film's mobile construction of Egyptian subjectivity that subverts the binaries of native and foreign, Eastern and Western, working-class and elite.

The film establishes a stark contrast between the moneyed elites and Ahmad's debased circumstances. Near the beginning of the film, on the sun-drenched grounds of a country estate, smartly dressed members of the elite celebrate Shamm al-nasim—the spring festival Mizrahi favors (as mentioned in chaps. 1 and 4). In the shade of a manicured arbor, 'Ali, the criminal, masquerading as a respectable member of the elite, uses sweet talk and lies to insinuate himself with Saniya. By contrast, in the following scene Ahmad makes his first appearance dressed in his auto mechanic's uniform, walking purposefully down the street of a lower-class district after dark. Along the way he greets a pair of Nubian men, as well as two modestly dressed women standing in the doorway to a building. After he disappears into the building, one of the women identifies him as the hardworking, devoted son of their ailing neighbor, Shafiqa.

The viewer's initial impression of Ahmad, then, is that of a working-class craftsman. But the apparent binaries established by these two back-to-back scenes do not hold up for long: our initial assumptions about Ahmad's place in the Egyptian social hierarchy are almost immediately called into question when we see him take a seat at a drafting table and begin drawing. A visit by a prospective employer, the director of an engineering firm, elicits Ahmad's education and employment history (related in the opening paragraphs above). The flashback sequence that accompanies this narration depicts Ahmad at his post in Italy, wearing a suit, overcoat, and hat, discussing a project in Italian with one of his employees. He is visually transformed from a member of the Egyptian working classes to a cosmopolitan, European-educated member of the elite professions (fig. 34).

The following scene continues to illustrate the ways that Ahmad straddles two social positions—the one he currently inhabits, and the one he previously occupied. After the director of the engineering firm leaves, Shahata ('Abd al-'Aziz Ahmad), the family's former servant, who has found work as a greengrocer, arrives delivering fresh vegetables. Upon seeing the drafting tools on the table, Shahata implores Ahmad to accept his new station and give up on his dreams of finding work as an engineer.

Rebuffing Shahata's advice, Ahmad shows him the plans for a waterworks project he is designing: "a great engineering project to light up the country and the villages using the power of the waters of the Nile to generate forty thousand horsepower." Ahmad promises a technological revolution to lead the modern Egyptian nation out of darkness into light—out of the darkness of poverty (an apartment lit by kerosene lamps, a crowded alley) into the light of modernity, development, and economic opportunity. Read this way, Ahmad's vision—enabled by his European education—follows a Western narrative equating technological development with enlightenment.[14] Ahmad fits the profile of the interwar Wafd intellectual described by Albert Hourani: a European-educated admirer of Western civilization who seeks to modernize Egypt.[15] In this way, A Rainy Night can be read as what Lucie

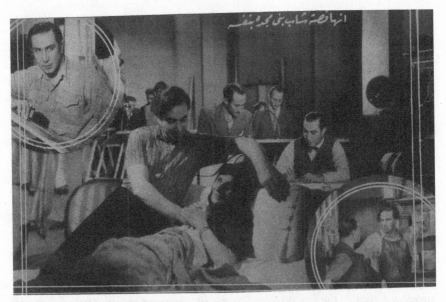

FIGURE 34. A collage, entitled "The Story of a Self-Made Man," shows Ahmad (Yusuf Wahbi) in his many guises: devoted son (center left); engineer at a firm in Italy (center right); mechanic (lower right); and engineer for colonial project in Sudan (upper left). Pressbook for *A Rainy Night* (Togo Mizrahi, 1939). Courtesy of the Rare Books and Special Collections Library, American University in Cairo.

Ryzova calls an effendi narrative—a narrative that becomes even more popular in Egyptian cinema during the following decade.[16]

Typical of effendi films, *A Rainy Night* is not a narrative about class mobility; rather, the film maps the restoration of an Egyptian social order disrupted by external forces. Ahmad was of a privileged background and lost his status, but he gets his break when he marries into an elite family. We learn that Shahata's family had served Ahmad's family for generations, and that Ahmad and Shahata were raised together "like brothers." Although the class and educational differences remain— Ahmad promises his benevolence to Shahata once he secures employment as an engineer—Ahmad's association with this simple, good, honest, plainspoken *ibn al-balad* grants him, by extension, the native authenticity that Shahata embodies.

Ahmad's difficulty in finding work is never explained; in the flashback sequence documenting his employment history, we are shown only a series of doors closing before him.[17] The Egyptian economy had taken a hit from the global depression. An unknown engineer whose family connections were lost with the death of his father might have a difficult time getting a foot in the door. We also see, in another scene, how Ahmad's foreign credentials become a source of suspicion rather than providing an advantage.

When Ahmad is working as an auto mechanic, a British customer comes into the garage and asks for him. The customer explains the problem in broken, heavily accented Arabic, and Ahmad responds, reassuringly, in English. A longtime employee of the garage storms into the manager's office and objects that the new employee is attracting all of the customers. He threatens to quit unless Ahmad is fired. The manager summons Ahmad and dismisses him on the grounds that "there is little work and our expenses are high." As Ahmad collects his pay, the disgruntled mechanic quips, "Go back home and work as an engineer."

Ahmad's multilingualism and his education—his training as an engineer—clearly threaten the garage hierarchy. But the particular language of the mechanic's rebuke demands closer examination. The Arabic phrase "*fi baitkum*" ("your home") utilizes the second-person plural, indicating a collective home to which Ahmad is being commanded to return. The collective to which he is presumed to belong remains unstated, but I propose we read this interaction as an echo of Ahmad's previous job loss under the Italian racial laws. In Ahmad's words: "One day, a law was passed that prohibited *foreigners* from working in the professions. They began to eliminate all *non-Italian* employees in manufacturing and commerce. Of course, *the law pertained to me, like everyone else* [my italics]." Fascist anti-Jewish laws promulgated in Italy between September and November 1938 excluded Jewish pupils from state schools, placed limitations on Jewish ownership of enterprises and property, and ordered the expulsion of foreign Jews.[18] Although Ahmad describes the laws as directed against "foreigners," the Italian racial laws were directed only at Jews. When we read these scenes together, we recognize the slippage between "foreigner" and "Jew," and identify the collective with which Ahmad is identified. We are asked, in other words, to read Ahmad's displacements as articulations of Jewish anxieties in the face of the rise of European fascism.

I am not arguing that A Rainy Night reflects anti-Jewish sentiment in Egypt. To the contrary, I believe the film, like Mizrahi's preceding works, endorses the liberal ideal of a pluralist Egypt. A Rainy Night renders visible—and universal—the threat of fascism, but locates the threat outside its borders. Instead, Mizrahi's art reflects his vision of the nation he inhabits, just as he creates within his films the pluralist nation he wants Egypt to be.

ITINERARY II, EGYPT-SUDAN: *A RAINY NIGHT* (1939)

In *A Rainy Night*, Ahmad escapes his complicated domestic arrangement by requesting assignment to a project in Omdurman, Sudan. Shahata, as promised, has accompanied him on the voyage as a personal assistant. The two dress in the garb of British explorers and work out of a hut with drafting tables and files (fig. 35).

Mizrahi's portrayal of Sudan under the Anglo-Egyptian Condominium romanticizes the colonial enterprise. Borrowing from common tropes in the metropole, Ahmad's journey from emasculated poverty to effendi masculinity[19] is effected

FIGURE 35. The bottom left image in this collage shows Ahmad (Yusuf Wahbi, left) and Shahata ('Abd al-'Aziz Ahmad, center) in Omdurman; also pictured, Ahmad dressed as an effendi (top right) and Saniya (Layla Murad, bottom right). Pressbook for *A Rainy Night* (Togo Mizrahi, 1939). Courtesy of the Rare Books and Special Collections Library, American University in Cairo.

through the trials of labor in the colony. The portrayal of Sudan in this albeit uncritical colonialist idiom problematizes the widespread political acceptance in interwar Egypt of Egypt's right to rule Sudan (as discussed in chap. 5). The Egyptian experience in Sudan is rendered through a British colonial lens—raising, but ultimately not answering, questions of colonial legitimacy, sovereignty, and territoriality of nation and state. I have been arguing that *A Rainy Night* attempts to define the boundaries of what it means to be Egyptian. The Sudan itinerary, I argue, serves to problematize the definition of Egypt's geographical boundaries.

According to the terms of the Anglo-Egyptian Condominium of 1899, Sudan fell under joint British and Egyptian administration. In 1924, following the assassination of Sir Lee Stack, the governor-general of Sudan and the commander in chief of the Egyptian Army, Egyptian troops were ordered out of Sudan, and other Egyptians working in Sudan followed.[20] Although Egypt's military involvement in Sudan was effectively terminated in 1924, Egypt's political and economic designs on Sudan remained in force.[21] The 1929 Nile Waters Agreement codified "the natural and historic rights of Egypt to the waters of the Nile," and set a fixed amount Sudan would be permitted to withdraw.[22] Under the terms of the Anglo-Egyptian Treaty, negotiated and ratified in 1936 and signed in Montreux, Switzerland, in 1937, Britain agreed to terminate its occupation of Egypt, with the exception of the Suez Canal zone. Two outcomes of the treaty are relevant for the discussion of this film: first, the agreement—never implemented—to reinstate Egyptian troops in Sudan; and second, the abolition of the Capitulations, which had granted special privileges to foreign nationals living in Egypt. Both of these developments raise questions about the boundaries of Egypt—the geographical boundaries of the state and the ethnonational boundaries of the nation—that I maintain are addressed in this film.

In *A Rainy Night*, Ahmad's employment in Sudan reflects Egyptian designs on Sudan and on the waters of the Nile. The location of Ahmad's project in Omdurman, on the west bank of the Nile across from Khartoum, places it near the important and economically successful Al Jazira (Gezira) Project, the centerpiece of which was the Sannar Dam, completed in 1925. The project's network of irrigation canals transformed the region into Sudan's agricultural center.[23] In 1932 the Egyptian parliament agreed to fund the construction of the Jabal al-Awliya' Dam south of Khartoum based on the understanding that "the increased water supplies were designated for [Egypt's] use only."[24] Construction of the dam was completed in 1936, it was first utilized in 1938, and the reservoir reached capacity in 1943.[25] In 1938, an Egyptian, 'Abd al-Qawi Ahmad, was appointed head of the Sudanese Irrigation Service.[26]

But it is pure cinematic fantasy that an Egyptian engineering firm would be contracted on a dam- or canal-building project in Sudan in 1939, or that an Egyptian engineer, even one with European (but not British) credentials like Ahmad, would be tapped to oversee such a project. The British designer of the Al Jazira project was Sir Murdoch MacDonald, who had previously served as adviser to the Egyptian government's Public Works Ministry, and in that capacity was also responsible for the construction of the Aswan Dam in 1921. The engineer overseeing the Al Jazira project, O.L. Prowde, was also British, and the construction was carried out by the British-owned Sudan Construction Company.[27] The Jabal al-Awliya' project was constructed by the firm of Gibson and Pauling.[28] Even during the renewal of waterworks projects in Sudan in the 1930s, according to David Mills, "Egyptian construction companies probably did not possess the requisite technical expertise for such a project at the time."[29]

As discussed in length in chapter 3, one of the characteristics of Mizrahi's Levantine cinematic idiom is a pluralist aesthetic. In order to achieve an inclusive vision of the expanded boundaries and racial identity of the nation, *A Rainy Night* carefully constructs visual parallels between the scenes set in Cairo and those set in Omdruman. There are two dancing scenes in the film that each occupy a different space in the narrative, but that share obvious visual parallels. In the first scene, a dancer (Tahiya Carioca) in a Cairo cabaret of 'Ali's is instructed to distract a Sa'idi patron whom 'Ali wishes to avoid; the camera cuts between the dancer's gaze and that of the male viewer (fig. 36). The second dance sequence takes place in the worker's encampment at the construction site that Ahmad is overseeing in

FIGURE 36. Dancer (Tahiya Carioca) in a Cairo nightclub. Screenshot from *A Rainy Night* (Togo Mizrahi, 1939).

Sudan. When a telegram arrives announcing that Saniya has given birth to a boy, Ahmad's Sudanese workers break into a spontaneous celebration featuring local instruments and a dancer (fig. 37). During the dance, the camera cuts away twice from the dancer (Zaynab al-Sudaniya) to show a male celebrant similarly pleased at watching this second dancer. The dancers wear similar costumes, adorned with shimmering discs. In these scenes, *A Rainy Night* foregrounds cultural practices shared between Cairo and Omdurman.

The camera does, at times, also cast an othering, Orientalist gaze upon Ahmad's Sudanese workers. As discussed in the previous chapter, Mizrahi's films reflect a somewhat ambivalent racial politics. Just as in *Seven O'Clock*, released two years earlier, the inclusion of black actors playing Nubian and Sudanese characters in *A Rainy Night* is somewhat problematic. The Sudanese characters are employed in physical or domestic labor. In one scene, a woman who later breaks into dance brings Ahmad a pot of tea and then sits docilely on the floor next to Ahmad's chair as they watch a camel train pass. Yet, unlike other Egyptian films of the era, where an occasional Nubian actor is cast as a servant, Mizrahi makes an effort to bring groups of Nubian and Sudanese actors to the screen. The Sudanese scenes in *A Rainy Night* are shot at Studio Wahbi in Giza, and the characters are played by Sudanese or Nubians living in greater Cairo. As Eve Troutt Powell notes, "The

FIGURE 37. Dancer (Zaynab al-Sudaniya) in worker's camp in Omdurman, Sudan. Screenshot from *A Rainy Night* (Togo Mizrahi, 1939).

Egyptian colonial experience in the Sudan was an encounter that took place in two territories: in the Sudan and in Egypt itself."[30] In *A Rainy Night*, the interplay on race asserts a pluralist Egypt as a counterpoint to Italian fascism.

Historians have noted the parallels between racial laws imposed in Italy's African colonies in 1936–37 and the promulgation of racial laws directed against Jews in Italy in 1938.[31] The primary distinction was that the fascist laws in Italy were directed against citizens rather than colonial subjects.[32] In contradistinction to the xenophobia of Italian fascism, Togo Mizrahi, in his pluralist idiom, adopts an Anglo-Egyptian colonial imaginary but utilizes it to render visible racial diversity in the Egyptian metropole.

A Rainy Night explores the limits of the Egyptian nation and Egyptian national identity. The itinerary from Milan to Cairo to Omdurman exposes traveling anxieties that I argue should be read in the context of political developments in and between those locales. The Milan itinerary exposes Jewish anxieties about fascism, whereas the Omdurman itinerary raises questions about Egypt's colonial entanglements while simultaneously asserting a multiracial Egypt in contradistinction to the fascist threat. *A Rainy Night* offers reflection on key issues animating Egyptian intellectuals in the 1930s: the film explores the contours and boundaries of Egyptianness; counters the threats to the Egyptian nation posed by fascism; and renders visible Egypt's colonial designs on Sudan. The film's antifascist sentiment is inflected with a particularly Jewish perspective. The film integrates these Italian-Jewish anxieties into its exploration of the limits of Egyptian identity.

ITINERARY III, EGYPT–PALESTINE–LEBANON: THE *STRAIGHT ROAD* (1943)

The Straight Road is a melodramatic morality tale tracking a wily female performer's corruption of an upstanding male citizen. While Jewish concerns effectively frame the narrative in *A Rainy Night*, the Jewish anxieties in this 1943 film are presented as an embedded allegory, and play out more in the visual realm than in the script.

The protagonist of *The Straight Road*, Yusuf Fahmi (Yusuf Wahbi), a bank executive, is portrayed as an honest man of moral fiber—stern with his children and strict with his employees. The melodramatic plot maps Yusuf's fall. Contemporaneous critics noted the film's similarities to Josef von Sternberg's *Blue Angel* (1930).

In honor of his promotion to general director, Yusuf throws an extravagant party at the Semiramis Hotel. Early in the evening, he bumps into a beautiful, well-dressed woman and spills her drink. He soon discovers that she is no guest. Rather, she is Suraya (Fatima Rushdi), the singer who is performing that night. In cahoots with her manager and lover, Ibrahim (Stefan Rosti), Suraya ensnares Yusuf in a plot to bilk him of his wealth. Once Yusuf's accounts are depleted Suraya breaks off relations with him, leaving him broke and devastated.

Yusuf, compelled by the bank's board of directors to personally deliver a large quantity of gold to the branch in Beirut, succumbs to temptation: he invites Suraya to run away with him. En route, in the height of a rainstorm, their car veers off a cliff along the coast of Palestine. News of the accident reaches Cairo. Although Yusuf's body is not recovered from the scene of the accident, he is presumed dead. His family and former colleagues mourn his loss.

Meanwhile, Yusuf has made his way to Beirut with Suraya and Ibrahim. The gold is stolen from his room, and he is forced to take a series of increasingly demeaning jobs at the theater where Suraya is booked to perform. Suraya and her entourage leave Yusuf behind when she tours the Levant. Upon their return several months later, a completely debased Yusuf overhears a conversation between Suraya and Ibrahim that reveals the full extent of their deception. Yusuf exacts his revenge and then flees back to Cairo, where he, too, meets his fate.

In the 1930s and 1940s, the banking industry was an economic sector in which the national anticolonial drama was playing out. Muhammad Tal'at Harb, the founder of Studio Misr, the major player in the film industry when *The Straight Road* was released, had founded Bank Misr in 1920, in the midst of the nationalist fervor following the 1919 Revolution.[33] As Joel Beinin has noted, "Tal'at Harb staged his business career as a nationalist drama, portraying himself as the promoter of national economic development."[34] A nationalist agenda was inscribed in Bank Misr's charter, which permitted only Egyptian citizens to purchase shares and serve on the board of directors. Under Harb's directorship, the bank invested in new companies to compete with the interests of foreign capital and diversify the Egyptian-owned sectors of the economy.

As discussed in chapter 1, under Harb, Bank Misr offered itself as the nationalist alternative to foreign financial institutions and those representing interests of the foreign-minority elites protected by the colonial administration, such as Al-Bank al-ahli al-misri, also known as the Egyptian National Bank, founded in 1898 by Sir Ernest Cassel in partnership with *mutamassir* (Egyptianized) capitalists, chief among them the Greek Constantine Salvagos from Alexandria, and members of the Jewish Suarès family from Cairo.[35]

In *The Straight Road*, Yusuf is employed by a fictional bank called Al-Bank al-watani al-misri. I have chosen render the name of this bank as "the Egyptian Nationalist Bank," to distinguish it from the actually existing Egyptian National Bank (Al-Bank al-ahli al-misri). This somewhat over-the-top translation—calling the former the "nationalist bank"—also highlights my claims about the pluralist nationalist agenda reflected in Togo Mizrahi's films.

In 1939 the outbreak of World War II prompted a run on banks, and Bank Misr faltered. Tal'at Harb was forced to resign as the bank's director, and in the subsequent decade the overtly nationalist rhetoric and public posturing decreased. Suspicions swirled that the "British and the Bank's Egyptian enemies used the temporary embarrassment of the Bank to oust the nationalistic minded Tal'at Harb and his supporters and to replace them with more amenable leaders."[36] Although scholars have debunked this conspiracy theory, both Harb's mystique and Bank Misr's nationalist symbolism remain intact. Robert Vitalis has demonstrated that, in practice, Bank Misr was no more a promoter of nationalization of the economy than its primary competitors, and all were navigating the intricate play of interests among political parties, the palace, and the British. He writes: "Business and politics in this key period in Egyptian history prove to have been more complicated than capitalists lining up in a tug of war over economic development, one side pulling the economy toward independent industrialization, the other straining to keep the economy locked in the grips of foreign capital."[37]

In other words, in 1943, when *The Straight Road* was released, the banking industry was a site where the interests of the foreign minorities, colonial powers, and Egyptian nationalists were seen to be in conflict. This unfolding drama will, then, serve as our portal into the lobby of Mizrahi's fictional "Egyptian Nationalist Bank." As Yusuf's driver enters the bank to make a delivery, we see him step into a wide hall with a tiled floor featuring a large Star of David in the center (fig. 38).

The presence of the Star of David is cryptic, since there is no evidence that we are to view this bank as a Jewish enterprise. Jews played actual and imagined

FIGURE 38. Lobby of "The Egyptian Nationalist Bank." Screenshot from *The Straight Road* (Togo Mizrahi, 1943).

roles in the banking industry (in Egypt and globally). Jews were involved in the founding of both the Egyptian National Bank and Bank Misr: the Suarès family was among the founders of the former, and Joseph Aslan Cattaoui, a Jewish Egyptian citizen, was a founding investor in the latter. But according to Robert Vitalis, by the time this film was made, the influence of Jewish and other minority capitalists was already on the decline.[38]

Mizrahi had previously depicted an explicitly Jewish-owned bank in his 1937 comedy *Al-'Izz bahdala* (*Mistreated by Affluence*, discussed in chap. 4). Two impoverished friends—Chalom, a Jew; and 'Abdu, a Muslim—receive a windfall and decide to found a bank, which they call Bank Chalom. The film's humor rests on the ways the pair are socially, linguistically, and professionally unprepared for their meteoric rise. Ultimately, the market crashes, the bank fails, and the two characters to return to their humble origins. In the 1930s, as discussed in chapters 3 and 4, Mizrahi directed three comedies starring the actor Chalom (Leon Angel) as a lower-class Egyptian Jewish character of the same name. Although both Mizrahi's comedies and his melodramas tend to revolve around plots of mistaken identity, playing on the shape-shifting nature of Levantines, markers of difference are transparent and factor into the plots of the comedies, but not the melodramas. Angel and his wife, Esther Cohen Angel (screen name: 'Adalat), retired from cinema in

1937.[39] Along with Chalom's departure from the screen, the overt representation of Jewish characters in Mizrahi's films disappeared.

In Mizrahi's films, difference or diversity is usually signaled by codes other than religion, such as ethnic names or foreign accents. For example, in *A Rainy Night* Ahmad sells his overcoat to a Greek used-clothing dealer: a multilingual sign identifies the merchant as George Mostakinopolo, and he speaks Arabic with a Greek accent.

The characterization of Yusuf in *The Straight Road* bears no distinctive religious markers; his first name is ambiguous, but in the absence of markers of difference, he is presumed Muslim. When Yusuf meets Suraya, she offers him a drink, and he demurs, claiming that he doesn't drink alcohol. Yusuf's moralizing—toward a wayward employee, and toward his family—is drawn from shared cultural values rather than specifically Islamic teachings.

But, by contrast, *The Straight Road* makes a point of explicitly identifying the members of the board of directors at the Egyptian Nationalist Bank as Muslims. In one of the most overt markers of religion in Mizrahi's oeuvre, when the senior executive who sent Yusuf on the mission to Lebanon learns of his protégé's death, he utters the Muslim statement of faith, the *shahada*. As a counterpoint, at a moment of crisis in *A Rainy Night*, Saniya prays for divine intervention to save her from 'Ali's blackmail. Her generically deist entreaty "*Ya rabb. Ya 'adl. Ya qadir 'ala kul shai'. Usturni, ya rabb* [O Lord. O Just One. O All Powerful. Protect me, O Lord]" could be uttered by an Egyptian Jew, a Christian, or a Muslim. In *The Straight Road*, the bank's owners are explicitly marked as Muslim.

How, then, do we understand the presence of a Star of David in the lobby of the bank? In the absence of Jewish characters, I maintain that the Star of David in *The Straight Road* visually signals the embedding of Jewish concerns in the narrative. Recall that Mizrahi is credited with the scenario, and Wahbi wrote the script. Mizrahi employs his creative license in the staging and shooting of the scenes.

Through the bank's entryway one can arrive at an allegorical reading of Yusuf's accident. Yusuf drives the car through torrential rain while Suraya tries to wipe condensation off the windshield. They can't see where they are going, and the car careens off a cliff. The only witnesses are the owners of a small seaside tavern, Abu Elias and Umm Elias, and their employee, Shukri.

Just as one cannot ignore a Star of David in the entry hall of a bank in the film of a Jewish director during World War II, one cannot ignore the significance in 1943 of Palestine as the radical rupture in the itinerary between Cairo and Beirut. The only planned stop along the itinerary depicted on-screen is the customs house in Isma'iliya. Directional signs just beyond the customs-house gate note the distances to Cairo and to the border of Palestine as the camera pans from the former, the point of origin, to the latter (fig. 39). The sign, notably, does not include the distance to their destination, Beirut.

FIGURE 39. Bilingual directional sign near the customs house in Isma'iliya indicating the distance to Palestine. Screenshot from *The Straight Road* (Togo Mizrahi, 1943).

The accident conveniently provides cover for the later loss of the gold. A telegram sent to the Egyptian Nationalist Bank states that the driver's body was not found but that a bag and a wallet belonging to Yusuf Fahmi were recovered. The article from the newspaper *Al-Jumhur* that Ibrahim reads out loud in Suraya's dressing room in Beirut notes that no trace of the body or the gold has been found. The two pieces of news, delivered in Cairo and Beirut, bracket the absence in Palestine, and grant it signification: on the one hand, news of Yusuf's presumed death, and on the other, revelation of Yusuf's survival but the demise of his identity.

Exchanging one identity for another, the character formerly known as Yusuf assumes the identity of a successful merchant (*tajir*), 'Abd al-Rahman Salim. The family name Salim, meaning "safe" or "whole," underscores the irony of Yusuf's predicament; he may be "safe"—uninjured, protected from the law—but he is not "whole." A member of Suraya's entourage reminds him that now he is a common thief—that if he were caught, he "would lose [his] name and honor." And Ibrahim assures him, "Yusuf Bey Fahmi died honorably. Then you became someone else. Who will recognize you?"

The only words that Yusuf utters in the scene are "I am uneasy." This uneasiness is an expression of unarticulated anxiety—the anxiety expressed by some Egyptian

Jewish and other Arab Jewish intellectuals about the role of the Zionist efforts in Palestine to build a Jewish state, and of the growing conflict between Jews and Arabs there, in unsettling their future in their home countries. In one notable example, Rene Qattawi (Cataoui), head of the Sephardi community of Cairo from 1943 to 1946, opposed Zionism and, along with the vice president of the Alexandria Sephardi community, sent a letter to the 1944 World Jewish Congress detailing the grounds for his opposition.[40] *The Straight Road*, through its interrupted itinerary, reveals an anxiety that Palestine is the cliff that Jews may drive off, causing Egyptian Jews to lose their homes, their jobs, and their identity.

CODA: LAYLA *BINT AL-BALAD*

In 1941 Yusuf Wahbi and Layla Murad appeared together on-screen for the second time, in *Layla bint al-rif* (*Layla the Country Girl*). Following the formula of *A Rainy Night*, *Layla the Country Girl* is a musical melodrama featuring a remarriage plot. Yusuf Wahbi plays Fathi, a Cambridge-educated surgeon (*sic*) turned playboy, who returns to his village in Upper Egypt and is pressured into marrying his cousin, Layla (Layla Murad). Upon their return to Cairo he ignores her, going out every night to parties with his friends, and continues carrying on with his mistress, a nightclub dancer.

But Layla's frumpy looks are deceiving. Just as she is about to request a divorce and return to the country, a friend from school—where they received a European-style education—discovers that Layla has returned to Cairo. The friend helps Layla update, modernize, and urbanize her look to turn Fathi's head. Layla—dressed in a ball gown and speaking French—surprises Fathi at an elegant party. Her plan to win Fathi's affections is foiled by the evil 'Izzat (Anwar Wagdi), who has his eye on Layla's substantial inheritance. Fathi falls prey to 'Izzat's deception and ends up divorcing Layla. Fathi later performs emergency surgery on 'Izzat, without knowing the identity of his patient. Grateful to Fathi for saving his life, 'Izzat comes clean and provides evidence of Layla's innocence. The film ends as Fathi races up to the village to proclaim his love to Layla before she is married again. In the final scene of the film, Fathi sweeps Layla off her feet to take her back to Cairo. Layla protests, "First, let me change out of my peasant clothes." Fathi responds, "I have only now understood the value of these clothes."

Layla Murad's character "Layla the Country Girl" is a true native daughter. Layla *bint al-rif* is Layla *bint al-balad*: Layla the country girl is Layla the true Egyptian girl. If an image of Layla in her peasant dress coupled with a sketch of a felucca on the Nile gracing the cover of the film's program (fig. 40) were not sufficient, Mizrahi drives the point home in the concluding scene. Fathi's car comes to a screeching halt in front of Layla's family home, where people are gathered to celebrate her wedding to another man. Before Fathi races inside, the camera captures

FIGURE 40. Pressbook for *Layla the Country Girl* (Togo Mizrahi, 1941). Courtesy of the Rare Books and Special Collections Library, The American University in Cairo.

the decorations. The front of the house is adorned with a string of Egyptian flags. In the shot of Fathi's arrival, a scene that anticipates the couple's happy reunion, the top of the screen is dominated by the repeated image of the Egyptian crescent and three stars. *Layla the Country Girl* thus begs to be read as national allegory. As Eyal Sagui-Bizawi writes, Layla "wins Fathi's heart and shows him the light, demonstrating how it is possible to act according to the 'Western' codes but also to remain loyal to the 'Eastern' Egyptian mores."[41] Egypt, according to the logic of the film, can embrace modernity, French education, and European style and still remain true to what is authentically Egyptian. Layla Murad, the Jewish singer who, like her character, received a European-style education, becomes the face of the modern, authentic Egyptian.

Layla Murad appeared in a series of "Layla" films. Following *Layla the Country Girl*, Layla again costarred with Yusuf Wahbi in another Togo Mizrahi production, *Layla bint madaris* (*Layla the Schoolgirl*, 1941), in which she once again played a young, innocent, and naive character, a girl. Layla Murad's popularity and star power grew exponentially over the course of her collaboration with Togo Mizrahi. In the following chapter, I explore the nature of female stardom in two of Togo Mizrahi's musicals: *Layla* (1942), starring Layla Murad, and *Sallama* (1945), starring Umm Kulthum.

Courtesan and Concubine

LOVE MATCHES AND MARRIAGE PLOTS

Togo Mizrahi's musical melodrama *Qalb imra'a* (*Heart of a Woman*, 1940) features two weddings. The first wedding opens with a montage following a visual idiom established in Mizrahi's film *Layla mumtira* (*A Rainy Night*, 1939; see chap. 6). The image of champagne pouring into crystal glasses is superimposed over fashionably dressed youth dancing in pairs. The unhappy bride, Khayriya (Amina Rizq), like her counterpart Layla in *A Rainy Night*, is resigned to the union. When the film opens, Khayriya, the daughter of a landowning family in the Egyptian countryside, is engaged to her first cousin, Amin (Anwar Wagdi), the orphaned son of a noble. But Amin spurns Khayriya when he learns that, unbeknownst to her, her family has lost its wealth. Khayriya's mother and her brother decide to hide their changed circumstances from Khayriya to spare her a second blow. Fayiz (Sulayman Naguib), a wealthy factory owner, falls in love with Khayriya, and persists in his desire to marry her even after learning that there will be no dowry. Khayriya, still in love with her cousin, unenthusiastically accepts his proposal.

While in *A Rainy Night* the montage of the nuptials is accompanied by Felix Mendelssohn's "Wedding March," the montage of Khayriya and Fayiz's wedding in *Heart of a Woman* is accompanied by nondiegetic strains of Arabic music. The scene then cuts to the inside of a tent, where we see the source of the music: a male signer accompanied by traditional instruments is entertaining the villagers. His inspiring performance (*tarab*) is periodically interrupted by the celebrants' interjection of praise and appreciation. Female dancers wear long-sleeved, high-necked, ankle-length black dresses—not the revealing, spangled costumes worn by dancers in *A Rainy Night*. Khayriya and Fayiz's cross-class, communal wedding party celebrates not only their nuptials but also Egyptian village culture. The wedding party reflects the groom's generosity, civic-mindedness, and appreciation of local traditions—characteristics the bride comes to appreciate over the course of the film.

In the second wedding, Amin weds Fatima (Aqila Ratab), the daughter of butcher, whose nouveau riche family seeks legitimation via her marriage with a member of the elite. The well-matched social climbers, Fatima and Amin, whose first on-screen dialogue is conducted in affected English, wed off-screen in Cairo. Seeking to arouse the jealousy of Amin's cousins, now living in genteel poverty, they throw a lavish, exclusive wedding party in the village. Two professional dancers, backed by a small orchestra, perform to Ravel's *Boléro*. Fatima offers to sing for her guests, but the song turns into a suggestive flirtation with Fayiz, Khayriya's husband.

The audience's sympathies are with Khayriya and Fayiz—and the fusion of modernity with tradition, wealth, and generosity that their union represents. Walter Armbrust views the entwining of patriarchal society with trappings of Western modernity in Egyptian cinema as an articulation of a culturally specific Egyptian modernity. Armbrust argues that the 1938 film *Yahya al-hubb* (*Long Live Love*), directed by Muhammad Karim and starring Muhammad ʿAbd al-Wahab and Layla Murad, presents a narrative of a modern love relationship in which familial love and romantic love work in consort, even when the parties' interests come into conflict.[1] In *Long Live Love*, the love match of the modern couple turns out to also be the perfect arranged marriage, endorsed by the two fathers.

In *Heart of a Woman*, the match is arranged by the lawyer who handles Khayriya's family affairs after the loss of the patriarch. Over time, Khayriya falls in love with the groom selected for her. Khayriya's esteem for Fayiz is sealed when she finally learns that Fayiz, aware of the family circumstances as she had not been, married her for love and not money. At the end of the film, Khayriya finds love, improves her social status, and achieves financial security. Upholding the cinematic conventions of the love match, *Heart of a Woman* also portrays marriage as a socioeconomic transaction.

In the 1940s, Togo Mizrahi departs from these love-marriage conventions in two musical films. *Layla* (1942), an adaptation of Alexander Dumas fils's novel *La dame aux camélias* (1848), stars Layla Murad in the role of a courtesan. *Sallama* (1945), an adaptation of ʿAli Ahmad Ba Kathir's novel *Sallamat al-Qass* (1941), stars Umm Kulthum in the role of a *qayna*, a singing slave girl. This chapter analyzes the performance of female sexuality and the sexuality of performance in these melodramas featuring two of the biggest female musical film stars in 1940s Egypt. These films, set in the past, lay bare the transactionality of the modern marriage plot and respond to significant changes in personal-status law in Egypt.

In what follows, I first discuss the social, legal, and educational transformations Egyptian women experienced in the late nineteenth and early twentieth centuries. In particular, I focus on the changes in women's lives affected by the success of two abolitionist movements: the late-nineteenth-century efforts to abolish slavery, and the movement to end the practice of legal prostitution in the first half of the twentieth century. These interrelated issues, affecting not only indentured women and sex workers, but also family structure among the elites, influenced the cinematic construction of the modern marriage plot, and provide a background for my discussion of the films that diverge from these norms. In the second section below, "Courtesan/Queen: *Layla* (1942)," I explore how the film *Layla* reflects upon female performance, casting Layla (star and protagonist) as cinema royalty. The film thereby levies an indirect critique on the sexual improprieties of Egypt's monarch. Layla, the courtesan, resembles the female social climbers in the modern marriage plot, like Fatima from *Heart of a Woman,* more than she resembles the Egyptian prostitutes at the center of the abolitionist movement. But I argue that *Layla* can be read as a critique of prostitution's debasement of the nation—a central tenet of the abolitionist movement. The final section of this chapter, "A Modern *Qayna: Sallama* (1945)," unpacks the sociosexual implications of Umm Kulthum's preference to play the role of the singing slave girl. I begin this section by reviewing the implied sexual politics of her two prior appearances as a *qayna:* in *Widad* (1936, Fritz Kramp) and *Dananir* (1940, Ahmad Badr Khan). In *Sallama,* Umm Kulthum's character is bought and sold multiple times, making her sexually available to multiple owners. My analysis unpacks the way the film maintains the honor of Sallama, the slave, in a manner consistent with modern marriage conventions. In addition to granting Sallama a safe space within the palace, I argue, Togo Mizrahi elicits queer Levantine performances from the actors who play Sallama's owners to diffuse the sexual threat they would otherwise pose.

ABOLITION OF SLAVERY AND LEGAL PROSTITUTION IN EGYPT

Women's roles in society and access to education in Egypt were significantly transformed in the first three decades of the twentieth century. Two laws, passed in 1923 and 1931, raised the marital age to sixteen for women and eighteen for men, respectively.[2] In 1929 the state extended universal elementary education to girls, opened secondary schools and teacher training programs for girls, and began admitting women into university.[3] By 1930 elite women were no longer secluded in the domestic sphere, and were widely abandoning the practice of veiling.[4]

In the 1940s, when *Layla* and *Sallama* were released, the processes that brought about the universal acceptance of conjugal marriage (and the abandonment of the Islamically sanctioned practice of concubinage), the dissolution of the harem, and the emergence of elite women into the public sphere were still part of the living memory in Egypt. The struggle for the abolition of legalized prostitution was still ongoing. Like other films produced in Egypt in the 1940s, neither *Layla* nor *Sallama* is overtly political. The two films neither explicitly represent nor directly comment upon the rapid changes in women's status that Egypt had experienced in the preceding decades. Both films are based on works of literature and peddle in common filmic tropes. Nevertheless, it is worth asking how these two films—about a prostitute and a slave, respectively—might have been read by contemporaneous audiences who were inhabiting those changed circumstances.

The changes in women's status effected in early-twentieth-century Egypt were driven by two abolitionist efforts: one against slavery and the other against legal prostitution. In Egypt, both the practice of slavery and that of prostitution were historically interrelated, and both are connected to the dissolution of the harem among the ruling elites. Beginning in Mamluk Egypt and continuing into the nineteenth century, the markets for slaves and sex workers were intertwined. Imported sex workers came from the same sources as slaves: Africa and the Caucasus.[5] Pimps sometimes purchased sex workers, and conversely, some slave merchants also operated brothels. Some African slaves were reportedly forced into prostitution by their masters.[6]

Despite state efforts in Egypt to outlaw the importation and sale of slaves beginning in the middle of the nineteenth century, the practice persisted until the turn of the twentieth century. Slavery in nineteenth-century Egypt, as in the rest of the Ottoman Empire, was sanctioned by and practiced according to Islamic law. Freeborn Muslims could not be enslaved; non-Muslims captured by slave traders in the Caucasus and sub-Saharan Africa were torn from their homes and families to supply the demand for slaves in Egypt. According to Liat Kozma's estimates, in nineteenth-century Egypt female slaves, employed largely for domestic labor, outnumbered male slaves three to one.[7] Male slave owners could take their female slaves as concubines. Children born from such unions were free and were considered eligible to inherit their father's property; concubines who bore children were freed upon the death of their master.[8]

Efforts to reduce or abolish slavery in Egypt through much of the nineteenth century met with limited success. The 1877 Anglo-Egyptian Slave Trade Convention, in conjunction with increased local policing efforts, served to slow the slave trade.[9] In the following two decades, slave ownership declined, and, according to Kozma, "the emerging Egyptian nationalist intelligentsia started condemning slavery as un-Islamic."[10] By 1895, when Egypt and Britain signed the Anti-Slavery Convention prohibiting all sales of slaves, even between individuals, both the number of enslaved people and the number of slave owners had significantly declined. Although no new slaves could be brought into Egypt or sold between families, Gabriel Baer finds evidence that slaveholding persisted until 1907.[11]

The abolition of slavery and the legalization and regulation of prostitution were effected contemporaneously. In 1882, following the British occupation of Egypt, colonial authorities implemented regulations to legalize and thereby regulate prostitution. The Comprehensive Law on Brothels was promulgated in 1896, a year after the Anti-Slavery Convention, and the year in which the opening scene of

Layla is set.[12] This law established a licensing system of brothels and sex workers, both under surveillance by the authorities. Prostitutes were subject to weekly medical exams, and brothels were permitted only in designated urban areas.[13]

In the first half of the twentieth century, public opposition to legal prostitution grew among a number of constituencies. According to Hanan Hammad and Francesca Biancani, "nationalists, religious authorities, local feminists, British purity movement advocates, and colonial administrators" all opposed legal prostitution, each group defending its position from a different perspective.[14] Elite women objected to prostitution on basis of hygiene, and as a means of opposition to the Ottoman-era capitulations under which residents with foreign citizenship were governed by a different legal standard than Egyptians. Professional women such as Labiba Ahmad and Munira Thabit also objected to prostitution, but they blamed the country's moral decline on Egyptians' embrace of Western consumerism.[15] According to Beth Baron, Egyptians across the political spectrum, "from the Muslim Brotherhood to the Egyptian Feminist Union," concurred that legal prostitution in Egypt "dishonored the nation."[16]

In response to these wide-ranging calls to abolish prostitution, a mixed Anglo-Egyptian commission was formed in 1932. The proposals laid out in the commission's 1935 report to further limit and regulate prostitution were put into effect in by a Ministry of Health decree in 1938. The regulation forbade the registration of new brothels and the licensing of additional prostitutes. The Egyptian parliament first addressed the issue of prostitution in 1939. Despite the increasing public and administrative opposition, with the increased number of British Commonwealth soldiers in Egypt, the sex market expanded during World War II.[17] In 1943, prostitution was abolished in provincial towns.[18] Legal brothels continued to operate in provincial capitals, including Cairo and Alexandria, until 1949, when prostitution was abolished nationwide by military decree. A law passed in 1951 officially criminalized sex work.[19]

In sum, according to Haytham Bahoora, Egyptian efforts to abolish legal prostitution were "concerned less with the marginalized figure of the prostitute than with symbolically restoring the nation's purity and overcoming colonial violation."[20] The film *Layla* was released in the midst of this nationalist abolition effort. Layla, the fictional courtesan, does not resemble the typical prostitute in Egypt. During the period between 1896 (the film's setting) and 1942 (its release date), sex workers hailing from a number of working-class backgrounds worked out of legal brothels or in illicit "*maisons de rendez-vous*" located in popular neighborhoods.[21] Layla, by contrast, lives the high life, supported by her aristocratic lovers, whom she visits in their country homes or entertains in her own apartment. Despite the characteristics that distinguish the filmic figure of the prostitute from those who plied their trade in Egyptian brothels, I take the anticolonial discourse of national purification as a point of departure for my analysis of the film *Layla*.

COURTESAN/QUEEN: *LAYLA* (1942)

In the first decades of Egyptian cinema production, star salaries made up a signifi-cant proportion of production budgets, since, as Jacob Landau notes of Arab cin-emagoers, "the public hankers first and foremost for the stars."[22] Over the course of her films with Togo Mizrahi, Layla Murad's star power grew exponentially. When Muhammad 'Abd al-Wahab offered the young singer a role in the film *Long Live Love* in 1938, she earned 350 Egyptian pounds for her appearance.[23] After the suc-cess of their first film collaboration, Togo Mizrahi reportedly offered Layla Murad a two-film contract for a combined 3,500 Egyptian pounds, but she insisted on 3,000 each. By the time Togo approached Layla about appearing in a fourth movie, *Layla*, he offered her a contract worth 7,000 Egyptian pounds.[24] The legendary rapid rise of Layla Murad's salary was an integral part of her image as a star.

With her rising star power, Murad also commanded greater control over pro-duction. Murad reportedly insisted upon reviewing the script of *Layla* with Miz-rahi prior to the start of shooting. Mizrahi had also intended to once again cast the veteran actor Yusuf Wahbi as her costar, but Murad insisted that the more youthful Husayn Sidqi play the role instead.[25]

Critics agree that Togo Mizrahi recognized and cultivated Layla Murad's star potential. In contrast to her performance in *Long Live Love*, under the shadow of Muhammad 'Abd al-Wahab, Murad emerges as a true leading lady in Mizrahi's *A Rainy Night*. The benefits of their collaborations were mutual: Layla Murad's popu-larity boosted Togo Mizrahi's career as well. Their fourth film together, *Layla*, was a huge success, running for nineteen weeks at the Cinema Cosmo.[26]

From his earliest film efforts, Togo Mizrahi cast some actors to play charac-ters who shared their name or their stage name. This phenomenon is most pro-nounced, and most successful, in the case of Layla Murad. The close association between the singer's name, the titles of her films, and the characters she played on-screen was unique in Egyptian cinema. The name "Layla" appeared in the title of seven of her movies, spanning her career. In addition, the first film she made with Togo Mizrahi, *A Rainy Night* (chap. 6), contained a play on her name. Her four additional films directed by Mizrahi were *Layla bint al-rif* (*Layla the Country Girl*, 1941); *Layla bint madaris* (*Layla the Schoolgirl*, 1941); *Layla* (1942); and *Layla fi al-zalam* (*Layla in the Dark*, 1944). Anwar Wagdi followed suit in choosing titles for three of the films he directed starring Murad: *Layla bint al-fuqara'* (*Layla the Poor Girl*, 1945); *Layla bint al-aghniya'* (*Layla the Rich Girl*, 1946); and *Layla bint al-akabir* (*Layla the Aristocratic Girl*, 1953). In these films, Layla was cast as an ingénue—a role she continued playing until well into her thirties. In what follows, I analyze the film *Layla* (1942) to explore the relationship between "Layla" and Layla: character and star, performance and performer.

Layla is based on *La dame aux camélias*, a story about a prostitute, Marguerite Gautier, who sacrifices herself to save the honor of the man she loves, Armand

Duval. Dumas adapted the story for the theater in 1852. Inspired by Dumas's play, Giuseppe Verdi began work on an opera that was to become *La Traviata* (1853). There have also been multiple film adaptations of the story, including several in the silent era featuring the biggest stars of the day. In 1934, Abel Gance—a mentor and early influence on Togo Mizrahi—codirected the first French sound film production of *La dame aux camélias*.[27] The first Hollywood adaptation of the sound era was *Camille* (George Cukor, 1936), starring Greta Garbo. Layla Murad loved the novel when she first read it, and was thrilled to have the opportunity to play the role of Marguerite. Referring to the part as her "dream role," Murad reread the novel in French and in Arabic translation to study the part.[28]

All versions of the story—novel, play, and film adaptations—share several core plot elements. The prostitute, suffering from tuberculosis, is pursued by an earnest young man.[29] While she is ill, he asks after her every day, but declines to identify himself. After her recovery, they meet. She tries to dissuade him from besmirching his good name by associating with her, but he rebuffs her admonitions, and they fall in love. They leave the city together and settle in the countryside, where she can recuperate. While living the high life, she had accumulated significant debts. Having distanced herself from the wealthy lovers who used to support her lifestyle, she secretly sells her belongings to pay off her remaining debt. The young man discovers her secret and decides to help support her with his family's money. The young man's father is thus alerted to his son's profligacy and what he deems his poor judgment. The father appeals directly to the former prostitute to leave his son for the sake of his future and the family's honor. She agrees and breaks with her lover in dramatic fashion so he won't wish to reconcile. The prostitute then returns to her former life, and ultimately succumbs to consumption. Her lover learns of her sacrifice. In the novel, the knowledge comes too late, but in the play and in most film adaptations, the lovers are granted a parting scene on her deathbed.

In Mizrahi's adaptation, the kept woman is a singer named Layla (Layla Murad). The young man, Farid (Husayn Sidqi), issues from a conservative Upper Egyptian landowning family.[30] The film is set in Cairo in 1896, an era often called the "veiled protectorate." Britain had occupied Egypt in 1882, after suppressing the 'Urabi Revolt. Egypt maintained its status as an autonomous province of the Ottoman Empire. But Britain held a de facto protectorate over Egypt.

The film's historical setting invites a reflection on the shifting perceptions of female performance in Egypt. The first woman appeared on the stage of a highbrow theater in Cairo in 1894 when a Jewish actress—also, by coincidence, named Layla—performed in a production at the Cairo Opera House.[31] The first actresses to perform in public were Jews and Christians. But within the first two decades of the twentieth century, Muslim women began joining, and eventually leading, performing troupes.[32] As Sherifa Zuhur writes in her study of Layla Murad's contemporary Asmahan, "[I]n the middle of the twentieth century, [the female singer] was never simply an individual, but also, and always a female body emitting poetic text through song."[33]

The film's setting also indexes Egypt's entrance into the cinematic era. The opening party represented in the film occurs in June 1896; in November of the same year the Lumière brothers arrived in Egypt to screen their moving pictures in both Alexandria and Cairo, mere months after the premiere in Europe. *Layla* draws attention to the star system introduced by the film industry and the respective shift it ushers in of the social valences attached to performance as well as to spectatorship.

The opening scene lays out these tensions—between women's public performance and confinement; and between Turkish influence and British power in Egypt. The sound of a waltz plays as the credits roll. The scene cuts to a hand holding an invitation to a party hosted by "Sulayman Pasha" on 3 June 1896. In the entry hall, a servant opens the French doors for arriving guests. As the scene cuts to the main hall, we catch a glimpse of the dance floor framed on the bottom by the balustrade of the musicians' balcony, and an arch supported by two columns. An ornate crystal chandelier hangs from the center of the ballroom, partially obstructing our view of the dancers. The architecture is modern, Western.

The camera then zooms in for a medium shot of the dancers. The dancing men are wearing tuxedos, and the women are in ball gowns. Only the men's headgear distinguishes between members of the elite. European men check their top hats at the door—a detail that serves as the basis of a comic interlude as the scene proceeds—while some of the Egyptian men keep a tarboosh on their heads.

As the music continues, the scene then cuts to the exterior, where we see carriages lined up discharging their passengers—all women in ball gowns wearing white yashmaks, Turkish-style veils. The music ends. The scene cuts back to the long shot of the main hall as dancers applaud the orchestra and exit the dance floor.

The first words of the film are uttered by an unidentified British official in military garb. He is shown, in partial profile, addressing the host—Sulayman Pasha, an elegantly dressed gentleman in a tuxedo and tarboosh. The British official exchanges pleasantries with the host, then asks, "Why are there no Egyptian women?"

The Egyptian women, Sulayman points out, sit upstairs "in the loge." The loge is constructed in the manner of a theater balcony. Seated like spectators of a performance, the women observe—and comment upon—the party below. They watch the proceedings through thin, translucent drapery, which is occasionally drawn aside for a better view. In keeping with the Western decor of the venue, the separate women's space is designed as a viewing balcony. It is not called a harem, nor is it constructed in the idiom of Islamic architecture—as appears in *Sallama*.

Layla's reputation precedes her. When she enters, the crowd gossips about her recent affairs. Farid is captivated by her. When he asks his friend Hamdi ('Abd al-Salam al-Nablusi) to make an introduction, Hamdi warns him that "she wrecks the homes [*bi-tikharab baytuh*] of those she meets." The commodification of Layla's body is signaled in her first song, "Min yishtiri al-ward minni"—"Who Will Buy a Flower from Me?" For the performance, she dons a vendor's tray full of cut flowers, which she tosses into the crowd as she sings. Her costume, however, is not that of a salesgirl. Her white lace gown is a modest—high-necked, long-sleeved—version of period French fashion, with corseted waist and full skirt. After Layla makes her grand entrance into the reception hall, a male guest proclaims to his female companions (in Arabic) that she "always dresses well," and then adds (in French), "*Chic.*" Reminiscent of a wedding gown, Layla's dress signifies the dichotomy of her character as heroine-whore. Layla, both as performer and as an Egyptian woman given access to the mixed space of the reception hall, stands out. Both within the diegesis and external to it, as the star performer Layla is an object of desire for the men, and of emulation for the women.

The film, I argue, further elevates Layla's status—both diegetically and extradi-egetically. Layla is visually and narratively aligned with symbols of the ruling family, casting both character and star as cinematic royalty. *Layla* accomplishes this alignment through the vernacular of fashion and via her mode of transportation.

In 1890s Egypt, elite women would have worn the Turkish-style veil when they were out in public—as are the women depicted arriving in carriages to attend Sulayman Pasha's party. Layla and her friend Zuzu (Zuzu Shakib) arrive together. Underneath their cloaks and the Turkish veil, they both wear elegant ball gowns. We are not given much of a view of the other Egyptian women: those populating the loge are seated behind a balustrade and partially obscured by the curtain. Some wear the yashmak, while others are coiffed and bareheaded. A woman—perhaps a servant—standing in the back of the loge wears a black hijab and a white face veil. Layla is shown in public only one other time in the film—during a carriage ride (discussed at greater length below)—and there, too, she is shown wearing a yashmak.

A great deal has been written about veiling in Egypt and the Islamic world in general. Photographs of women's demonstrations from 1919 show Egyptian women—many of them elites—wearing black robes draped over their head and body, accompanied by a translucent white veil covering their faces from the bridge of the nose down. In May 1923, returning from a women's conference in Rome, Huda Sha'arawi and Saiza Nabarawi publicly removed their face veils upon descending from the train in Cairo. Other politically engaged elite women followed suit.[34]

In 1940s Egyptian cinema, veiling (or the lack thereof) indexes a web of social cues. In films set in the present, lower-class urban women, or fellahin, are shown veiled in public, wearing traditional *baladi* head coverings, and wrapped in a black *milaya* (a long wrap draped over the head and shoulders).[35] When at the end of *Layla* the maid goes begging for money to buy Layla medicine, she is dressed in a black wrap and a white face veil. Layla's veil in the film, by contrast, comprises two pieces of white fabric—one draped around the head, and a second one draped loosely around her head and neck—with her face uncovered.[36]

When *Layla* was released in 1942, the only women wearing the yashmak paired with Western fashion were members of the royal family and women of the court. The most visible female member of the royal household was the young queen, Farida. In 1938, the recently installed, youthful King Farouk married Safinaz Zul-ficar, the daughter of an elite Egyptian-Circassian family, who adopted the name Farida. Images of the royal couple regularly graced the pages of the strictly cen-sored local press. In keeping with the practices of modern royalty, Farida was fre-quently shown at charity events and at state functions. During these occasions as an official representative of the state, she wore the Turkish-style yashmak.[37]

Within a month of *Layla*'s premiere, the queen appeared twice on the cover of the weekly popular journal *Al-Ithnayn*. On 16 March 1942, the journal pub-lished a reproduction of the queen's official portrait commemorating the royal couple's fourth wedding anniversary (fig. 41). The cover of the 4 May 1942 issue of *Al-Ithnayn* features a photograph of the queen visiting an orphanage in a fashion-able dress, with a stylish finger wave peeking out from under her veil.[38] The week of *Layla*'s premiere, *Al-Ithnayn* included a two-page spread about the women who attended the opening of parliament, viewing the proceedings from box seats. The notable women are identified as the daughters and wives of ministers and politi-cal elites. The copy accompanying the photographs compliments the women's ele-gance and fashion choices: "[T]he ladies were noticeably elegant. We saw the latest hairstyles as well as the most modern designs." In all of these pictures, the queen and the ladies of the court wear smart skirt suits—the height of 1940s fashion—and a white Turkish-style yashmak.[39]

The advertisement that ran in *Al-Ithnayn* on 6 April 1942, the week of *Layla*'s premiere, featured the characters Layla and Zuzu dressed as they were upon their arrival at Sulayman Pasha's party, wearing this same style of veil (fig. 42).[40] The image is a publicity photo, not a still from the final cut of the film. They are shown in an interior space: behind them a picture frame—image obscured—hangs on a wall that is horizontally bisected by a chair rail. Peeking out behind Layla's shoulder is a lone white flower—a camellia, with which her character is associated. The image makes an effective advertisement for an escapist costume drama released at a time of domestic and international crisis; we see popular actresses dressed in elegant fin-ery. But, the ad's visual identification with the ruling family, I argue, is also unmis-takable. First, the image pairs haute couture with the yashmak, the Turkish veil. Second, the title of the film is bordered by an ornate oval frame, much like the frame of the royal portrait—and more generally associated with Farouk and his family.

The advertisement promotes both the film itself and Layla's star image. The ad copy reads: "Togo Mizrahi, the producer of the three big hits *A Rainy Night*, *Layla the Country Girl*, and *Layla the Schoolgirl* closes out the cinema season with his new, outstanding film *Layla*." The titles of the first three films are listed in an angled column, bordered on the right by a line connecting the words to the image of Layla Murad appearing as the eponymous character, Layla. Other ver-sions of the advertisement also include this repetition of the titles, linking star

FIGURE 41. Portrait of Queen Farida on the cover of *Al-Ithnayn*, 16 March 1942.

and character. Visually and textually, the connection between character and star promotes the idea of Layla Murad as cinema royalty.

Layla's mode of transportation also contributes to the identification of Layla with royal symbols. In the opening scene, other female guests are shown arriving at Sulayman's party in two-seater carriages with the hood pulled up to partially

FIGURE 42. Opening-week ad for *Layla*, featuring Layla Murad (right) and Zuzu Shakib. *Al-Ithnayn*, 6 April 1942.

obstruct public view of the passengers. Layla, by contrast, rides in a large open carriage. In distinction from the other arriving guests, two uniformed, dark-skinned servants carrying staffs run barefoot alongside the pair of horses pulling Layla's carriage.

In the 1890s, when the film is set, state officials and wealthy families would employ foot guards, known as *amshagiyya*, to run in front of horse-drawn carriages to clear a path through the crowded streets. With the advent of the automobile, *amshagiyya* became all but obsolete.[41] By the late 1920s, members of the urban elite who had previously employed *amshagiyya* to accompany their carriages had widely adopted the new mode of transportation. The royal family continued to employ *amshagiyya* for ceremonial occasions into the early years of Farouk's reign. In 1937, Farouk was transported to his investiture via royal carriage, accompanied by both cavalry and *amshagiyya*.[42] In 1942, when *Layla* was released, the only remaining *amshagiyya* were those employed by the palace for ceremonial purposes.

In the film, on the night of Sulayman Pasha's party, Layla's carriage is the only one accompanied by *amshagiyya*. The primary function of the *amshagiyya*—as becomes evident in their second appearance—is to support the identification of the character Layla with the royal court, and the identification of Layla Murad as cinema royalty.

In the film, Layla, after recuperating from her first illness, takes a ride with Zuzu in the open carriage. When Farid learns of Layla's outing, he eagerly runs to catch a glimpse of her. Farid's guardian, 'Abd al-Mas'ud (Bishara Wakim), follows after him. They stop short as they catch sight of the approaching carriage. Farid signals to 'Abd al-Mas'ud to keep silent. Shot in broad daylight, Layla's carriage is in clear view as it travels at a moderate pace down a wide street, accompanied by a pair of *amshagiyya* (fig. 43). First, we see a tight two-shot of Layla and Zuzu; then the scene cuts to a long shot of the approaching carriage. There are no pedestrians, no donkey carts, no throngs of vendors that the *amshagiyya* must part for the carriage to pass through. Like the footmen accompanying the royal carriage as it processes along a cleared parade route, Layla's *amshagiyya* position themselves next to, rather than in front of, the horses.

At the conclusion of the scene, the camera tracks back slightly as the carriage approaches, and then pans to follow it as it passes, catching the back of Farid's and 'Abd al-Mas'ud's heads as they, too, turn to watch Layla go by. The two specta-tors stand in awe—frozen as if at attention—as the procession passes. The music swells; throughout this scene the audience hears a nondiegetic reprise of the open-ing waltz. The passing of Layla's carriage is rendered a spectacle.

The opening sequence and this carriage scene are the only times in the film that Layla wears the Turkish veil, and also the only times the film depicts *amshagi-yya*. Multiple other carriages are shot in motion in the film without *amshagiyya*. After the summer vacation, Farid leaves his family home by carriage, and twice is

FIGURE 43. *Amshagiyya* accompany Layla's carriage. Screenshot from *Layla* (Togo Mizrahi, 1942).

shown departing by carriage from the home he shares with Layla in the country. A doctor arrives by carriage to treat Layla. Farid's father arrives and departs by carriage, framing his dramatic interaction with Layla. The film also features a carriage chase. At one point Farid storms out and rides off into the night on a simple buckboard. Layla follows after him, jumping into an enclosed carriage, a thin black veil pinned, as if in haste, to the back of her head. In this scene, as she rushes to reconcile with Farid by renouncing her reliance on the financial support of other men, Layla no longer wears the yashmak, and her carriage proceeds without the services of the *amshagiyya*. Within the diegesis, the loss of these royal symbols maps the character's disavowal of wealth in favor of happiness. But for the audience, the star, Layla Murad, remains associated with the trappings of royalty.

The film visually constructs its heroine in the image of the ruling Egyptian-Turko-Circassian elites. I have articulated what this gesture says about Layla, the character and the star, but it is less clear what it might say about the ruling family. Egyptian censors would hardly have tolerated any criticism of the ruling family, or any depiction of a despotic ruler that could have stood in for the Egyptian monarch. The film was produced during a period of intensification of World War II. Egypt maintained nominal neutrality in the conflict, although it was a base of operations for Allied troops, and was the site of key battles. In July

1941, a German air raid on Alexandria caused substantial damage, including four hundred casualties. A covert Italian operation in Alexandria harbor in December 1941 disabled two British ships.[43] On 4 February 1942, the British intervened in an Egyptian parliamentary dispute, giving Farouk an ultimatum: either accept formation of a government led by the Wafd Party, or abdicate. He accepted the formation of a new government to stay in power, but with his power significantly weakened vis-à-vis the British. King Farouk publicly reiterated Egypt's noncombatant status at the opening of parliament on 30 March 1942—restating that according to the terms of the Anglo-Egyptian treaty, Britain was responsible for the protection of Egypt.[44]

Layla is unique among Egyptian films of the era for representing the recent past—a past still in living memory. Further, the film takes the unprecedented step—for the era—of including a British official in the opening scene. Egyptian historical films of the 1930s and 1940s tended to be set in the distant past to avoid running afoul of the censors. Perhaps because the film was an adaptation of a popular work of literature, it was given surprising latitude by the censors. Taken together, the historical proximity and the presence of the British officer in the opening scene invite viewers to draw parallels between a fictional representation of the past and the politics of the present.[45]

While King Farouk was politically impotent in the face of the British, rumors abound about his virility in the conduct of his private affairs. King Farouk was known to attend wild parties and engage in illicit liaisons with women. The rowdy party Layla hosts in the film echoes rumors of royal debauchery.

Selective use of anachronisms in the film draws attention to the parallels between the fictional past and current affairs. While the film does not for the most part aim for period authenticity, Layla's costumes evoke 1890s fashions. Many of Layla's dresses, including the white gown she wears in the opening scene, feature tight bodices and sleeves that puff at the shoulder—reminiscent of period corseted waistlines and gigot sleeves. By contrast, when she sings "Bi-ti-buss li kidda leh?" ("Why Do You Look at Me That Way?"), her dress—also white—features a 1940s waistline and neckline. Throughout the film, evening gowns worn by extras in the party scenes are more 1940s than 1890s, but the guests' costumes at Layla's party are strikingly more revealing than those worn by the guests in the opening scene. Collectively, then, costumes at Layla's party read as contemporary—not period. A contemporaneous reviewer noted another anachronism—style of dancing.[46] The party scene, shot largely from the point of view of the upstanding character Farid, casts a critical eye on the excesses and moral laxity of the elites, and the scene's anachronisms encourage viewers to make the connection to the present.

Although some of the biggest scandals broke later in King Farouk's reign, including his affair with the Egyptian actress known as Camelia (née Lilian Cohen), by 1942 relations between the monarch and Queen Farida were already strained.[47]

Is Farid's attraction/repulsion to the debauchery perhaps a gesture toward spurned Queen Farida, who struggled to maintain her honor in the face of her husband's philandering?

While telling a crass story, Layla, to illustrate a point, lifts her dress. Farid looks on horrified. When they have a private moment alone, Farid asks, "Why do you speak that way? Only beautiful words should issue from that beautiful mouth and those beautiful lips."

Layla starts to respond, and he silences her. Raising his hand in front of her mouth, Farid implores her, "Don't speak. Don't say a word. I thought you were different."

Layla echoes, "Different?"

"Please, let's leave it with what I thought. Leave me to my imagination."

"Imagination?"

The oud player interrupts, and takes Layla away to prepare to perform the song "Why Do You Look at Me That Way?" The performance permits Farid to live in the world of his imagination as beautiful words and music issue from Layla's lips. The lyrics pivot some of the attention from the auditory to the visual, the relationship between female performer and male spectator:

> Why do you look at me that way?
> Tell me, what are your intentions? Why do you look at me that way?
> Are you trying to tempt me?
> Or did you feel sorry for me and wish to console me?
> Or did you see the love asleep in my heart? Did you want to engage my heart and
> awaken my love?[48]

Layla sings the opening refrain and the first verse directly to Farid. As she sings this verse, Layla is shot in close-up, over Farid's shoulder, interrupted by a brief reaction shot. In the opening scene, Farid mistakenly thought Layla was singing directly to him; here, there is no ambiguity. Formulaic features of love songs abound in "Why Do You Look at Me That Way?" 'Ali Jihad Racy notes that these formulae "are emotionally effective not despite, but because of their tendency to generalize, abstract, and stereotype."[49] Layla's performance of the first verse inverts the typical formula. Since the verse is sung by a prostitute to an honorable young man, the temptation to which the lyrics allude is not sexual desire, but rather the temptation to become emotionally engaged, to fall in love.

The second verse reverts to form. During the instrumental interlude between verses, the camera pans to follow Layla strolling through the crowd, then cutting back to Farid's gaze. She delivers the second verse to Hamdi, hands on her hips, as if indignant. He turns to look at her, his back to the camera. At the end of the verse, feigning disgust at his desire to "pick a flower" seen "blooming on the branches" as a "salve for his grief," she throws her handkerchief at his chin, in lieu of a slap in the face, and storms off into the crowd. Continuing with the theme of grief, Layla directs the third verse to an anonymous seated male guest. Between each verse, the camera cuts to a shot of Farid's longing gaze.

While the first three verses are addressed to a singular "you," the final verse is delivered in the plural. This verse is shot with an unmediated view of Layla: the spectators are positioned behind her, blurry, beyond the focal point of the camera. She faces the camera as she sings, looking slightly off-center in the medium distance, not directly at the camera—refusing to return the audience's gaze.

> Why are your eyes thirsty, always seeking someone to quench their thirst?
> Why are your hearts confused, not finding anything to satisfy them?
> I make you laugh, I entertain you, I carouse with you, I console you.
> Then you take what beauty gives, and me, what do I get from you in return?

At the end of the verse, Layla steps out of the frame, and the camera focuses in on the guests standing behind her. The crowd of both men and women respond to the song's final question, "What do I get from you in return?," by chanting, "Money, money, money." Just before the start of the song, Hamdi had quipped to Farid that for nice words from Layla one pays their weight in gold.

Layla's performance of "Why Do You Look at Me That Way" closely resembles Fatima's performance of "Illi wayak al-fulus" ("You Who Have Money") at her engagement party in *Heart of a Woman*. The fiancée and fiancé—Fatima, a butcher's daughter, and Amin, the impoverished orphan of a pasha, respectively—have been deceiving one another about their respective financial situations and social statuses. Wearing a white dress, Fatima sings to the assembled guests. The two party scenes are similarly shot: medium shots or close-ups of the singer interspersed with reaction shots between verses. As Fatima passes among the guests, she reaches into one man's suit jacket and extracts a bill, which she tosses away. "With money," she proclaims, "I could buy myself a million fiancés." When Amin starts looking concerned, she reassures him that she is ventriloquizing: "Everyone's opinion, except mine."

Layla the courtesan and Fatima the social-climbing bride are not so different after all. Layla, unlike Fatima, finds her love match, and seeks to reform herself, but is thwarted by social convention. *Layla* may not directly address the abolitionist debates swirling around Egypt at the time of the film's release, but it addresses the question of national honor that underpins the nationalist abolitionist movements. *Layla* also lays bare the transactionality of the modern marriage plot.

A MODERN QAYNA: SALLAMA (1945)

A few weeks after *Layla* opened, the magazine *Rose al-Yusuf* reported on Umm Kulthum's reaction to the film. Umm Kulthum attended a screening with a friend. While they were waiting in the theater for the film to begin, her companion said she had heard that Togo Mizrahi had thoroughly succeeded in Egyptianizing the story of *La dame aux camélias*. Umm Kulthum expressed her doubts about adapting the story to "the Egyptian mold." But after watching the scene where Farid's mother tells him that she prepared *mulukhiyya*, a traditional Egyptian dish, for his return home, Umm Kulthum turned to her companion and exclaimed, "It's true, Togo really managed to Egyptianize the story!"[50] A little over two years later, Umm Kulthum signed on to make a film with Togo Mizrahi. Mizrahi has been acknowledged for capturing Umm Kulthum's most affective performance on-screen.[51] Umm Kulthum was already a star performer in the 1930s, when the Egyptian film industry began to develop. Umm Kulthum "cultivated sophistication and respectability" and "styled herself as an elegant exponent of Egyptian romanticism."[52] Umm Kulthum's public persona "fuse[s] two nationalist symbols prevalent at the time: economic nationalism, on the one hand and 'cultural authenticity' on the other."[53] Studio Misr contracted with Umm Kulthum to star in its first production. As Ifdal Elsaket has noted, "The nationalist aura that surrounded Umm Kulthum was fundamentally shaped not only by the film characters she portrayed . . . but also by her off screen link to Studio Misr."[54]

Between 1936 and 1947 Umm Kulthum starred in six feature films. Umm Kulthum commanded significant creative control, insisting on playing a role in developing her character and the scripts for the films in which she starred.[55] Three out of six of her films are set in an imagined imperial Islamic court of the past, and feature Umm Kulthum in the role of a *qayna*, a singing slave girl: Kramp's *Widad*, Badr Khan's *Dananir*, and Togo Mizrahi's *Sallama* (1945).[56] Virginia Danielson quotes an interview in which Umm Kulthum articulated her preference for playing the role of *qayna*: "There is sincerity in the character of the slave girl and modesty is a mark of historical heroines. I value sincerity and I incline to modesty."[57] Umm Kulthum also preferred playing characters who were also singers, to avoid some of the awkwardness in musicals that arises when characters spontaneously break into song.[58] As such, her slave-girl character was not the standard domestic worker or *jariya*; rather, she was a *qayna* (*qiyan*, pl.).[59] *Qiyan* were female slaves trained as singer-poets. The practice of training slave girls as entertainers appears to have begun in the Umayyad period (661–750 CE), reaching its pinnacle under the Abbasids (750–1258 CE). Two of Umm Kulthum's characters were based on known *qiyan*: Dananir al-Barmakiyya (late eighth to early ninth century CE), author of *Kitab mujarrad al-aghani* (*The Book of Choice Songs*);[60] and Sallamat al-Qass (d. after 740), who was known as a composer, oud player, and Qur'an reciter.[61] *Qiyan*, like other female slaves, were considered concubines, sexually available to their owners. As Fuad Matthew Caswell describes them: "The *qiyan* were the select class of entertainers—chosen, educated, trained and 'finished' with the object of entertaining the better class of people and presenting themselves as objects of desire in refined social and artistic surroundings."[62]

In order to understand Umm Kulthum's role in *Sallama*, I begin by reviewing her prior appearances as a *qayna*. I trace how each film addresses the sociosexual dilemmas the figure of the female slave poses for modern Egyptian viewers. My analyses unpack the intersection of Umm Kulthum's association with the nation and her appearance as a *qayna*. I conclude with a discussion of how Mizrahi utilizes the queer Levantine idiom to navigate the complications imposed by the plot of *Sallama*.

Widad: The Singing Slave Girl and the Nation

In Fritz Kramp's *Widad*, the title character (Umm Kulthum) is a slave owned by a wealthy merchant, Bahir (Ahmad 'Allam), who buys her extravagant gifts as expressions of his love. He invests all his capital in a shipment of new merchandise, but the caravan is sacked, and he loses his investment. Bahir sells off his possessions, moves to a smaller house, and turns over his shop to a wealthy uncle in the interest of servicing his debts. Having lost the faith of his creditors, Bahir has no capital to invest in a new venture and is caught in a cycle of poverty. Widad insists that Bahir sell her, too, to generate funds so he can return to his livelihood.[63] Widad is brought to the slave market and ultimately sold to a respectable older man, Radwan, whose rakish nephew Sa'id can barely control his desire for her. On his deathbed, Radwan grants Widad her freedom. Upon Radwan's death, Widad tries to escape before Sa'id hears the news. But Sa'id catches Widad alone in a dark stairway. After this frightening encounter, the film abruptly cuts to Widad's escape to Cairo via felucca. When she arrives, Widad discovers that Bahir has once again succeeded in commerce. Widad returns to Bahir as a free woman, of her own free will. The film ends with an embrace between the reunited lovers.

Widad is set in Islamic Cairo in some vague period of the past.[64] There are no titles to help the viewer situate the film in time. But commerce in the film is conducted with Ottoman-era currency phased out in the nineteenth century, the mahbub. Trade, in the film, is conducted entirely with the East: Bahir's awaited caravan originates in Damascus. There is no sign of European merchants or merchandise. We are meant to understand that the film is set in a period prior to the French invasion in 1798, in an imagined, protected, and isolated Islamicate sphere.[65]

Nevertheless, even without the nationalist fanfare surrounding Studio Misr and the film's production, Widad begs to be read as national allegory in the context of the modern anticolonial struggle. Bahir's caravan is attacked at Tell el-Kebir, on the edge of the eastern Egyptian desert. Egyptians would recognize Tell el-Kebir as the site of the devastating defeat of the nationalist uprising led by Ahmad 'Urabi in 1882. Further, Bahir's debilitating burden of debt parallels national circumstances; Egypt's debt to foreign powers undermined its sovereignty. In *Widad*, female sacrifice permits the astute, hard-working Egyptian man to regain his independence from his creditors and return to rule over his domain. Widad, too, secures her independence, and returns to her love as his equal.

But what of the *qayna*'s sexual availability to her owners? Elsaket claims that *Widad* "does not allow room for speculation about her potential sexual infidelity":

she nurses her elderly, infirm owner "like a daughter," and shuns his son "to maintain her 'honour.'"⁶⁶ While the film downplays the possibility of a sexual encounter between Widad and Radwan, it nevertheless depicts Widad alone in a bedroom with three different men: Bahir, Radwan, and Saʿid. Widad repels Saʿid's advances while Radwan is still alive, but their last encounter in a dark staircase is threatening, and, I argue, should be read as a prelude to implied rape.

On the night of his uncle's death, Saʿid is shown in his quarters drinking, cavorting with women, listening to music, and watching scantily clad belly dancers. Framed by the backlit doorway, the servant, his back to the camera, whispers the news to Saʿid. The camera then cuts to a close-up of Saʿid's face as, in the melodramatic idiom of silent Hollywood cinema, he adopts a conniving expression. Drunk, he staggers out to find Widad. Widad has packed a small satchel of her belongings and donned a *milaya*. She attempts to escape via a dark staircase. Saʿid hears her before sees her. The two exchange few words:

> Saʿid: Who's there? Widad?
> Widad: Yes, Widad.
> Saʿid: Where are you going? [*He looks at her satchel, reaches for it, and she hides it behind her back.*] What are you hiding?
> Widad: I owe you nothing.

Saʿid grunts, "*Eh?*" (Is that so?) as he reaches for her and she backs away. Saʿid's verbal response effectively dismisses Widad's claim. His body language is threatening, and she backs away in fear.

Following this menacing encounter, the scene cuts abruptly to a shot of a felucca's sail in broad daylight. As the camera tilts down the sail to show the boat, we hear the crew and passengers singing a love song that begins: "Take me to my beloved's village, the longing and distance torture me. *Ya habibi,* my heart is with you." The camera cuts to Widad sitting silently, surrounded by singing and clapping passengers. At no point in the scene does Widad join the other passengers in song. She has drawn her *milaya* across the lower half of her face, and her eyes nervously dart around. No other women aboard the felucca cover their faces. Widad is a free woman, with documents to prove, it, and she is returning to her beloved. What is she hiding with her excessive display of modesty in this scene, if not the shame of what implicitly transpired off-screen?⁶⁷

Within a few years of *Widad*'s release, rape or seduction narratives had become commonplace in Egyptian melodrama. According to one estimate, "in the 1942–43 season, more than 50 percent of Egyptian films presented seduced or raped women."⁶⁸ Viola Shafik argues that this proliferation of rape and seduction narratives should be read in the context of the "strong national sentiments" in the years prior to the 1952 Free Officers revolt.⁶⁹ As Beth Baron has extensively documented, dating back at least as far as 1919, the nationalist Egyptian press commonly depicted Egypt as a woman, and British occupation was viewed as a "rape of the nation."⁷⁰

Kay Dickinson identifies 'Aziza 'Amir's *Layla* (Vedat Örfi and Stefan Rosti, 1927), widely hailed as the first Egyptian feature film, as establishing the filmic idiom of the nationalist allegory "Egypt as a Woman."[71] Sa'id's implied rape of Widad, then, plays an important symbolic function in the film's allegorical representation of the national struggle.[72]

Dananir—Loyalty and Monogamy

While *Widad* presents an allegory of Egypt's struggle for independence, Ahmad Badr Khan's *Dananir* articulates nationalist sentiment somewhat more obliquely. When the film opens, Dananir, a Bedouin orphan, is living with her adoptive family. Her singing catches the attention of Ja'far, the vizier of the caliph Harun al-Rashid, while he is on a hunting expedition accompanied by poet Abu Nuwas. Ja'far purchases Dananir from her adoptive father—a bag of coins changes hands—so she can accompany him to the capital and study music. Ja'far promises to look after Dananir.

Unlike Umm Kulthum's characters in the other *qayna* films, Dananir is unambiguously monogamous. She and Ja'far are devoted to one another. When the caliph inquires about purchasing her, Ja'far refuses. The caliph prevails upon Ja'far to "send her to him" upon request. This conversation transpires after Dananir's first and only performance before the caliph. While the context suggests that the caliph wishes to send for Dananir to perform in his court, the request is left open-ended, as is Ja'far's reluctant, ambiguous gestural response.

The film maps Ja'far's fall. At the beginning, Ja'far serves as the powerful vizier of Harun al-Rashid. The film ends following his execution by order of the caliph. After Ja'far's death, Dananir defies the caliph twice—first by audibly mourning for Ja'far, and then by refusing to join his harem. The caliph spares her his wrath, and she returns to her adoptive father, who has lost his wealth and his eyesight.

Ja'far is portrayed as a good, kindhearted, and loyal figure. We see Ja'far's compassion early in the film when he agrees to free an elderly and infirm prisoner, Yahia Ibn 'Abd Allah al-'Alawi. Al-'Alawi was imprisoned for plotting against the caliph. By freeing al-'Alawi, Ja'far oversteps the bounds of his power, angering Harun al-Rashid.

Jealous plotters in the court seek to overthrow Ja'far, sowing doubt about his loyalty in the mind of the caliph. Ja'far is a member of the Baramika (also known as the Barmakids), a family of Persian origin who became influential in the Abbasid court. The plotters, like the caliph, are Hashimi—deriving their legitimacy as descendants of the prophet's tribe. The fight against Ja'far is also characterized as a consolidation of power. In the minds of the Hashimis, the Barmakids are interlopers, and Ja'far has usurped their power. To make clear the extent of the power conflict, after Ja'far's execution, the caliph's troops set upon the Barmakid quarter and kick the residents out of the city.

While *Dananir* is based on historical figures, the film's depiction of the power struggle between Ja'far and the caliph is, as Viola Shafik notes, "neither realistic

nor put into a proper historical context. . . . The events are forced into the senti-
mental corset of melodrama. The history forms the extraordinary frame of a quite
ordinary drama."[73] But the film's detachment from historical sources makes it a
better vehicle for articulating contemporary political grievances. The caliph's com-
plaints against Ja'far would have resonated with the Egyptian viewing public. After
the caliph has learned about Ja'far's treachery, he looks around the fairgrounds,
where a sporting match has just been held, and asks who owns the land. Confirm-
ing that it belongs to the Barmakid Ja'far, who also owns the land surrounding
Baghdad, the caliph concludes: "See how we made them [the Barmakids] rich and
impoverished our own!" When a member of the court tries to defend Ja'far for his
generosity to the poor, the caliph retorts that it is a bribe to win over the peasants.
The caliph's words undermine Ja'far's credibility: he is attributed characteristics of
both the reviled landowning class and the foreign-minority opportunists.

Another scene suggests that Ja'far's detractors see his internationalism as a
source of his treachery. The caliph receives emissaries from Charlemagne before a
gathering of notables in his court. He asks Ja'far to read aloud the letter from the
king of the Franks. The letter praises the caliph and thanks him for "securing
the road for the pilgrims to Jerusalem." The letter continues: "We are assured of the
Franks' safety in your nation, as you are well known for your justice and spreading
of peace and toleration among the people. Peace be upon you." As Ja'far is rolling
up the scroll, the camera cuts to a group of plotters, and one whispers, "Which
one of them is in charge here?" Only after they grumble their dissatisfaction with
Ja'far's power—justifying their position with a Qur'anic citation[74]—does the camera cut back to the royal visit, at which point the caliph responds: "Inform your
king that I am keen to spread equality, with no racial or religious discrimination."
If we are to believe the plotters, the caliph's statement of tolerance and coexistence
reflects the interests of Ja'far (and by extension the Barmakids) rather than those
of his own tribe and nation.

Viola Shafik also outlines another way the film evokes a sense of cultural pride.
She argues that *Dananir* "feed[s] the myth of a legendary golden age of Islam,
which in turn underlines the splendor of Arab Muslim culture in general and
serves as a cultural reaffirmation."[75] The dialogue, she notes, is "embroidered with
quotations from the great poet Abu Nuwas."[76] Bucking the trend for presenting
film dialogue in spoken dialect, the characters in *Dananir* speak literary Arabic
(*fusha*). Shafik claims that language use in the film "serves as a bridge to a mythi-
cally transfigured past."[77]

Sallama—The Virgin Concubine

Togo Mizrahi's film *Sallama* is based on the historical novel *Sallamat al-Qass*, written by 'Ali Ahmad Ba Kathir, first published serially in *Al-Thaqafa* starting in June
1941,[78] and issued as a book in 1943.[79] In the novel Ba Kathir retells and adapts a
narrative tradition about an encounter between a *qayna*, Sallama, and a holy man,

'Abd al-Rahman al-Qass. Both characters are based on historical figures: Salla-mat al-Qass served in the court of the Umayyad caliph Yazid Ibn 'Abd al-Malik (720 to 724 CE), where, in addition to performing, she composed elegies to both Yazid and his son; 'Abd al-Rahman b. Abi 'Ammar is identified as a transmitter of hadith.[80] Ba Kathir's novel is derived from earlier Islamic retellings of what Marlé Hammond calls the folktale of Sallama and the Priest.[81]

In the film adaptation, Sallama (Umm Kulthum) starts out as a slave (jariya), indentured to a strict elderly couple, Umm al-Wafa' (Esther Shattah) and Abu al-Wafa' ('Abd al-Warith 'Ashir). Sallama and another jariya, Shawq (Zuzu Nabil), are charged with domestic labor and tending sheep. The family live in a quarter of Mecca dominated by the palace of the merchant Ibn Suhayl (Fu'ad Shafiq). As the open-ing voice-over establishes, Ibn Suhayl engages in nightly debauchery, disturbing the peace of the pious townsfolk. The music that issues from the palace sparks Sallama's desire to sing. Sallama learns a song from a fellow shepherd, which she sings as she returns to town, followed by an appreciative audience. Abu al-Wafa' encounters the crowd as he leaves the mosque. Angered, he sells Sallama on the spot.

Sallama ends up as a qayna in Ibn Suhayl's harem. 'Abd al-Rahman al-Qass (Yahya Shahin), an upstanding young man who has captured Sallama's heart, goes to the palace to purchase her back for her former owners. When he arrives, Ibn Suhayl stops the ongoing revelry in deference to the young man's piety. Sallama learns that 'Abd al-Rahman is in the palace, and to get his attention, she recites verses from the Qur'an from behind a screened balcony. The two meet in the courtyard, sparking the chaste romance between them. 'Abd al-Rahman resolves to purchase and free Sallama so they can marry, but his plans are thwarted when Ibn Suhayl goes bankrupt and Sallama is sold to Ibn Abi Rumana ('Abd al-'Aziz Khalil), a member of the caliph's court, where she receives further musical train-ing. After a conflict with Habbaba (Rafi'a al-Barudi), another singer in the caliph's court, Sallama runs away, finding refuge with a Bedouin tribe.[82] 'Abd al-Rahman locates her and then approaches Ibn Abi Rumana to purchase her freedom. But when he learns that Sallama has since been sold to the caliph, he gives up hope of marrying her and volunteers for the caliph's army. In the climactic scene, Sallama is called to perform before the caliph ('Abd al-Qadir al-Masiri) on the same day that 'Abd al-Rahman is gravely wounded while leading a successful battle. 'Abd al-Rahman is summoned to the palace, where he dies in Sallama's embrace. Her voice silenced by her grief, Sallama spends the rest of her days wandering in 'Abd al-Rahman's footsteps.

Marlé Hammond posits that the film Sallama "argue[s], in no uncertain terms, that woman's voice is not 'awra, and that women should be allowed to perform, and even broadcast, Qur'anic incantation before mixed audiences, just as they should be allowed to sing secular songs without having their virtue questioned."[83] Hammond glosses "'awra" as "a term that applies to any part of the body of a man or a woman which could incite sexual desire" and, thus, should be covered.[84]

Hammond supports her reading of the film by unpacking the signification of two key scenes: the performance of the film's most famous song, "Ghani li shwayi shwayi" ("Sing to Me Little by Little"); and Umm Kulthum's recitation from the Qur'an. Hammond reads "Sing to Me Little by Little" as a "polemical pro-music manifesto" directed at fellow Muslims who oppose women singing in public, chief among them Sallama's owner Abu al-Wafa'.[85] Hammond further argues that the response to Sallama's song within the film's diegesis supports the right of women to sing in public and derides those who oppose women singing.[86]

Hammond also asserts that "the filmmakers go to great lengths to disassociate Umm Kulthum's Qur'anic recitation with any suggestion of worldly seduction. This they achieve first and foremost by removing the image of Sallama, who elsewhere in the film is portrayed as an object of desire from the camera frame."[87] Engaging in a shot-by-shot analysis of the recitation scene, Hammond notes that Sallama's male listeners assume a pious demeanor, and look up or away from Sallama as she recites. However, when taken in its diegetic context, Sallama's Qur'anic recitation does constitute an act of seduction—albeit one motivated by honorable intentions. Sallama loves 'Abd al-Rahman and wishes to attract his attention. The verses she recites reflect the piety of her intentions.

According to Hammond, the premodern source texts for the story of Sallama and the Priest all cite aya ("verse"; pl. ayat) 43:67: "On that Day, friends [akhilla'] will become each other's enemies. Not so, the righteous."[88] Hammond argues that the inclusion of this aya "promote[s] a message of sexual abstinence."[89] Ba Kathir incorporates this verse into his novel as the parting words uttered by Sallama and 'Abd al-Rahman before she is sent to the caliph in Damascus. In the film, though, Sallama instead recites ayat 38–42 from Surat Ibrahim:

> Our Lord, You know well what we conceal and what we reveal: nothing at all is hidden from God, on earth or in heaven. Praise be to God, who has granted me Ishmael and Isaac in my old age: my Lord hears all requests! Lord, grant that I and my offspring may keep up the prayer. Our Lord, accept my request. Our Lord, forgive me, my parents, and the believers on the Day of Reckoning.[90]

In these verses Ibrahim addresses Allah with a supplication and statement of devotion. The passage opens with a declaration of Allah's universal knowledge. It then speaks of lineage: Ibrahim asks for forgiveness for his parents and thanks Allah for his descendants.[91] The choice of text contextualizes Sallama's recitation as seduction, situating her desire in the context of procreation. Reading the ayat proscriptively within the diegesis of the film, Sallama expresses her desire for 'Abd al-Rahman as a desire to increase the number of believers, and, through their mutual devotion to Islam, to pass on Allah's teachings. The choice of this aya, which names both of Ibrahim's sons, Ishmael and Isaac, also stresses the shared heritage of Muslims and Jews.

In many ways, a film based on Ba Kathir's novel is a curious choice for Togo Mizrahi to take on. Even at this early stage in his career, Ba Kathir's writings evidenced his "Arab-Islamic nationalist thinking."[92] Ba Kathir, a Yemeni diaspora writer, was never fully embraced by the Egyptian literary establishment—a factor critics have variously attributed to his pan-Arab and pan-Islamic sympathies at a time of nationalist, anticolonial fervor; his interest in depicting Islamic narratives and exploring morality in Islamic terms, at a time when secularism and socialism were ascendant; and his foreign origins.[93]

Sallama reflects Mizrahi's vision as director and producer, but not as a writer. In signing on to direct *Sallama*, Mizrahi agreed to all of Umm Kulthum's conditions, including matters of character, scenario, cast, songs, and music.[94] The screenplay for *Sallama* was composed by poet Bayram al-Tunsi, based on Ba Kathir's novel.[95] The shot composition and editing choices, however, reflect Mizrahi's vision. My reading of *Sallama* seeks to tease out how Mizrahi's distinct film idiom addresses some of the issues presented in Umm Kulthum's other *qayna* films.

As already discussed, while Umm Kulthum was drawn to the character of the *qayna*, the films needed to address the shifting notions of marriage, as well as the contemporary discomfort with slave ownership and the *qayna's* sexual availability to her owners. *Widad*, I have argued, includes an implied rape that is intended to be read in the context of national allegory. In *Dananir*, the eponymous character has only one owner, and the film depicts their relationship as one of mutual attraction and admiration, despite the obvious power difference between them. In *Sallama*, the screenplay demands that the *qayna* be sold multiple times—each time for a significantly increased price—making her sexually available to multiple men. But it is crucial to Umm Kulthum's image that her character maintain honor as her 1940s audience would understand the term. I argue that to diffuse the threat to Sallama's virginity posed by her male owners, Mizrahi adopts the queer Levantine performance of masculinity evident in his comedies (chap. 4).

Of Umm Kulthum's three *qayna* films, only *Sallama* makes an explicit issue of the protagonist's virginity. Near the beginning of the film, 'Abd al-Rahman articulates his concerns to Abu al-Wafa', Sallama's and Shawq's prior owner: "I would have bought them instead of someone who will beat them, harm them [yu'adhahun], and get them drunk. They are innocent, tender youths [fatatan sadhajatan raqiqatan]." In the first sentence, 'Abd al-Rahman's fears about the slaves' safety is not explicitly gendered: he articulates concern about physical abuse and exposure to prohibited alcoholic beverages. But the second sentence lays bare his specific concern—for the preservation of the girls' "innocence." In this context, his use of the verb yu'adhahun articulates his fear that they are at risk of sexual molestation specifically. As a point of contrast, consider the opening scene of *Widad*, in which the slave and owner, alone in a bedroom, share an affectionate embrace. In *Dananir*, the slave's sole owner purchases her directly from her father; Dananir's innocence is implied, but the film doesn't make an issue of it. By contrast, I contend that the preservation of the protagonist's virginity is a central concern in *Sallama*. A *qayna*'s value is pegged to her virtuosity as a singer—not her virtue. But *Sallama*, both narratively and visually, takes pains to protect the protagonist from men's sexual desires. This concern is imposed on the diegesis to satisfy modern sensibilities about marriage and generic expectations of melodramatic cinema.[96]

By contrast with the other *qayna* films, Sallama never appears in a scene alone with a man; even her encounters with the upstanding 'Abd al-Rahman are chaperoned by Shawq.[97] But the film goes further in constructing an impregnable space to protect Sallama. Within Ibn Suhayl's palace, Sallama is granted a private chamber that is characterized as a place of refuge, shielding Sallama from the risks and temptations of court life. From the time Sallama enters Ibn Suhayl's palace, the camera is privy to communal space within the harem. The first mention of a private room occurs in the context of Sallama's encounter with drunk, lascivious, and belligerent guests. One guest (Stefan Rosti) tries to force Sallama to take a drink, and she slaps him repeatedly in the face. In response, Ibn Suhayl politely suggests that she take leave to rest in her private quarters. Following her departure, the debauchery resumes, and scantily clad dancers once again take the stage. The scene then cuts to Sallama indignantly storming into her room accompanied by Shawq. Sallama angrily removes her hat and her earrings, and then sits on a bench to remove her shoes. The modesty of Sallama's undressing scene, even in this private space, stands in stark contrast to the exhibitionism of the scantily clad dancers that immediately precedes it.

Shawq rebukes Sallama for fraternizing with the guests, and sagely advises her to seek shelter in her room: "If you sing another time, after you perform, return to your room like a sensible person." Upon her next encounter with 'Abd al-Rahman, Sallama assures him that he need not worry about her exposure to corrupting influences. Echoing Shawq's advice, she tells him: "If I sing again, I will return to my room after my performance."

Sallama is not shown performing for Ibn Suhayl again, but she can't avoid the drunken crowd. One night, after she sings of her love for 'Abd al-Rahman on the balcony, while she is returning to her room, she is confronted by the guest she had slapped. Grabbing Sallama, he menacingly threatens her, telling her that this time she can't escape. Shawq helps her get away, and they seek refuge in the harem, where they hide behind a curtain in a locked room. The drunken guest and a sidekick chase Sallama and Shawq. Banging on the door, he threatens, "Even if this door were made of iron, I would break it down." His sidekick grabs a spear, and the two men, grunting, ram the door with the large phallic object. But they fail to penetrate the women's private space. Ibn Suhayl, informed of the guests' breach into the restricted space of the harem, arrives in time to disarm the men.

The guests' wolfish behavior serves to highlight Ibn Suhayl's inefficacy and effeminacy. Throughout the film Ibn Suhayl commands little respect from the

FIGURE 44. Fu'ad Shafiq (left) as the merchant Ibn Suhayl. Screenshot from *Sallama* (Togo Mizrahi, 1945).

members of his court. His profligacy on lavish entertainment drives him into bankruptcy; he is forced to sell everything to pay off his debts. The character's folly is also communicated by the campy performance of effeminacy given by veteran character actor Fu'ad Shafiq (fig. 44). Take, for example, the scene in which Ibn Suhayl is introduced. The camera enters Ibn Suhayl's palace with a traveling shot following a *jariya* carrying an inlaid wooden box; we hear, but do not yet see, a female singer (Su'ad Zaki) accompanied by an orchestra. As the *jariya* moves from entryway to reception hall, we see an architecture of opulence—columns, soaring archways, spacious rooms. The camera pauses when she joins a cluster of domestic slaves waiting on a jovial Ibn Suhayl, who is in the process of applying perfume to himself. Another *jariya* shakes the bottle into his hands, whereupon he applies the scent by touching his face lightly with only his fingertips in an effeminate gesture. Then he purses his lips twice. This facial tic—a sort of pantomime of the act of chewing—is a campy affectation he exhibits throughout the film. He then turns his back to the camera and unwraps one end of his sash, swishing it with his hand as he walks away.

Ibn Abi Rumana, Sallama's third owner, has a much smaller role, but like Ibn Suhayl, he, too, is depicted as inept: he provokes discord among the *qiyan*; and Sallama manages to escape from his harem. 'Abd al-'Aziz Khalil, outfitted in an extravagant costume, gives a campy performance as Ibn Abi Rumana (fig. 45).

FIGURE 45. 'Abd al-'Aziz Khalil as the caliph's courtier Ibn Abi Rumana. Screenshot from *Sallama* (Togo Mizrahi, 1945).

When facing 'Abd al-Rahman, the poor holy man, both wealthy slave owners are reduced to stuttering. Ibn Suhayl, embarrassed, stammers out a string of lies as he tries to cover up his impious ways. Ibn Abi Rumana stammers his surprise that 'Abd al-Rahman has located his fugitive slave. This behavior, in combination with their dress and demeanor, emasculates Sallama's owners, diffusing the sexual threat they pose.

In *Sallama*, Mizrahi elicits comic performances by Sallama's male owners that echo the performativity of identity and the gender instability central to the contemporaneous costume comedies starring 'Ali al-Kassar. In the 1940s, Mizrahi directed three al-Kassar films based loosely on the tales of the Thousand and One Nights: *Alf Layla wa-Layla* (*One Thousand and One Nights*, 1941), *'Ali Baba wa-l-arba'in harami* (*'Ali Baba and the Forty Thieves*, 1942), and *Nur al-Din wa-l-bhhara al-thalatha* (*Nur al-Din and the Three Sailors*, 1944). The films feature princes and princesses in elaborate costumes, as well as lavishly constructed palace sets. Like the earlier collaborations between Mizrahi and al-Kassar, these films also feature plots of mistaken identity. In *'Ali Baba*, al-Kassar's character dresses like a member of a band of thieves to help save a captured princess who does not know her true identity. *Nur al-din* features al-Kassar playing two roles: an evil prince; and his double, a poor baker. In *One Thousand and One Nights*, a convoluted narrative involving multiple cases of mistaken identity, al-Kassar, playing his signature character 'Usman, carries on the cross-dressing antics from his earlier films (chaps. 3 and 5). *One Thousand and One Nights* establishes clear, gendered spatial boundaries: the entry to the women's spaces—the princess's chamber, and the harem occupied by the female slaves—are policed. 'Usman gains access to the princess's chamber in the guise of a doctor; but two guards with swords stand outside the entrance to the harem, threatening to slit the throat of any man who dares enter. Dressed as a woman, 'Usman's sidekick ('Ali 'Abd al-'Al) is sold as a *jariya* to dance before the prince. 'Usman sneaks into the palace, ending up, inadvertently, in the harem. To escape the angry guards, he, too, dresses as a woman—donning a white face veil to cover his beard; and then he is also called upon to perform. Al-Kassar's slippage between pauper and prince, good-hearted 'Usman and his evil twin, male and female, is fundamental to the films' plots and their characterization of the folkloric past. I argue that Mizrahi employs this idiom of Levantine exchange in *Sallama,* too.

In *Sallama,* in addition to the effeminate representation of the slave owners, the presence of a male servant (Muhammad Kamil) in the women's quarters—presumably a eunuch—also indexes queer gender identities.[98] Neither of Umm Kulthum's other *qayna* films' plots and their includes a eunuch. The figure of the eunuch in *Sallama* reflects popular conceptions of the Islamic harem created and reinforced by cinema—particularly the Orientalist imagery of Hollywood.

In keeping with the performances of the effeminate slave owners, the eunuch in *Sallama* is presented as a comic figure. Sallama hatches a plot to escape from Ibn Abi Rumana's palace. At night the eunuch sleeps by the door to guard the harem. To escape, Sallama and Shawq must remove the key from under his arm. In their efforts they accidentally tickle him, and he giggles in his sleep. After two attempts, Shawq tickles his nose. Giggling again, he reflexively lifts his hand to his face, and Shawq grabs the key. After unlocking the door, Sallama places the key upright in his left hand. Instead of retreating immediately, she reaches for his staff, placing it erect in his right hand. The scene draws attention to the eunuch's condition—only in his dreams can he experience jouissance.

While the characters of the eunuch and Sallama's two wealthy owners could fit right into one of 'Ali al-Kassar's One Thousand and One Nights comedies, Yahya Shahin, by contrast, presents his pious, honest character, 'Abd al-Rahman al-Qass, with the (humorless) dignity the role demands. Shahin has the dashing good looks of a leading man. He represents a version of masculinity legible to the modern audience. Unlike the elaborate costumes of the wealthy slave owners, 'Abd al-Rahman wears the timeless dress of the fellahin (fig. 46). Romantic notions of the immutability of the fellahin abound—both in Egyptian culture and in Orientalist representations of the Egyptian countryside. In this case, 'Abd al-Rahman's costume promotes the identification of the modern audience with the character.

FIGURE 46. Collage: 'Abd al-Rahman al-Qass (Yahya Shahin) in peasant dress (left, center); Umm Kulthum as Sallama (lower right). Pressbook for *Sallama* (Togo Mizrahi, 1945). Courtesy of the Rare Books and Special Collections Library, The American University in Cairo.

'Abd al-Rahman elevates his desire by expressing himself in verse. The poem "Qalu: Uhibb al-Qass Sallama" ("They Say al-Qass Loves Sallama"), composed by Ba Kathir for the novel, adheres to traditional poetic form.[99] The short poem is modified for the film. The first line (in both versions) reads: "They say al-Qass loves Sallama / He is the pure, pious ascetic." In the film, *al-nasik*, the world for "pious," is changed to *al-wara'*—a term that also implies timidity or cautiousness. In the original poem, the second line reads: "As if only the brazen, lethal seducer could already know desire." By contrast, the version in the film eliminates the direct reference to seduction and changes the gender of the subject, replacing the line with the words: "As if only a brazen girl could know the taste of desire and love." The poem is then set to music and sung by Umm Kulthum in Sallama's voice. The power of the characters' longing in the novel is reduced to the tepid, commonly accepted tropes of love and desire acceptable in popular song.

'Abd al-Rahman makes clear that he wishes to purchase Sallama to remove her from the system that makes women sexually available to multiple men. In articulating his love for Sallama, 'Abd al-Rahman expresses his desire to buy her so he can free her, and marry her "according to the law of Allah." Of course, Islamic law also sanctions relations between free Muslim men and concubines. In this turn of phrase, we see how the love match between a 'Abd al-Rahman and Sallama—free man and enslaved woman—is transformed into companionate marriage.

A SUCCESS RUMORED TO BE A FAILURE

News that Egypt's greatest singing star had agreed to appear in a film by the director of popular and successful musicals was warmly received in the Egyptian press. Mizrahi and Umm Kulthum publicly expressed their mutual admiration, and their pleasure at having the opportunity to work together. In the pages of the film's pressbook, Mizrahi and Umm Kulthum lavish praise on one another. Umm Kulthum also published a letter in *Al-Sabah* the week after *Sallama's* premiere, describing Mizrahi as "the only director who truly knows the cinema."[100] One can only imagine that this assessment did not sit well with Ahmad Badr Khan, who had directed three of her four previous movies—or with other Egyptian directors who aspired to work with her.[101]

The collaboration between Umm Kulthum and Mizrahi sparked the jealousy of competing studios, who appear to have launched a campaign to undermine its success. In the same issue of *Al-Sabah*, a second letter about the film was printed just to the right of Umm Kulthum's letter to Mizrahi, where its gossipy content would be read first. The letter, signed by an anonymous cinema producer, asserts that "Umm Kulthum's appearance in a film directed and produced by a creative genius like Togo Mizrahi would destroy all other musicals, and wouldn't leave them a market or revenues."[102] The letter accuses producers who had musical films in the pipeline of attempting to dampen public enthusiasm for *Sallama* by calling the film a failure and by denigrating both Umm Kulthum's performance and Mizrahi's directing. One particularly juicy rumor suggested that *Sallama* had failed because Umm Kulthum took charge of directing some scenes. The letter ends by challenging the Cinema Producer's Union to respond.[103] The following week, another article by the anonymous cinema producer appeared, entitled "How the Plot against *Sallama* and Umm Kulthum by Directors of Cinema Companies Was Discovered . . . and How It Failed." Without naming names, the producer accuses his peers—including the director of a large Egyptian film company—of sending representatives to shout out disapproving comments during the film, and to loudly voice critical opinions after screenings.[104]

Studio Misr—at whose cinema *Sallama* premiered—was also accused of depressing ticket sales.[105] Most of Mizrahi's films throughout his career had opened at Cinema Cosmo. During the 1944–45 season, when *Sallama* appeared, Cinema Cosmo was monopolized by films produced by Mizrahi's Egyptian Films Company.[106] However, Mizrahi opted to premiere *Sallama* at Cinema Studio Misr. The cinema was the site of a lavish opening party, as well as a special screening for King Farouk.[107] Although Cinema Studio Misr denied undermining the film, ticket sales for *Sallama* during its opening run were surprisingly low. One source attributes the low turnout to poor timing: the film was released amid school exams.[108] A contemporaneous investigation by *Al-Sabah* cast doubt on Studio Misr's involvement in the affair,[109] but accusations of Studio Misr's complicity continued to circulate for months.[110] Mizrahi and Studio Misr publicly made amends. Mizrahi published a letter to the editors of Al-Sabah objecting to the accusations levied against Studio Misr.[111] Cinema Studio Misr, in turn, offered to project any of Mizrahi's films on its screen for a three-week run.[112] When members of the Cinema Producer's Union issued a statement of unity a month after Sallama's premiere, Mizrahi was among the signatories.[113]

Sallama ultimately moved to Cinema Cosmo for its second run during the month of Ramadan and the feast of Eid al-fitr.[114] After its opening run, Sallama's domestic and international ticket sales soared. Hasan 'Amr, at the time of the film's release a film student and aspiring filmmaker, recalls that it was during the sluggish first two weeks that Mizrahi negotiated the terms for foreign distribution. Sallama, according to 'Amr, was the most expensive film production of its day, with a budget five times that of any other Egyptian film. Concerned about recuperating the costs associated with producing the film, Mizrahi sold the film reels to the Iraqi distributor for a fixed fee of 5,000 dinars rather than taking a percentage of ticket sales. The film went on to be a smash success in Egypt and other Arab countries. According to 'Amr's recollection, ticket revenues from Iraq alone amounted to 100,000 dinars. Despite the success of the film, 'Amr reports that Mizrahi suffered a breakdown over the lost revenue, and spent three months recuperating at the Behman Psychiatric Hospital in Cairo.[115] Mizrahi's family denies this rumor.

Sallama represents both the pinnacle of Mizrahi's career as a filmmaker and a turning point. Sallama is the final film Togo Mizrahi directed in its entirety. The plots and subterfuge of his peers may have contributed, at least in part, to Mizrahi's decision to quit directing. Following Sallama, Mizrahi turned his attention exclusively to film production.

Even before filming Sallama, Mizrahi had begun producing films by other directors. During the 1945–46 season, Mizrahi's Egyptian Films Company produced five films. Mizrahi's collaboration with director Yusuf Wahbi continued with the production of Al-Fanan al-'azim (The Great Artist, 1945) and Yad Allah (The Hand of God, 1946). Two projects Mizrahi produced ran into unanticipated complications. On 2 April 1945, director Kamal Salim died, leaving unfinished his final project, Qissat gharam (Love Story, 1945). Mizrahi invited director Muhammad 'Abd al-Gawad to complete the film, although the press reported that Mizrahi had taken a turn at directing some scenes.[116] During the filming of Malikat al-gamal (The Beauty Queen, 1946), director Niyazi Mustafa is said to have walked off the set. Mizrahi stepped in as director to complete the film. The Beauty Queen, released on 25 April 1946 without directorial credit, was the last film Mizrahi directed. Husayn Fawzi's Akspris al-hubb (Love Express, 1946) was the last film produced by the Egyptian Films Company.

In December 1946 Mizrahi was accused of supporting the production of a Zionist film. Following these rumors, as discussed in chapter 2, it appears that Mizrahi was blackballed by the Egyptian film industry. Despite his efforts to make a comeback in 1949, Togo Mizrahi never directed or produced another film in Egypt. In 1952, he transferred the directorship of Studio Mizrahi and the Egyptian Films Company to his brother, Alfred. In 1961 the Egyptian Films Company was sequestered, and Togo Mizrahi lost the rights to his films. Yet, seventy-five years after he wrapped production on *Sallama*, Togo Mizrahi's films remain popular, and continue to influence the work of other artists. The concluding chapter assesses Togo Mizrahi's enduring legacy.

8

Frames of Influence

Anouar Sedki, the frustrated star of the film *I Sacrifice My Honor*, vents his pent-up rage at the film's director, Kayro Jacobi. "It's always like that with you others," Sedki barks. "We, the Egyptians . . . you duped us, you cheated us out of our salary, you made us wait long hours in dressing rooms and stifling studios, you insulted us with your arrogance. But everything comes to an end, and one day—"

Jacobi interrupts, "What do you mean by 'you others'? Explain."

"You others, *khawagat.*"

Jacobi responds, "*Khawalat?* No one has ever done that to me."[1]

Sedki and Jacobi are characters in a novel by Paula Jacques, *Kayro Jacobi, juste avant l'oublie* (*Kayro Jacobi, Just before Oblivion*, 2010). The eponymous character, a Jewish Egyptian cinema director and producer, was inspired by the life and work of Togo Mizrahi.[2]

For her francophone readers, Jacques glosses the colloquial Arabic word play between actor and director as follows: "*khawagat* = foreigners; *khawalat* = inverts [*sic*], homosexuals."[3] In this scene, set in 1952, the fictional actor, Anouar Sedki, spouts Egyptian nationalist-inflected stereotypes at the Jewish director, calling him a duplicitous *khawaga*. Kayro Jacobi parries the actor's use of the epithet "*khawagat*" with the queer "*khawalat.*" Jacobi's retort mimics the way Togo Mizrahi disarmed exclusionary nationalist discourses with the pluralist, queer Levantine. The scene succinctly indexes both the historical context—the inimical environment for Jews in Egypt in the mid–twentieth century—and Jacobi's/Mizrahi's queer Levantine cinematic idiom.

The novel is framed by the voice of Norma Jacobi, who laments her husband's drift into obscurity. In a chapter dated January 2007, Norma muses: "Kayro Jacobi was a first-class artist. It is a fact. And then what? What place does he now occupy in the cruel memory of history? Nowhere. Nothing. *Fini.*"[4] *Kayro Jacobi* traces the historical and cultural forces that led to the mass emigration of the majority of Egyptian Jews in the mid–twentieth century, and reflects upon its costs on the personal level. The novel is part of Jacques's efforts to preserve Egyptian Jewish cultural heritage through her literature.[5] *Kayro Jacobi* particularly aims to rescue Togo Mizrahi's reputation from oblivion.

Togo Mizrahi's slide into obscurity was not merely a function of his departure from Egypt, or of the passage of time. For a time, Egyptian authorities actively sought to disassociate Togo Mizrahi's name from his films. But Mizrahi's movies were not forgotten. With the advent of television in Egypt in 1960, the state broadcast service regularly aired feature films.[6] Even at the height of the conflict between Egypt and Israel, the films of the accused Zionist sympathizer Togo Mizrahi played on Egyptian state television. Although they excised Togo Mizrahi's name from the credits of his films, the Egyptian broadcast authorities did not ban the films themselves.[7] To the contrary, Egyptian state television continued to broadcast Mizrahi's movies. These broadcasts both satisfied existing demand for Mizrahi's films and introduced new audiences to his movies decades after their production.

After the 1979 peace accord between Egypt and Israel, Egyptian television ceased censoring Togo Mizrahi's name. Filmmaker Ahmad Kamil Mursi, a protégé of Togo Mizrahi, recalls seeing a broadcast of *Layla fi al-zalam* (*Layla in the Dark*, 1944) in 1979 that listed Mizrahi's name in the credits. "At that moment," Mursi writes, "I thought that things had finally been made right."[8]

Recognizing that the restoration of Mizrahi's credits on state television signaled a broader domestic policy shift, Mursi set out to rehabilitate the reputation of his former mentor. He published a laudatory retrospective of Mizrahi's career in the cinema journal *Al-Sinima wa-l-nas* (*Cinema and the People*). Focusing on Mizrahi's artistic accomplishments as a director and his business acumen as a producer, Mursi wrests the man's legacy from the politics of the Arab–Israeli conflict. Mursi writes that Mizrahi was "a Jew by religion" but "an authentic Egyptian artist."[9] Having worked in Mizrahi's studio, Mursi was aware of Mizrahi's contributions to building an Egyptian cinema industry. He sought to set the record straight, and to give Mizrahi the credit due to him.

This book, *Togo Mizrahi and the Making of Egyptian Cinema*, has aimed to rescue Mizrahi's reputation from obscurity by documenting the myriad ways Mizrahi contributed to the development of Egyptian cinema in the 1930s and 1940s. The press in Mizrahi's day amply covered his efforts and their impact. However, tracking Mizrahi's lasting influence is a less straightforward endeavor. One could point to the members of the Togo cinema family—people like 'Abd al-Halim Nasr, Mahmud Nasr, and Ahmad Kamil Mursi, who continued to make movies in Egypt for decades after Mizrahi's departure. To illustrate Mizrahi's lasting impact in the realm of cinema, I have selected a series of "frames of influence"—screenshots from visual media—produced between the 1950s and the 2000s in Egypt, Israel, and Syria. This admittedly idiosyncratic selection attempts to provide a sense of the temporal scope and geographic scale of Mizrahi's impact. The first frame of influence speaks to Mizrahi's continued influence on Egyptian cinema even after his departure. The other examples map Mizrahi's influence on filmmakers beyond Egypt's borders.

FRAME 1: *HASAN AND MARIKA* (EGYPT, 1959)

The effort to erase or downplay Togo Mizrahi's contributions to Egyptian cinema played out in a number of spheres in Egypt—not just on state television. In 1967, critic Samir Farid gave an interview in which he divided Egyptian cinema production into two schools: an Alexandria school associated solely with Togo Mizrahi; and a Cairo school associated with all the major filmmakers of Egyptian cinema's golden age. As I argued in chapter 1, Farid's characterization of the two schools effectively relegates Mizrahi's oeuvre to the sidelines of Egyptian film history. But despite Farid's contentions, elements of the Levantine cinematic idiom that Togo Mizrahi championed continued to live on in Egyptian cinema—an idiom perhaps best personified by the prolific and beloved comic actor Isma'il Yasin.

Throughout his long career, Isma'il Yasin embraced and perpetuated the comic tradition of his mentors, Fawzi al-Gazayirli and 'Ali al-Kassar. Isma'il Yasin began his career as a monologist and singing comic,[10] and featured in early Egyptian radio broadcasts.[11] In 1935, Yasin joined 'Ali al-Kassar's troupe, an affiliation that lasted over a decade. Yasin then made his first forays into cinema with members of Fawzi al-Gazayirli's troupe.

In the 1940s, Isma'il Yasin was featured in three films directed by Togo Mizrahi. Yasin appeared alongside 'Ali al-Kassar in two costume comedies directed by Mizrahi: *'Ali Baba wa-l-arba'in harami* (*Ali Baba and the Forty Thieves*, 1942), and *Nur al-Din wa-l-bahhara al-thalatha* (*Nur al-Din and the Three Sailors*, 1944). Yasin also appeared in Mizrahi's pastoral comedy *Tahiya al-sitat* (*Long Live Women*, 1944) and makes a cameo appearance in *Al-Tariq al-mustaqim* (*The Straight Road*, 1943).

Beginning in 1954, Isma'il Yasin appeared in a string of films in which—like Chalom and Layla Murad—he played an eponymous character who shared the actor's screen name.[12] Yasin is also remembered for cross-dressing on-screen. Indeed, one critic writes that Yasin "institutionalized the role of drag queen" in Egyptian cinema with his performance in *Al-Anisa Hanafi* (*Miss Hanafi*, Fatin 'Abd al-Wahab, 1954)[13]. But *Miss Hanafi* was neither Yasin's first appearance in drag, nor his last.

In the 1959 film *Hasan wa-Marika* (*Hasan and Marika*, Hasan al-Sayfi), Isma'il Yasin's cross-dressing takes on a distinctly Levantine character. Two Egyptian, and nominally Muslim, men, Hasan (Isma'il Yasin) and Fahlawi ('Abd al-Salam al-Nablusi), are competing for the affections of Marika (Maha Sabri), a Greek Egyptian woman. But the young woman's father, Yanni (Stefan Rosti), has other ideas. He imports a prospective husband from Greece. Hasan plots ways to disrupt this match. In one scene, Hasan dresses as a lower-class Egyptian woman and offers Yanni his services as a maid. Hasan is seeking to enter the apartment in order to court Marika. Instead, Hassan attracts Yanni's affections (fig. 47).

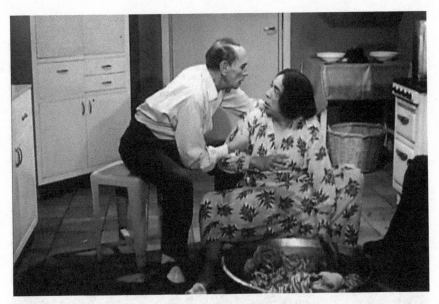

FIGURE 47. Yanni (Stefan Rosti, left) leans in to kiss Hasan (Isma'il Yassin), who is dressed as a woman. Screenshot from *Hasan and Marika* (Hasan al-Sayfi, 1958).

In *Hasan and Marika,* critic Joel Gordon sees a "society in transition," as Greek-Egyptians begin to emigrate en masse, like the Italians and Jews before them.[14] Following the 1956 Suez conflict, Gordon can find "virtually no characters we might identify as representative of the once thriving minority populations" in Egyptian cinema, with the exception of *Hasan and Marika.*[15]

Hasan and Marika's Levantine cinematic idiom, with its plot of mistaken identity, and Yasin's comic style reflect Togo Mizrahi's influence. Contrary to Samir Farid's claim, Togo Mizrahi's "Alexandria school" of filmmaking was not a dead end. The queer Levantine cinematic idiom that Mizrahi cultivated lives on in Yasin's films. Even as identifiably Levantine characters disappeared from the screen, Yasin persisted. Isma'il Yasin continued to perform his signature comic style with its queer Levantine inflections until just before his death in 1972.

FRAME 2: *CINEMA EGYPT* (ISRAEL, 1998)

Togo Mizrahi's influence is readily apparent in Rami Kimchi's documentary *Sinema mitsrayim* (*Cinema Egypt,* 1998). This biographical film traces the life of Kimchi's mother, Henriette Azar, a Jew born in Mit Ghamr, a small city in the Nile Delta, who, as a youth, moves to the Egyptian city of Alexandria, and then immigrates to Israel in the 1950s. In retelling his mother's story, Kimchi intercuts clips from Mizrahi's *Layla the Country Girl* (1941; chap. 6). For Kimchi, Layla's move from an Egyptian village to Cairo in *Layla the Country Girl* functions as an analogue to Henriette's move from the Nile Delta to the city of Alexandria.

FIGURE 48. Poster in Hebrew for Togo Mizrahi's *Layla the Country Girl,* featuring Layla Murad. Screenshot from *Cinema Egypt* (Rami Kimchi, 1998).

Kimchi and his mother had a fraught relationship in his youth, but they forged a bond by watching television together, particularly Israeli television's weekly Friday-afternoon broadcasts of Arab movies.[16] Kimchi relates that when he was a film student, his mother would expectantly ask him his opinion about classic Egyptian films they watched together. At the time, he dismissed them as "stupid and made in poor taste." In retrospect, he realizes that as an "arrogant cinema student," he failed to appreciate what his mother loved about the movies. He concedes: "Now I know that Mother revealed to me then her most vulnerable feelings—the loves of her childhood that she was forced to turn her back on all these years." The title of the film comes from the name of the cinema—Cinema Misr—located across the street from Henriette's childhood home in Mit Ghamr, where, from her bedroom, she would listen to the movies as she went to sleep at night.

Cinema Egypt is Kimchi's effort to make amends with his mother, to come to terms with his family history, and to reconsider his prior disdain for Egyptian cinema. Kimchi rents out a shuttered Israeli cinema, Cinema Armon, and arranges a private screening for his mother. The film they watch is *Layla the Country Girl.* On the empty marquee, Kimchi hangs a poster, in Hebrew, for the screening (fig. 48). For Kimchi and his mother, *Layla the Country Girl* serves as a point of connection between generations. In the documentary, Kimchi muses that Togo Mizrahi's film provides the only surviving remnant of the cosmopolitan world his mother inhabited in Egypt.

FRAME 3: *PASSION* (SYRIA, 2005)

Muhammad Malas's 2005 film *Bab al-maqam* (*Passion*), set in Aleppo, tells the story of Iman (Salwa Jamil), a woman who loves to sing. Her passion: the songs of Umm Kulthum. Visually and thematically, *Passion* owes little (or nothing) to the idioms of commercial Egyptian genre cinema. Mizrahi's influence is evident nonetheless.

The film is based on events documented in the Syrian press about a woman murdered by male relatives. To her suspicious uncle, brother, and cousins, her love of singing was an irrefutable sign that she had committed adultery. In addition to the film's powerful indictment of honor killings, critic Samirah Alkassim also sees the film levying a critique of the "metaphoric murder of culture happening in Syria and the Arab world at large." Alkassim reads the film as a national allegory for Syria, a country "dishonorably killed by its leaders and political systems."[17] This criticism is effected through a nostalgic pan-Arab lens. In one scene, protesters against the American invasion of Iraq in 2003 hold up posters of Gamal Abdel Nasser, recalling a unified pan-Arab identity prior to the Baathist dictatorships.

This transnational and nostalgic orientation is evident in *Passion*'s representation of Arab musical traditions of the past as well. The record shop where Iman meets Badiʿa, a retired wedding singer, is adorned with images of musicians long deceased. One wall features photographs of local early-twentieth-century masters of *tarab*: ʿAli Darwish, ʿUmar al-Batsh, and Bakri al-Kurdi.[18] Another wall is adorned with photographs of Umm Kulthum, Muhammad ʿAbd al-Wahab, Layla Murad, and Asmahan. These musical stars, who recorded in Egypt, have enduring, transnational appeal.

In a romantic interlude in *Passion*, Iman's husband (Usama al-Sayyid Yusuf) implores her to sing "Ghani li shwaya shwaya" ("Sing to Me Little by Little") (fig. 49). Umm Kulthum debuted this song in Togo Mizrahi's film *Sallama* (1945) (chap. 7). *Sallama* features Umm Kulthum in the role of a *qayna*, a singing slave girl. As discussed in the previous chapter, critic Marlé Hammond has argued that *Sallama* vociferously defends the idea that women's singing in public is permissible according to Islamic teachings.[19] Hammond's argument derives from her reading of the scene where Sallama finds her voice. At the outset of the film, Sallama serves as a simple *jariyya*, a domestic slave. Her owner, Abu Wafaʾ, takes the strident position that women's voices should not be heard in public. When Abu Wafaʾ catches Sallama singing in public, he rashly vows to sell her. ʿAbd al-Rahman al-Qass, the respectable young man who has captured Sallama's heart, counsels restraint, advocating for the permissibility of women singing. In *Sallama*, what provokes the debate about women singing in public is this same song, "Sing to Me Little by Little." Umm Kulthum recorded hundreds of songs over the course of her career. Malas chose this song for Iman to sing to her husband in a moment of intimacy on the night before she is murdered.

Even though throughout the film Iman sings only in the privacy of her apartment, her voice carries out the windows, into the stairwell and garden of

FIGURE 49. Iman (Salwa Jamil) sings "Sing to Me Little by Little." Screenshot from *Passion* (Muhammad Malas, 2005).

the building, and beyond into the street, where it reaches the ears of her spying uncle. The heinous act carried out by Iman's male relatives in *Passion* is provoked by the same male logic employed by Abu Wafaʾ in *Sallama:* that a woman's singing voice audible in public is objectionable. Referencing Togo Mizrahi's *Sallama,* Muhammad Malas's *Passion* levies an affective critique of patriarchal control over women's bodies and voices.

FRAME 4: YOUTUBE

The final image captures not only a film, but also the frame through which the film is viewed. YouTube has become the medium of choice for disseminating classic Egyptian films. By any measure, Togo Mizrahi's films command an impressive audience on streaming media.

Counting the number of films that pop up on streaming Internet video sites and tallying the number of views is, to be sure, a highly speculative and anecdotal measure of enduring popularity. Although streaming media provides an invaluable resource for scholars and aficionados of early Egyptian cinema alike, it is an unstable format. Films are posted haphazardly, and many are removed suddenly, without notice. YouTube may track views for the duration of a posting, but for scholars, the way users employ the platform to post old Arabic movies doesn't generate reliable statistics of viewership over the long term.

With that caveat, a quick scan of viewer statistics on YouTube nevertheless provides ample evidence of the enduring popularity of Mizrahi's films. *Layla the*

FIGURE 50. ʿAli al-Kassar (center) and Ahmad al-Haddad (left) in 'Usman and 'Ali (Togo Mizrahi, 1938). Screen capture from YouTube, 28 May 2019.

Schoolgirl (1941), starring Layla Murad, garnered over 19,000 views over a period of eight months.[20] Mizrahi's Chalom and ʿAbdu comedy *The Two Delegates* (1934) was viewed nearly 30,000 times in a year and a half.[21] The ever-popular Umm Kulthum racked up over 140,000 views for *Sallama* during a two-and-a-half-year period.[22] Between January 2016 and May 2019, Mizrahi's film *'Usman and 'Ali* (1938) was viewed over a million times (fig. 50).[23]

The availability of films streaming on the Internet is closely connected to television broadcasts. As already noted, Togo Mizrahi's films regularly screened on Egyptian television in the 1970s. By the mid-1990s, when I started collecting videos of Egyptian films, Togo Mizrahi's movies were sufficiently popular to warrant the release of several titles on VHS. In the early 2000s many of Mizrahi's films were sold on VCD or DVD. The media conglomerate Rotana released a restored and subtitled DVD of *Layla the Schoolgirl*. Classic Egyptian films, including Mizrahi's movies, also continue to be broadcast on local television stations in Arab countries, satellite networks, and subscription services. Films are posted to YouTube by viewers who capture and upload videos, many of which bear the logos of the channels from which the unauthorized copy was made. In both absolute and relative terms, Mizrahi's films are well represented on YouTube.

Mizrahi was a prolific filmmaker. Compounding his productivity is the fact that a remarkable percentage of Mizrahi's films survived into the television era. In the 1930s, Togo Mizrahi directed sixteen films—two silent and fourteen sound. Nine of Mizrahi's fourteen sound films from the 1930s have survived and are readily viewable on YouTube for anyone with an Internet connection. By contrast, in the same decade Muhammad Karim directed five films—one silent and four sound. Of these 1930s films, Karim's three blockbuster musicals starring Muhammad 'Abd al-Wahab have survived. Assia Dagher's Lotus Films produced eight sound films in the 1930s, all directed by Ahmad Galal; only two have been made available to stream on the Internet. In the same decade, the Lama brothers' Condor Films produced nine films; none are available.[24]

There is an element of luck and good fortune in the survival rate of Mizrahi's films. Ibrahim Lama's studio experienced two fires, one in 1942 and the other in 1951; on both occasions, the films in production were destroyed and had to be reshot.[25] Other Lama brothers films may have been lost to the conflagrations as well, and hence would not have survived into the era of television broadcast. Although Studio Mizrahi did not experience loss on that scale, two of Mizrahi's films are known to have caught fire in the course of screenings.[26] While Mizrahi was attuned to the flammability of nitrocellulose, he also viewed the medium as safe when handled with proper precaution. When the Egyptian Ministry of the Interior opened an inquiry about the safety of film, Mizrahi insisted that audiences could be kept safe if cinemas agreed to employ two projectionists who could, between them, remain vigilant during screenings.[27]

Not only is nitrocellulose highly flammable; it also decomposes and has proven difficult to preserve. Over the long and celebrated history of the cinema industry, there has been no sustained, centralized effort to properly store and systematically archive film in Egypt.[28] According to one estimate, as much as 50 percent of Egypt's cinema heritage has been lost.[29] Even the films that survive have deteriorated due to poor storage conditions. Given this situation, it is quite remarkable how many of Togo Mizrahi's films are still available to be watched today.

Popularity alone does not explain why Mizrahi's films survived the punishing effects of time and poor storage conditions. But popularity does account for the continued availability of Mizrahi's films in a variety of formats. Mizrahi's movies are still screened on classic-film stations, and uploaded to YouTube by viewers who enjoy them and wish to share them. To this day, Togo Mizrahi's movies are watched by hundreds of thousands—if not millions—of viewers around the globe.

WRITING TOGO MIZRAHI INTO THE HISTORY OF EGYPTIAN CINEMA

In 1942, Mizrahi published an article in *Al-Sabah* entitled "Tarikh al-sinima fi Misr" ("The History of Egyptian Cinema").[30] The article is in part history, and in part a snapshot of the vibrancy of the Egyptian cinema industry at the time. The article begins, "Cinema production in Egypt began before the Great War. In 1913 [*sic*] the first studio was established in Alexandria at 3 Nuzha Street."[31] Films in the first two decades of the twentieth century were produced in glass structures and were lit by sunlight, and Mizrahi notes that the conditions in Egypt were advantageous for cinema production. Mizrahi relates that an Italian company founded the first studio and production company in Egypt, SITCIA, but that the effort was short-lived. He then honors 'Ali al-Kassar, 'Aziza Amir, and Muhammad Karim as well as the Lama brothers for their contributions to cinema production in the 1920s.[32] According to Mizrahi, since the establishment of the cinema industry in its then-current form—beginning, in his estimation, in 1929—it had become an important engine for the Egyptian economy.[33]

Mizrahi doesn't get all of the historical facts straight: 'Aziz Bandarli and Umberto Dorés established a studio in 1907: SITCIA (the Italian Cinematographic Society) was founded in 1917.[34] However, the article provides insights into how Mizrahi viewed Egyptian cinema history. Mizrahi identifies Alexandria as the site of the first locally produced films. By Mizrahi's account, the studio era starts in 1929, before the establishment of Studio Misr in 1934. Mizrahi also sees foreigners and noncitizen residents as an integral part of the history of Egyptian cinema. By contrast, the dominant narratives of Egyptian cinema history are Cairo-centric and narrowly define what it means for a film to be considered "Egyptian."

The second half of the article reflects Mizrahi's public-relations efforts on behalf of the cinema industry as a whole. In 1942, according to Mizrahi, there were twenty film-production companies in Egypt, ten of which were committed to producing films full-time and year-round. The six active studios operated a total of ten sound stages, and between them employed approximately one thousand people, including hundreds of artisans and technicians. By Mizrahi's accounting, the industry poured 500,000 Egyptian pounds into the economy annually, and paid 40,000 Egyptian pounds to the government in taxes.[35]

According to Mizrahi, locally produced films dominated the cinemas, especially outside of the big cities—although it is worth noting that World War II suppressed distribution of Hollywood and European films in Egypt, and imports of foreign films resumed after the war. Mizrahi cites international demand for Egyptian films as another marker of the industry's success. He provides a long list of countries where Egyptian films were distributed in 1942: Sudan, Iraq, Iran, Syria, Lebanon, Palestine, Transjordan, Turkey, India, and Somalia. The war, Mizrahi notes, also temporarily halted distribution of Egyptian films to Tunisia, Algeria, Morocco, Ethiopia, and Libya. Mizrahi also celebrates that some films found an audience across the ocean in Brazil, Argentina, and the United States. Mizrahi caps off his boosterism of the film industry by signing the article as member of the board of directors of the Egyptian Chamber of Commerce, Giza Directorate.

Mizrahi was too modest to write himself into the narrative of Egyptian cinema history. In this article—and in his other published pieces—Mizrahi takes credit neither for his role in the founding of the industry, nor for his contributions to its subsequent growth. Nevertheless, Togo Mizrahi played an active role in developing the cinema industry in Egypt in the 1930s and 1940s. Mizrahi was involved in efforts to establish professional syndicates in cinema. He used his influence to lobby parliament for industry protection. As a business owner, he joined the chamber of commerce to advocate on behalf of the local cinema industry. When he spoke to the press, he used his fame not to promote his own films, but rather to represent the industry as a whole. In his published essays, he touted the achievements of Egyptian cinema, and raised public awareness of issues hampering the development of the Egyptian cinema industry, particularly drawing attention to the challenges facing independent studios. He also used the press to pressure cinemas to screen more locally produced films, and to engage in business practices that would encourage development of a range of local idioms. Mizrahi always cast his promotion of cinema's cultural and economic potential in patriotic terms. Mizrahi viewed his role as director, producer, and studio owner as contributing to the endeavor of building a viable and vibrant film industry in Egypt in the 1930s and 1940s.

The success of Mizrahi's films can, in part, be attributed to his ability to attract some of the best talent in Egypt—both in front of and behind the camera. He brought to the silver screen popular veteran actors of the stage, like 'Ali al-Kassar, Fawzi al-Gazayirli, Yusuf Wahbi, and Amina Rizq. Mizrahi's musicals featured some of the top recording stars of the era. He directed what is widely regarded as Umm Kulthum's best performance on-screen. Mizrahi's name is closely linked to Layla Murad, who, over the five films they made together, became a huge box-office success. He fostered the performances of actors whose careers blossomed in the 1940s and 1950s, such as Isma'il Yasin, Tahiya Carioca, 'Aqila Ratab, and Anwar Wagdi. All of these stars continue to draw audiences today.

Mizrahi was a skilled craftsman and astute businessman, whose attention to detail was put in the service of producing entertainment. Mizrahi directed many box-office hits, and his films were widely praised by critics. He wrote, directed, and produced socially conscious comedies and melodramas. While his big-budget musicals peddle escapist fantasies of wealth and luxury, these films, too, engage in social and cultural critique. But more than that, Mizrahi made movies that are satisfying to watch.

The influence of Mizrahi's cinematic idiom is evident in Egyptian filmmaking long after he wrapped production on his last movie in 1946. His work continues to influence filmmakers and writers outside of Egypt. As the contemporaneous box-office successes and contemporary popularity on YouTube attest, Togo Mizrahi produced movies with enduring audience appeal. The Egyptian films of this Jewish Italian Egyptian filmmaker continue to delight generations of audiences in Egypt and around the world.

Togo Mizrahi Filmography

TABLE 1 Arabic films directed by Togo Mizrahi

Film	Director	Producer	Writing	Studio	Cinematography	Music	Songs	Lyrics	First Screening	Cast
Al-Hawiya, al-kukayin (Labîme ou: Cocaïne)¹ (The Abyss, or Cocaine)	Togo Mizrahi	Togo Mizrahi	Togo Mizrahi	–	Alvise Orfanelli	–	–	–	19 November 1930, American Cosmograph, Alexandria	Félix Mizrahi (as 'Abd al-'Aziz al-Mashriqi), Fatma Hassan Shawki, 'Abdallah Sabit
05001	Togo Mizrahi	Egyptian Films Company	–	–	Alvise Orfanelli	–	–	–	11 April 1932, Cinema Olympia, Alexandria	Leon Angel (as Chalom)
Awlad Misr (Les fils d'Egypte) (Children of Egypt)	Togo Mizrahi	Egyptian Films Company	–	Togo Mizrahi	Alvise Orfanelli	–	–	–	6 April 1933, Cinema Lido al-Watani, Alexandria	Ginan Raf'at; Togo Mizrahi (as Ahmad al-Mashriqi); Félix Mizrahi (as 'Abd al-'Aziz al-Mashriqi)
Al-Manduban (Les deux délégués)(The Two Delegates)	Togo Mizrahi	Egyptian Films Company, Togo Mizrahi	Togo Mizrahi; Leo Angel (assistant)	–	Alvise Orfanelli	Zakariya Ahmad	Badi' Khayri	–	16 May 1934, Cinema Fu'ad, Cairo	Siham, Fawzi al-Gazayirli; Ihsan al-Gazayirli; 'Abdu Muharram; Leon Angel (as Chalom)
Al-Duktur Farhat (Le docteur Farahat) (Doctor Farahat)	Togo Mizrahi	Togo Mizrahi	Togo Mizrahi	–	'Abd al-Halim Nasr	'Izzat al-Gahli	–	–	7 March 1935, Cinema Cosmograph, Alexandria	Fawzi al-Gazayirli; Amina Muhammad; Ihsan al-Gazayirli; Ahmad al-Haddad

Al-Bahhar *(The Sailor)*	Togo Mizrahi	Togo Mizrahi	Togo Mizrahi	—	'Abd al-Halim Nasr	—	—	19 September 1935, Cinema Diana Palace, Cairo	Amina Muhammad; Fawzi al-Gazayirli; Ihsan al-Gazayirli; Togo Mizrahi (as Ahmad al-Mashriqi); Muhammad al-Siba'i
100,000 gineh *(One Hundred Thousand Pounds)*	Togo Mizrahi	Togo Mizrahi	Togo Mizrahi	—	'Abd al-Halim Nasr	'Izzat al-Gahli	—	27 February 1936, Cinema al-Nahda, Cairo	'Ali al-Kassar; Zuzu Labib; Amina Muhammad; Hasan Salih, Ahmad al-Haddad
Khafir al-darak (alt. Ghafir al-darak) *(Le haffir du quartier) (The Neighborhood Watchman)*	Togo Mizrahi	Egyptian Films Company—Togo Mizrahi; Max Harari	'Ali al-Kassar and Togo Mizrahi	—	'Abd al-Halim Nasr	—	—	29 October 1936, Cinema al-Nahda, Cairo	'Ali al-Kassar, Zuzu Labib, Zakiya Ibrahim; Bahiga al-Mahdi, Hasan Salih, Ahmad al-Haddad
Al-'Izz bahdala *(Les deux banquiers) (Mistreated by Affluence)*	Togo Mizrahi	Togo Mizrahi	Togo Mizrahi	—	'Abd al-Halim Nasr	'Izzat al-Gahli	—	7 January 1937, American Cosmograph, Alexandria	Zuzu Labib; Esther Angel (as 'Adalat); Ruhiya Fawzi; Ahmad al-Haddad; Leon Angel (as Chalom)
Al-Sa'a 7 *(À 7 heures) (Seven O'Clock)*	Togo Mizrahi	Egyptian Films Company—Togo Mizrahi & Co.	'Ali al-Kassar and Togo Mizrahi	—	'Abd al-Halim Nasr	—	—	28 October 1937, Cinema Cosmograph, Cairo and Alexandria	'Ali al-Kassar; Bahiga al-Mahdi; Hasan Rashid; Ibrahim 'Arafa

(continued)

(TABLE 1 *continued*)

Film	Director	Producer	Writing	Studio	Cinemato-graphy	Music	Songs	Lyrics	First Screening	Cast
Al-Tiligbaf (*Le télégramme*) (*The Telegram*)	Togo Mizrahi	Togo Mizrahi & Co.	Togo Mizrahi	Egyptian Films Company —Togo Mizrahi	'Abd al-Halim Nasr	–	–	–	10 February 1938, Cinema Cosmo, Cairo	'Ali al-Kassar, Bahiga al-Mahdi, Zakiya Ibrahim
Ana tab'i kidda (*C'est mon caractère*) (*It's My Nature*)	Togo Mizrahi	Togo Mizrahi & Co.	Togo Mizrahi	Egyptian Films Company —Togo Mizrahi	'Abd al-Halim Nasr	Ahmad Sabra	–	–	24 March 1938, Cinema Cosmo, Cairo	Fu'ad Shafiq; Zuzu Shakib; Stefan Rosti; Bahiga al-Mahdi
'Usman wa-'Ali (*Osman et Ali*) (*'Usman and 'Ali*)	Togo Mizrahi	Egyptian Films Company —Togo Mizrahi & Co	Togo Mizrahi	–	'Abd al-Halim Nasr	–	–	–	3 November 1938, American Cosmograph, Alexandria	'Ali al-Kassar; Bahiga al-Mahdi
Layla mumtira (*A Rainy Night*)	Togo Mizrahi	Egyptian Films Company	Togo Mizrahi (scenario); Stefan Rosti (dialogue)	–	Sammy Brill	Muhammad al-Qasbagi; Riyad al-Sunbati; Farid Ghasn	'Ali Shukri; Husayn Hilmi al-Ministrali	–	9 March 1939, American Cosmograph, Alexandria	Yusuf Wahbi; Layla Murad
Salafini 3 gineh (*Prête-moi trois livres*)(*Lend Me Three Pounds*)	Togo Mizrahi	Egyptian Films Company	–	Studio Wahbi, Giza	'Abd al-Halim Nasr	–	–	–	28 September 1939, Cinema Cosmo, Cairo and Alexandria	'Ali al-Kassar; Bahiga al-Mahdi

Title	Director	Production Company	Writer	Studio	Cinematographer	Music		Premiere	Cast
Al-Bashmaqawil (The Chief Contractor)	Togo Mizrahi	Egyptian Films Company	Badiʿ Khayri (dialogue)	Studio Bacos, Alexandria	ʿAbd al-Halim Nasr	Farid Ghasn	–	18 January 1940, Cinema Cosmo, Cairo	Fawzi al-Gazayirli; Mimi Shakib; Ihsan al-Gazayirli
Qalb imraʾa (Coeur de femme)(Heart of a Woman)	Togo Mizrahi	Egyptian Films Company	–	–	ʿAbd al-Halim Nasr	–	–	11 April 1940, Cinema Cosmo, Alexandria	Sulayman Naguib; Amina Rizq; Dawlat Abyad
Al-Fursan al-thalatha (Les 3 Mousquetaires) (The Three Musketeers)	Togo Mizrahi	Egyptian Films Company	Togo Mizrahi (story); Badiʿ Khayri (script)	–	ʿAbd al-Halim Nasr	–	–	27 May 1940, Cinema Royal, Cairo	Fawzi al-Gazayirli, ʿAqila Ratab, Ihsan al-Gazayirli
Layla bint al-rif (Layla the Country Girl)	Togo Mizrahi	Egyptian Films Company	Togo Mizrahi	–	ʿAbd al-Halim Nasr	Riyad al-Sunbati; Zakariya Ahmad	Mahmud Husayn Ismaʿil; Badiʿ Khayri	5 January 1941, Cinema Cosmo, Cairo	Yusuf Wahbi, Layla Murad
Alf Layla wa-Layla (One Thousand and One Nights)	Togo Mizrahi	Egyptian Films Company	Togo Mizrahi (story); Badiʿ Khayri (script)	–	ʿAbd al-Halim Nasr	ʿIzzat al-Gahli; Farid Ghosn	–	20 March 1941, Cinema Cosmo, Cairo	ʿAli al-Kassar, ʿAqila Ratab

(continued)

(TABLE 1 continued)

Film	Director	Producer	Writing	Studio	Cinematography	Music	Songs	Lyrics	First Screening	Cast
Layla bint madaris (*Layla the Schoolgirl*)	Togo Mizrahi	Egyptian Films Company	Togo Mizrahi	–	'Abd al-Halim Nasr	Riyad al-Sunbati; Muhammad al-Qasbagi; Zakariya Ahmad	–	Badi' Khayri; Ahmad Rami	16 October 1941, Cinema Cosmo, Cairo	Yusuf Wahbi; Layla Murad
Layla	Togo Mizrahi	Egyptian Films Company	–	–	'Abd al-Halim Nasr	Muhammad al-Qasbagi; Riyad al-Sunbati	–	Ahmad Rami	2 April 1942, Cinema Cosmo, Cairo	Layla Murad, Husayn Sidqi
'Ali Baba wa-l-arba'in harami (*'Ali Baba and the Forty Thieves*)	Togo Mizrahi	The Egyptian Films Company, Togo Mizrahi	–	–	George Sad; Mahmud Nasr	Riyad al-Sunbati; 'Izzat al-Gahli	–	Riyad al-Sunbati; 'Izzat al-Gahli	1 October 1942, Cinema Cosmo, Cairo	'Ali al-Kassar; Layla Fawzi; Muhammad 'Abd al-Mutlib; Isma'il Yasin
Al-Tariq al-mustaqim (*The Straight Road*)	Togo Mizrahi	Egyptian Films Company	Togo Mizrahi (scenario); Yusuf Wahbi (dialogue)	–	'Abd al-Halim Nasr	Riyad al-Sunbati; Muhammad al-Qasbagi; Fawzi al-Haw	–	Badi' Khayri	30 September 1943, Cinema Cosmo, Alexandria	Yusuf Wahbi; Fatima Rushdi; Amina Rizq

Tahiya al-sitat (*Long Live Women*)	Togo Mizrahi	Egyptian Films Company, Togo Mizrahi	Togo Mizrahi (scenario)	–	'Abd al-Halim Nasr	–	Muhammad Amin	Husayn al-Sayid	4 November 1943, Cinema Cosmo, Alexandria	Layla Fawzi, Anwar Wagdi, Madiha Yusra, Isma'il Yasin, Muhsin Sarhan, Muhammad Amin
Layla fi al-zalam (*Layla in the Dark*)	Togo Mizrahi	Egyptian Films Company, Togo Mizrahi	–	–	'Abd al-Halim Nasr	–	Muhammad al-Qasbagi	Ahmad Rami, Zaki Ibrahim, Ma'mun al-Shinawi	24 February 1944, Cinema Cosmo, Cairo	Layla Murad, Husayn Sidqi, Amina Rizq, Anwar Wagdi
Kidb fi kidb (*Lies upon Lies*)	Togo Mizrahi	Egyptian Films Company	–	–	'Abd al-Halim Nasr	Mustafa al-Sayyid; Ahmad Sabra	Muhammad Fawzi al-Haw; Ahmad Sabra	–	14 September 1944, Cinema Cosmo, Alexandria	Baba 'Izz al-Din; Anwar Wagdi
Nur al-Din wa-l-bahhara al-thalatha (*Nur al-Din and the Three Sailors*)	Togo Mizrahi	Egyptian Films Company	–	–	George Sa'd	–	Riyad al-Sunbati; Ibrahim Hamuda	Fathi Qura	23 November 1944, Cinema Cosmo, Cairo	'Ali al-Kassar; Layla Fawzi; Ibrahim Hamuda
Sallama	Togo Mizrahi	The Egyptian Films Co.	Bayram al-Tunsi (script and songs); 'Ali Ahmad Ba Kathir (story)	–	'Abd al-Halim Nasr	–	Zakariya Ahmad; Riyad al-Sunbati	–	9 April 1945, Cinema Studio Misr, Cairo; Cinema Ritz, Alexandria	Umm Kulthum; Yahya Shahin

TABLE 2 Greek films directed by Togo Mizrahi[2]

Film	Director	Scenario	Writing	Cinematography	Music	Lyrics	First Screening	Cast
Doktor Epaminondas[3] (Doctor Epaminondas)	Togo Mizrahi	–	Togo Mizrahi	–	Giannis Kyparissis	–	1937	Anna Kalouta, Maria Kalouta, Paraskevas Oikonomou
Otan o svzygos taxidevi (When the Husband Is Away)	Togo Mizrahi	–	Manos Filippidis	–	–	–	1937	Anna Kalouta; Maria Kalouta, Manos Filippidis
Prosfigopoula (The Refugee Girl)[4]	Togo Mizrahi	Togo Mizrahi	Dimitris Bogris	'Abd al-Halim Nasr	Kostas Giannidis	Savvidis	1938	Sophia Fembo; Manos Filippidis
Kapetan Skorpios (Captain Scorpion)[5]	Togo Mizrahi	–	–	–	Giannis Kyparissis	–	1939	Anna Kalouta, Maria Kalouta, Paraskevas Oikonomou

TABLE 3 Films produced by Togo Mizrahi

Film	Director	Producer	First Screening
Al-Riyadi (Le sportif)(The Athlete)	Leon Angel (as L. Nagel) and Clement Mizrahi	Egyptian Films Company, Togo Mizrahi	18 November 1937, Cinema Cosmo, Cairo
Ibn al-haddad (Son of a Blacksmith)	Yusuf Wahbi	Egyptian Films Company	1 October 1944
Shari' Muhammad 'Ali (Muhammad 'Ali Street)	Niyazi Mustafa	Egyptian Films Company	21 December 1944
Al-Mazahir (Manifestations)	Kamal Salim	Egyptian Films Company	25 January 1945
Al-Fanan al-'azim (The Great Artist)	Yusuf Wahbi	Egyptian Films Company	25 October 1945
Qissat gharam (Love Story)	Kamal Salim; Muhammad 'Abd al-Gawad	Egyptian Films Company, Togo Mizrahi	December 1945
Yad Allah (The Hand of God)	Yusuf Wahbi	Egyptian Films Company	31 January 1946
Malikat al-gamal (The Beauty Queen)	Niyazi Mustafa; Togo Mizrahi (released without director credit)	Egyptian Films Company, Togo Mizrahi & Co.	25 April 1946
Aksbris al-hubb (Love Express)	Husayn Fawzi	Egyptian Films Company, Togo Mizrahi & Co.	December 1946

NOTES

NOTES ON TRANSLATION AND TRANSLITERATION

1. Copyright, Herbert D. Katz Center for Advanced Judaic Studies at the University of Pennsylvania. All rights reserved.

1. TOGO MIZRAHI, AGENT OF EXCHANGE

1. I have adopted Viola Shafik's translation of the film's title from Arabic into English. Viola Shafik, *Popular Egyptian Cinema: Gender, Class, and Nation* (Cairo: American University in Cairo Press, 2007). The title could alternately be translated as *Too Much Wealth Is a Nuisance*. The French title of the film at the time of its release was *Les deux banquiers* (*The Two Bankers*).

2. For more on the notion of the *effendiyya*, see chap. 3 and Lucie Ryzova, *The Age of the Efendiyya: Passages to Modernity in National-Colonial Egypt* (Oxford: Oxford University Press, 2014). See also Wilson Chacko Jacob, *Working Out Egypt: Effendi Masculinity and Subject Formation in Colonial Modernity, 1870–1940* (Durham, NC: Duke University Press, 2011).

3. The other two films are *Layla mumtira* (*A Rainy Night*, 1939) and *Layla fi al-zalam* (*Layla in the Dark*, 1944).

4. The film's program, too, was published in both Arabic and French.

5. Susan Hayward, "Framing National Cinemas," in *Cinema and Nation*, ed. Mette Hjort and Scott MacKenzie (London and New York: Routledge, 2000), 101.

6. Magdy el-Shammaa sees the posters as self-promotion, consistent with a practice Mizrahi pioneered in Egypt of embedding advertisements and product promotions in his films. Magdy Mounir el-Shammaa, "Shadows of Contemporary Lives: Modernity, Culture, and National Identity in Egyptian Filmmaking" (PhD diss., UCLA, 2007), 49n71.

179

7. Mizrahi's paternal grandmother, Sarah Aghion, was a member of a branch of the influential Jewish family that emigrated from Italy and settled in Egypt in the eighteenth century. See the website "Les Fleurs de l'Orient," which catalogues genealogy of Ottoman Jews: https://www.farhi.org/genealogy/index.html, accessed 23 May 2019. See also Cutler Brock, "Aghion Family," in Encyclopedia of Jews in the Islamic World (Leiden: Brill, 2010).

8. Gudrun Krämer, The Jews in Modern Egypt, 1914–1952 (Seattle: University of Washington Press, 1989), 4, 221.

9. Joel Beinin, The Dispersion of Egyptian Jewry: Culture, Politics, and the Formation of a Modern Diaspora (Berkeley: University of California Press, 1998), 2.

10. Krämer, Jews in Modern Egypt, 4, 221.

11. Ibid., 4.

12. For an assessment of nostalgia among Egyptian minority diaspora writers, see Robert Mabro, "Nostalgic Literature on Alexandria," in Historians in Cairo: Essays in Honor of George Scanlon, ed. George T. Scanlon and Jill Edwards (Cairo: American University in Cairo Press, 2002), 237–65.

13. Mark Cohen, "The Neo-Lachrymose Conception of Jewish-Arab History," Tikkun 6 (1991): 55–60. For analysis of the implications of this thesis and a list of proponents, see Beinin, Dispersion of Egyptian Jewry, 14–17, 277n26.

14. Jacob M. Landau, Jews in Nineteenth-Century Egypt (New York: New York University Press, 1969).

15. Linguist Gabriel Rosenbaum controversially argues that there are enough idiosyncrasies in Egyptian Jewish speech patterns that it should be considered a dialect, which he calls Egyptian Jewish Arabic (EJA). (For a discussion of the speech of Egyptian Jews in Mizrahi's films, see chap. 3.) Gabriel Rosenbaum, "Elements and Evidence of Spoken Judeo-Egyptian Arabic in Old Egyptian Movies," in Jewish Languages—Languages in Contact Conference (Hebrew University of Jerusalem, 2016); Gabriel Rosenbaum, "'Aravit yehudit meduberet ba-mitzrayim ha-modernit: Marhivim 'Ivriyim ve-lo-takaniyim," Massorot 12 (2002): 117–48.

16. To complicate matters, following the dissolution of the Ottoman Empire, Jews throughout the region claiming some family connection to Italy sought Italian nationality as well. Krämer, Jews in Modern Egypt, 17, 36.

17. Ibid., 18–22. For a brief introduction to the cultural activity of the Egyptian Ashkenazi community, see Leonard Prager, "Yiddish Theater in Egypt," Bulletin of the Israeli Academic Center in Cairo 15 (1992).

18. Krämer, Jews in Modern Egypt, 27; David Bunis, Joseph Chetrit, and Haideh Sahim, "Jewish Languages Enter the Modern Era," in The Jews of the Middle East and North Africa in Modern Times (New York: Columbia University Press, 2003).

19. Krämer, Jews in Modern Egypt, 28.

20. For more on the Egyptian Jewish bourgeoisie, see Dario Miccoli, Histories of the Jews of Egypt: An Imagined Bourgeoisie, 1880s–1950s (London: Routledge, 2015).

21. Jacqueline Kahanoff, "Childhood in Egypt," in Mongrels or Marvels: The Levantine Writings of Jacqueline Shohet Kahanoff, ed. Deborah A. Starr and Sasson Somekh (Stanford, CA: Stanford University Press, 2011), 4.

22. André Aciman, Out of Egypt: A Memoir (New York: Farrar Straus Giroux, 1994), 172.

23. Ziad Fahmy, "Jurisdictional Borderlands: Extraterritoriality and 'Legal Chameleons' in Precolonial Alexandria, 1840–1870," *Comparative Studies in Society and History* 55, no. 2 (2013); Will Hanley, *Identifying with Nationality: Europeans, Ottomans, and Egyptians in Alexandria* (New York: Columbia University Press, 2017); Sarah Abrevaya Stein, *Extraterritorial Dreams: European Citizenship, Sephardi Jews, and the Ottoman Twentieth Century* (Chicago: University of Chicago Press, 2016).

24. Hanley, *Identifying with Nationality.*

25. Shimon Shamir, "The Evolution of the Egyptian Nationality Laws and Their Application to the Jews in the Monarchy Period," in *The Jews of Egypt: A Mediterranean Society in Modern Times,* ed. Shimon Shamir (Boulder, CO: Westview Press, 1987), 33–67.

26. Stein, *Extraterritorial Dreams.*

27. Ibid.; Hanley, *Identifying with Nationality.*

28. Krämer, *Jews in Modern Egypt,* 222. Rami Ginat, *A History of Egyptian Communism: Jews and Their Compatriots in Quest of Revolution* (Boulder, CO: Lynne Rienner Publishers, 2011). Beinin, *Dispersion of Egyptian Jewry,* 142–78.

29. Miccoli, *Histories of the Jews of Egypt;* Najat Abdulhaq, *Jewish and Greek Communities in Egypt: Entrepreneurship and Business before Nasser* (London: I.B. Tauris, 2016).

30. Juan Cole, *Colonialism and Revolution in the Middle East: Social and Cultural Origins of Egypt's 'Urabi Movement* (Princeton, NJ: Princeton University Press, 1993), 225–26.

31. Krämer, *Jews in Modern Egypt,* 94–95.

32. Beinin, *Dispersion of Egyptian Jewry,* 46.

33. Ibid.

34. Ibid.

35. Ibid., 34.

36. Sasson Somekh, "Participation of Egyptian Jews in Modern Arabic Culture, and the Case of Murad Farag," in *The Jews of Egypt: A Mediterranean Society in Modern Times,* ed. Shimon Shamir (Boulder, CO: Westview Press, 1987), 130–40.

37. Sasson Somekh, "Farag, Murad," in *Encyclopedia of Jews in the Islamic World* (Leiden: Brill, 2010).

38. Israel Gershoni and James Jankowski, *Redefining the Egyptian Nation, 1930–1945* (Cambridge and New York: Cambridge University Press, 1995).

39. See, e.g., Ahmad Ra'fat Bahjat, *Al-Yahud wa-al-sinima fi Misr* ([Cairo]: A.R. Bahjat, 2005).

40. Deborah A. Starr, *Remembering Cosmopolitan Egypt: Literature, Culture, and Empire* (London: Routledge, 2009); Yaron Shemer, "From Chahine's *al-Iskandariyya . . . leh* to *Salata baladi* and '*An Yahud Misr*: Rethinking Egyptian Jews' Cosmopolitanism, Belonging and Nostalgia in Cinema," *Middle East Journal of Culture and Communication* 7, no. 3 (2014): 351–75; Mary Youssef, *Minorities in the Contemporary Egyptian Novel* (Edinburgh: Edinburgh University Press, 2019).

41. Wa'il 'Abd al-Fatah, "Mukhrij min Misr, am qanbala yahudiyya mufakhakha?," *Al-Mustaqbil,* 10 November 2005, 20.

42. A recent article explores similar questions about early Iranian cinema: Golbarg Rekabtalaei, "Cinematic Governmentality: Cinema and Education in Modern Iran, 1900s–1930s," *International Journal of Middle East Studies* 50, no. 2 (2018). Mohannad Ghanamaweh examines nationalist discourse in Egypt during the silent era., "Entrepreneurship in

a State of Flux: Egypt's Silent Cinema and Its Transition to Synchronized Sound, 1896–1934" (PhD diss., UCLA, 2020).

43. "Hafla sinimatujrafiyya 'ilmiyya wa-mufida," *Al-Ahram*, 12 July 1923, 5. Reproduced in Ahmad al-Hadari, *Tarikh al-sinima fi Misr*, vol. 1, *Min bidayat 1896 ila akhir 1930* (Cairo: Nadi al-sinima bil-qahira, 1989), 167–69.

44. Ibid.

45. Hadari, *Tarikh al-sinima fi Misr*, 1:167–74.

46. For more on Bayumi, see Muhammad Kamil al- Qalyubi, *Muhammad Bayumi al-ra'id al-awwal li-l-sinima al-misriyya* ([Cairo]: Akadimiyat al-funun, Wahdat al-isdarat, 1994). Al-Qaliyubi (Mohamed El-Kalioubi) also directed a documentary about Bayumi that also chronicles the discovery of Bayumi's films: *Muhammad Bayumi, waqa'i' al-zaman al-da'i'* (*Mohamed Bayumi, Chronicle of a Lost Time*, 1991).

47. "Hafla sinimatujrafiyya 'ilmiyya wa-mufida," 5. Reproduced in Hadari, *Tarikh al-sinima fi Misr*, 1:167–69.

48. "Fi bilad Tut 'Ankh Amun awl sharit 'an Misr," *Al-Suwar al-mutaharika*, 26 July 1923, 21. Reproduced in Hadari, *Tarikh al-sinima fi misr*, 1:169–70.

49. Hadari, *Tarikh al-sinima fi Misr*, 1:169.

50. Ouissal Mejri, "The Birth of North African Cinema," in *Africa's Lost Classics: New Histories of African Cinema*, ed. Lizelle Bisschoff and David Murphy (London: Legenda, 2014), 29.

51. Samir Farid, "Periodization of Egyptian Cinema," in *Screens of Life: Critical Film Writing from the Arab World*, ed. Alia Arasoughly (Saint-Hyacinthe, Quebec: World Heritage Press, 1996), 5.

52. Diya' Mar'i, "Al-Ajanib fi al-sinima al-misriyya," in *Al-Sinima al-misriyya: Al-Nash'a wa-l-takwin*, ed. Hashim Nahhas (Cairo: Al-Majlis al-a'la li-l-thaqafa, 2008), 260–61.

53. In a recent entry to the debate, the splashy journal *Rawi: Egypt's Heritage Review* hedges on this issue. Its time line of Egyptian cinema refers to *In the Land of Tutankhamun* as "the first full-length feature film in Egypt." *Layla* is identified as "the first 'Egyptian' full-length feature" (scare quotes in the original). "Timeline of Egyptian Cinema, 1896–1980s," *Rawi: Egypt's Heritage Review*, no. 9 (2018): 86–87.

54. Kay Dickinson, "'I Have One Daughter and That Is Egyptian Cinema': 'Aziza Amir Amid the Histories and Geographies of National Allegory," *Camera Obscura*, no. 64 (2007): 145.

55. *Al-Ahram*, 1 November 1927, cited in Hadari, *Tarikh al-sinima fi Misr*,1:219. The article transliterates the English word "propaganda" into Arabic.

56. Dickinson, "'I Have One Daughter,'" 140–41.

57. "Jama'a al-nuqqad takawan far'a laha fi al-Iskandariyya," *Fann al-sinima*, 12 November 1933, 29.

58. Mar'i, "Al-Ajanib fi al-sinima al-misriyya," 240–41.

59. Dickinson, "'I Have One Daughter,'" 165.

60. Ibid.

61. Mar'i, "Al-Ajanib fi al-sinima al-misriyya," 21–22.

62. Ernest Gellner, *Nations and Nationalism* (Ithaca, NY: Cornell University Press, 1983); Benedict Anderson, *Imagined Communities: Reflections on the Origin and Spread of Nationalism* (London: Verso, 1983); Homi K. Bhabha, *The Location of Culture* (London: Routledge, 1994).

63. Mette Hjort and Scott MacKenzie, Introduction to *Cinema and Nation*, ed. Mette Hjort and Scott MacKenzie (London and New York: Routledge, 2000), 4.

64. Paul Willemen, "The National Revised," in *Theorising National Cinema*, ed. Valentina Vitali and Paul Willemen (London: British Film Institute, 2006), 36.

65. In the same volume of essays, Philip Rosen articulates the point about the intertextual nature of cinema. He analyzes Burch's work on 1920s and 1930s Japanese cinema that examines the "transformative integrations of many foreign practices." Philip Rosen, "History, Textuality, Nation: Kracauer, Burch and Some Problems in the Study of National Cinemas," in *Theorising National Cinema*, ed. Valentina Vitali and Paul Willemen (London: British Film Institute, 2006), 24.

66. Willemen, "The National Revised," 33.

67. Ibid.

68. Hadari, *Tarikh al-sinima fi Misr*, 1:219.

69. Dickinson, "'I Have One Daughter,'" 138.

70. Hadari, *Tarikh al-sinima fi Misr*, 1:220.

71. "Istudiyu Misr Filim," *Fann al-sinima*, 13 January 1934, 30.

72. "Panel Titles Help U.S. Pictures in Near East," *Variety*, 21 November 1933.

73. *Al-'Arusa*, 7 August 1929, p. 6. Cited in Hadari, *Tarikh al-sinima fi Misr* 1:329. *The Jazz Singer* (Alan Crosland, 1928) premiered in Egypt at the American Cosmograph cinema in Alexandria on 20 December 1928. Regular screenings of sound films began in earnest in Autumn 1929. Hadari, *Tarikh al-sinima fi Misr*, 1:294, 331.

74. "Ila dur al-sinima," *Fann al-sinima*, 29 October 1933, 18.

75. Walter Armbrust, *Mass Culture and Modernism in Egypt* (Cambridge and New York: Cambridge University Press, 1996), 114.

76. "Iftitah sinima fu'ad," *Fann al-sinima*, 12 November 1933, 4. *The White Rose* eventually played at Cinema Fu'ad in January 1934. Armbrust, *Mass Culture and Modernism in Egypt*, 243n49.

77. "iftitah al-kusmugraf al-amriki bi-l-iskandariyya," *Fann al-sinima*, 5 November 1933, 5–6.

78. "Sinima al-Kusmugraf bi-l-Qahira," *Al-Sabah*, 15 October 1934.

79. "Sinima al-Kusmugraf al-jadida wa-l-aflam al-misriyya," *Al-Sabah*, 2 November 1934. Josy Films was established by Joseph Mosseri in 1915; the company operated numerous cinemas; was involved in film distribution, including RKO; and opened a studio in 1932. Miccoli, *Histories of the Jews of Egypt*, 81; Krämer, *Jews in Modern Egypt*, 43. (RKO detail from *Jaridat Juzi*, no. 51 [2 October 1931]: 8.) One source states that Togo Mizrahi had a financial stake in Josy Films, but I haven't seen this claim corroborated. Ahmed Kamel, "The Jewish Community of Egypt," *Egyptian Mail*, 2 September 2006.

80. Andrew J. Flibbert, *Commerce in Culture: States and Markets in the World Film Trade* (New York: Palgrave Macmillan, 2007), 44.

81. Sabry Hafez, "The Quest for / Obsession with the National in Arabic Cinema," in *Theorising National Cinema*, ed. Valentina Vitali and Paul Willemen (London: British Film Institute, 2006), 235–36.

82. Ahmad Badr Khan, *Sinima*, (Cairo, 1936), cited in Hafez, "National in Arab Cinema," 236.

83. Group of Cinema Critics, "Nihna insar li-l-sharikat al-sinima'iyya al-misriyya," *Fann al-sinima*, 29 October 1933, 7.

84. Muhammad Karim and Mahmud Ali, *Mudhakkirat Muhammad Karim: 50 sana sinima* (Cairo: Kitab al-idha'a wa-al-tilifizyun, 1972), 200–201. Cited in Armbrust, *Mass Culture and Modernism in Egypt*, 114.

85. Viola Shafik, "Egyptian Cinema," in *Companion Encyclopedia of Middle Eastern and North African Film*, ed. Oliver Leaman (London: Routledge, 2001), 25.

86. "Studiyu Misr yashtari dar jadida," *Al-Ithnayn*, 4 April 1938, 16.

87. Shafik, "Egyptian Cinema," 26.

88. Robert Vitalis, *When Capitalists Collide: Business Conflict and the End of Empire in Egypt* (Berkeley: University of California Press, 1995).

89. Ifdal Elsaket, "The Star of the East: Umm Kulthum and Egyptian Cinema," in *Stars in World Cinema: Screen Icons and Star Systems across Cultures*, ed. Andrea Bandhauer and Michelle Royer (London: I.B. Tauris, 2015).

90. Vitalis, *When Capitalists Collide*, 230.

91. For more on the nationalist discourse on economic endeavors in this era, see ibid.

92. Flibbert, *Commerce in Culture*.

93. Quoted in "Mu'tamar al-sinima fi Misr," *Al-Sabah*, 31 January 1936, 68.

94. This sort of protectionist argument was not unique to Egypt. For a discussion of the theoretical and practical validity of this argument in support of the development of national cinema, see Ian Jarvie, "National Cinema: A Theoretical Assessment," in *Cinema and Nation*, ed. Mette Hjort and Scott MacKenzie (London and New York: Routledge, 2000).

95. Ahmad al-Hadari, *Tarikh al-sinima fi Misr*, vol. 2, *Min bidayat 1931 ila akhir 1940* (Cairo: Al-Hay'a al-misriyya al-'amma li-l-kitab, 2007), 247–49.

96. Munir Muhammad Ibrahim, *Al-Sinima al-misriyya fi al-thalathiniyat (1930–1939)* (Cairo: Wizarat al-thaqafa, Sunduq al-tanmiyya al-thaqafiyya, 2002), 91–92.

97. Ibid.

98. "Mu'tamar al-sinima al-misriyya," *Al-Sabah*, 22 January 1937, 71.

99. Ibid.

100. A.M.H., "Al-Sharikat al-ajnabiyya tahtal sina'at al-sinima al-mahaliyya," *Fann al-sinima*, 3 February 1934.

101. Ibid.

102. Ad for *Sadat al-adghal*, *Al-Sabah*, 14 February 1936, 56.

103. In February 1938, Studio Misr entered the dubbing business with the release of an Arabic version of *Mr. Deeds Goes to Town* (1936, Frank Capra, dir.). "Hollywood Nataqat," *al-Ithnayn*, 7 February 1938. Hashim al-Nahhas, Al-Huwiya al-qawmiya fi al-sinima al-'Arabiya: Dirasa istitla'iya mustaqbaliya (Cairo: Al-Hay'a al-misriyya al-'amma li-l-kitab, 1986). Studio Misr eventually signed a contract with Columbia Pictures to dub other hits.

104. Ad for *Sadat al-adghal*, *Al-Sabah*, 14 February 1936, 56. For a brief discussion of the film, see Ibrahim, *Al-Sinima al-misriyya fi al-thalathiniyat*, 123.

105. Compare the popular slogan of 1919, "*misr li-l-misriyyin*," with the tagline for Cinema al-Nahda, "*sinima al-lati inshaha misri li-l-misriyyin*."

106. This idiom reappears in Egyptian films from the 1940s. Ifdal Elsaket, "Jungle Films in Egypt: Race, Anti-Blackness, and Empire," *Arab Studies Journal* 25, no. 2 (Fall 2017): 8–32.

107. The dubbed version of the film was released in February 1936; the Anglo-Egyptian treaty that redefined the relationship between the United Kingdom and Egypt was negotiated and ratified in the second half of the same year.

108. Egypt passed a law on the censorship of cinema in 1904. Shafik, "Egyptian Cinema," 33.

109. The censored projects were *Layla bint al-sahra'* (*Layla Daughter of the Desert*, Bahiga Hafiz, 1937; released as *Layla al-Badawiyya* [*Layla the Beduin*] in 1944) and *Lashin* (Fritz Kramp, 1938).

110. Hafez, "National in Arabic Cinema," 234–35.

111. Shafik, "Egyptian Cinema," 66–67.

112. Flibbert lists several notable examples of this commonly accepted view. Andrew Flibbert, "State and Cinema in Pre-Revolutionary Egypt, 1927–1952," in *Re-Envisioning Egypt 1919–1952*, ed. Arthur Goldschmidt, Amy J. Johnson, and Barak A. Salmoni (Cairo: American University in Cairo Press, 2005), 461n3.

113. Walter Armbrust, "The Golden Age before the Golden Age: Commercial Egyptian Cinema before the 1960s," in *Mass Mediations New Approaches to Popular Culture in the Middle East and Beyond*, ed. Walter Armbrust (Berkeley: University of California Press, 2000), 292.

114. Ibid., 301.

115. Shafik, "Egyptian Cinema."

116. Vitalis, *When Capitalists Collide*. See also Elsaket, "The Star of the East."

117. Joel Gordon, *Revolutionary Melodrama: Popular Film and Civic Identity in Nasser's Egypt* (Chicago: Middle East Documentation Center, 2002).

118. Iman 'Amr, "Al-Taghyirat al-tarikhiyya wa-atharha 'ala sinima al-thalathiniyat," in *Al-Sinima al-misriyya: Al-Nasha wa-l-takwin*, ed. Hashim al-Nahhas (Cairo: Majlis al-'ala li-l-thaqafa, 2008), 72–73.

119. I don't wish to denigrate the film, which is also widely acclaimed for its realist construction of lower-class struggles as well as its technical achievements. For an analysis of the film and its reception, see Armbrust, *Mass Culture and Modernism in Egypt*, 100–106.

120. Ahmad Ra'fat Bahjat, ed., *Misr: Mi'at sana sinima* (Cairo: Mihrajan al-Qahira al-sinima'i al-dawli al-'ishrun, 1996).

121. Pressbook for *Al-Bahhar*, Mahmoud Qassim Cinema Collection, Rare Books and Special Collections Library, American University in Cairo.

122. Ibrahim, *Al-Sinima al-misriyya fi al-thalathiniyat*, 91–92.

123. Hadari, *Tarikh al-sinima fi Misr*, 2:249.

124. Tojo Mizrahi, "Al-Muntij al-misri huwa al-muntij al-kamil fi al-'alam," *Al-Sabah*, 19 November 1942.

125. "Un Thé," *La tribune juive*, 14 October 1936.

126. "Juhud al-ustaz Togo Mizrahi fi 'alam al-sinima," *Al-Sabah*, 8 October 1937.

127. Ibrahim Dasuqi and Sami Hilmi, *Madrasat al-Iskandariyya li-l-taswir al-sinima'i* (Alexandria: Maktabat al-Iskandariyya, 2013), 24–25.

128. Ibid., 25.

129. Muhammad Awad and Sahar Hamouda, eds., *The Birth of the Seventh Art in Alexandria: Catalogue* (Alexandria: Bibliotheca Alexandrina, 2007), xi. In addition to the print catalogue, the Bibliotheca Alexandrina website hosts an open-access digital archive containing much of the same material: Biblotheca Alexandrina, "The Birth of the Seventh Art in Alexandria," http://www.bibalex.org/alexcinema/index.html.

130. Awad and Hamouda, *Birth of the Seventh Art*, xii.

131. Hayward, "Framing National Cinemas," 101.

132. Ibid.

133. Willemen, "The National Revised," 18; Hayward, "Framing National Cinemas," 101.

134. Vitali and Willemen, *Theorising National Cinema*, 36.

135. Deborah A. Starr, "Masquerade and the Performance of National Imaginaries: Levantine Ethics, Aesthetics, and Identities in Egyptian Cinema," *Journal of Levantine Studies* 1, no. 2 (2011): 31–57.

136. For a longer discussion of the performativity of the Levantine, see ibid.

137. Deborah Starr, *Remembering Cosmopolitan Egypt: Literature, Culture, Empire* (London: Routledge, 2009).

138. See, for example, Amanda Anderson, "Cosmopolitanism, Universalism, and the Divided Legacies of Modernity," in *Cosmopolitics: Thinking and Feeling Beyond the Nation*, eds. Pheng Cheah and Bruce Robbins (Minneapolis: University of Minnesota Press, 1998), 265–89; and David Harvey, "Cosmopolitanism and the Banality of Geographical Evils," *Public Culture* 12, no. 2 (2000): 529–64.

139. Robert Mabro, "Alexandria 1860–1960: The Cosmopolitan Identity," in *Alexandria, Real and Imagined*, ed. Anthony Hirst and Michael Silk (Aldershot, Hampshire: Ashgate Publishing, 2004), 247–62.

140. For an extended analysis of the "cosmopolitan" in the context of colonial and post-colonial Egypt, see Starr, *Remembering Cosmopolitan Egypt*, 1–28.

141. On-screen, the title of the latter film appears as "*khafir al-darak*," meaning "police sentry" in Modern Standard Arabic. In some print ads the title is rendered "*ghafir*," which also means "guard" or "night watchman" in Egyptian colloquial Arabic.

142. The name in the Arabic title is Farhat. The film's credits in French render this name as Farahat. I have chosen the latter spelling for the English title as Mizrahi's preferred romanization.

143. Viola Shafik, *Arab Cinema: History and Cultural Identity* (Cairo: American University in Cairo Press, 1998), 103.

2. TOGO MIZRAHI, WORK OVER WORDS

1. Quoted in Togo Mizrahi, "Khitab maftuh min al-ustaz Togo Mizrahi ila nujum wa kawakib aflamuh al-misriyya," *Al-Sabah*, 17 January 1941, 32.

2. Ibid.

3. "Mukhriju al-aflam al-misriyya, liman yakun al-tafawuq haza al-mawsum?," *Al-Sabah*, 18 January 1945, 23.

4. Mizrahi, "Khitab maftuh," 32.

5. Jacques Mizart, correspondence with author, 24 September 2013.

6. Sami Hilmi, *Al-Shakhsiya al-sakandariyya fi al-sinima al-misriyya* (Alexandria: Maktabat al-Iskandariyya, 2007), 39.

7. In 1904, Jacques is listed as director of transit for the company, whose name is listed in French as "Société des entrepôts." Stefano Poffandi, ed., *Indicateur égyptien administratif et commercial* (Alexandria: A. Moures, 1904), 385.

8. See the website Les Fleurs de L'Orient, which catalogues the genealogy of Ottoman Jews: www.farhi.org/genealogy/index.html, accessed 23 May 2019. See also Cutler Brock, "Aghion Family," in *Encyclopedia of Jews in the Islamic World* (Leiden: Brill, 2010).

9. Gudrun Krämer, *The Jews in Modern Egypt, 1914–1952* (Seattle: University of Washington Press, 1989); Sarah Abrevaya Stein, *Extraterritorial Dreams: European Citizenship, Sephardi Jews, and the Ottoman Twentieth Century* (Chicago: University of Chicago Press, 2016); Shimon Shamir, "The Evolution of the Egyptian Nationality Laws and Their Application to the Jews in the Monarchy Period," in *The Jews of Egypt: A Mediterranean Society in Modern Times*, ed. Shimon Shamir (Boulder, CO: Westview Press, 1987): 33–67; Ziad Fahmy, "Jurisdictional Borderlands: Extraterritoriality and 'Legal Chameleons' in Precolonial Alexandria, 1840–1870," *Comparative Studies in Society and History* 55, no. 2 (2013): 1–25; Will Hanley, *Identifying with Nationality: Europeans, Ottomans, and Egyptians in Alexandria* (New York: Columbia University Press, 2017).

10. I am grateful to Joseph Viscomi for clarifying this process. Joseph Viscomi, correspondence with author, 15 June 2017. For more detail, see Joseph Viscomi, "Out of Time: History, Presence, and the Departure of the Italians of Egypt, 1933–Present" (PhD diss., University of Michigan, 2016).

11. Zvi Ben-Dor Benite, "Global Experiments in Mizrahi Thought: 'Asia,' 'Europe' and the 'East' in the Writings of Hayyim Ben-Kiki," in *Symposium on Jewish Thought in Arab Societies, 1880–1960* (Beersheba, Israel: Ben Gurion University, 2014).

12. Certificate of the Grand Rabbinat, Communauté Israélite à Alexandrie. Act 370, vol. 10. 2 June 1920. From files of Jacques Mizart.

13. Jacques Mizart, correspondence with author, 24 September 2013; *Annuaire des juifs d'Égypte et du Proche-Orient* (Cairo: Société des éditions historiques juives d'Égypte, 1942), 269–70.

14. *Annuaire des juifs d'Égypte*, 269–70. While the *Annuaire* from 1942 is a contemporaneous source, I have not been able to corroborate his degree. Neither the University of Milan nor the Università Commerciale Luigi Bocconi of Milan has records for any students by the name of Mizrahi. Gaia Riitano, Centre Apice, University of Milan, correspondence with author, 5 February 2018; Tiziana Dassi, Biblioteca e Archivi Università Bocconi, correspondence with author, 30 June 2017. I am grateful to Dario Miccoli for helping me understand the Italian university system at the time.

15. Certificate signed by J. Rolo 15 April 1940, courtesy of Jacques Mizart.

16. Certificate dated 20 February 1926, courtesy of Jacques Mizart.

17. *Annuaire des Juifs d'Égypte*, 269–70; Mahmud 'Ali Fahmi, "Sinima Togo Mizrahi (1930–1946): Dirasa naqdiyya," in *Al-Sinima al-misriyya: Al-Nash'a wa-l-takwin*, ed. Hashim al-Nahhas (Cairo: Al-Majlis al-a'la li-l-thaqafa, 2008), 153.

18. Jacques Mizart, interview with author, 16 May 2017. Shooting for *Le fin du monde* took about a year, beginning in mid-1929. Alan Larson Williams, *Republic of Images: A History of French Filmmaking* (Cambridge, MA: Harvard University Press, 1992), 163–64.

19. *Annuaire des juifs d'Égypte*, 269–70; Alfred Mizrahi, "Togo Mizrahi, raconté par son frère, Alfred Mizrahi," in *La sortie au cinéma: Palaces et ciné-jardins d'Égypte, 1930–1980*, ed. Marie-Claude Bénard (Marseille and Aix-en-Provence: Éditions Parenthèses, MMSH, 2016), 19. Ahmad al-Hadari mentions four short films shot in Egypt in 1929, but he does not include any production information. One of the films, *Iftitah istad al-Iskandariyya* (*Opening of the Alexandria Stadium*), premiered at the Muhammad 'Ali Theater in Alexandria on 20 November 1929. (Al-Hadari cites from an issue of *La Réforme* 20 [November 1929].) Ahmad al-Hadari, *Tarikh al-sinima fi Misr*, vol. 1, *Min bidayat 1896 ila akhir 1930* (Cairo: Nadi al-sinima bi-l-qahira, 1989), 330. Muhammad 'Ali Fahmi notes that Togo Mizrahi was

a fan of the Nadi al-itihad al-sakandarani soccer team. A few years later, Mizrahi was responsible for signing the team's captain and star player, Sayyid Huda, to act in a film he was producing, *Al-Riyadi* (*The Athlete*, 1937). Fahmi, "Sinima Togo Mizrahi," 166–67. Several key scenes in *The Athlete* were shot at the Alexandria stadium. Given these later developments, it is possible to speculate that Mizrahi could have been responsible for the 1929 short *Opening of Alexandria Stadium*.

20. Fahmi refers to the company as Al-Sharika al-sinima'iyya al-'alamiyya (the International Film Company). Fahmi, "Sinima Togo Mizrahi," 153.

21. Mizrahi, "Togo Mizrahi, raconté par son frère," 19.

22. Ahmad Kamil Mursi, "Shawamikh 'alam al-sinima al-misriyya: Togo Mizrahi," *Al-Sinima wa-l-nas*, no. 11 (1979): 24–25, 55.

23. Mizrahi, "Togo Mizrahi, raconté par son frère," 19.

24. Hilmi, *Al-Shakhsiya al-sakandariyya*, 39.

25. Jacques Mizart, correspondence with author, 19 June 2017.

26. Togo appears in *Doctor Farahat* credited as 'Abd al-'Aziz al-Mashriqi. Some sources suggest Togo may also have appeared in *The Abyss, or Cocaine*. Ahmad al-Hadari, "Istudiyu Misr . . . Madrasa sinima'iyya fi al-thalathiniyat," in *Al-Sinima al-misriyya: Al-Nash'a wa-al-takwin*, ed. Hashim al-Nahhas (Cairo: Al-Majlis al-a'la li-l-thaqafa, 2008), 368.

27. Jacques Mizart, interview with author, 16 May 2017.

28. In turn, Alfred (1920–2000) raised the children of his brother Félix (1903–1957), including Jacques Mizart, who generously agreed to share family history with me, as well as documents and photographs. Jacques Mizart, correspondence with author, 24 September 2013.

29. The portrait of Mizrahi featuring dramatic, cinematic lighting (fig. 2) was taken by Dorés, who was both a celebrated photographer and an early pioneer of Egyptian cinema. Dorés photographed many high-profile members of the Egyptian elite, including the royal family.

30. Quoted in Ibrahim Dasuqi and Sami Hilmi, *Madrasat al-iskandariyya li-l-taswir al-sinima'i* (Alexandria: Maktabat al-Iskandariyya, 2013), 84.

31. Ibid., 84–85.

32. Ibid., 85. A brief item in *Al-Sabah* in November 1934 mentioned Mizrahi's recent return from Italy and announced his plans to begin shooting a film starring al-Gazayirli. "Togo Mizrahi wa-l-Gazayirli," *Al-Sabah*, 2 November 1934, 39.

33. Muhammad Awad and Sahar Hamouda, eds., *The Birth of the Seventh Art in Alexandria: Catalogue* (Alexandria: Bibliotheca Alexandrina, 2007).

34. Sammy Brill shot *Layla mumtira* (*A Rainy Night*, 1939), and George Sa'd shot *Nur al-Din wa-l-bahhara al-thalatha* (*Nur al-Din and the Three Sailors*, 1944).

35. Quoted in Dasuqi and Hilmi, *Madrasat al-Iskandariyya li-l-taswir al-sinima'i*, 86.

36. Quoted in Hilmi, *Al-Shakhsiya al-sakandariyya*, 40.

37. Mursi, "Shawamikh 'alam al-sinima al-misriyya."

38. Ibid., 24–25.

39. Munir Muhammad Ibrahim, *Al-Sinima al-misriyya fi al-thalathiniyat (1930–1939)* (Cairo: Wizarat al-thaqafa, sunduq al-tanmiya al-thaqafiyya, 2002), 133.

40. Liat Kozma, "White Drugs in Interwar Egypt: Decadent Pleasures, Emaciated Fellahin, and the Campaign against Drugs," *Comparative Studies of South Asia, Africa and the Middle East* 33, no. 1 (2013): 89–101.

41. To confuse matters further, Muna Ghandur refers to the film by the title "*Al-Kukayin.*" Muna Ghandur, *Sultanat al-shasha: Ra'idat al-sinima al-misriyya* (Beirut: Riyad al-Rayyis li-l-kutub wa-l-nashr, 2005), 132.

42. Ahmad al-Hadari questions whether the film was ever released. Hadari, *Tarikh al-sinima fi Misr*, 1:367. *Variety*, by contrast, reports a screening of the film, deeming it the first Egyptian sound film: "Foreign Film News: Egypt's First Talker Production on Screen," *Variety*, January 8 1930.

43. "Riwayat al-kukayin," *Al-Dunya al-musawwara*, 18 May 1930.

44. Ibid.

45. "Al-mukhadarat," *Al-Dunya al-musawwara*, 4 May 1930.

46. American Cosmograph, ed., "Program for Thursday 19 to Wednesday 25 February 1931" (Cairo: American Cosmograph, 1931), courtesy of Nicole and Maureen McManamny. In addition, the film *Al-Dahaya* (*The Victims*, Ibrahim Lama, 1932) also addresses the issue of drug use.

47. Plot summary from Fahmi, "Sinima Togo Mizrahi," 157–60. Al-Hadari reproduces images and captions published in *al-Sabah* 13 March 1931. See Hadari, *Tarikh al-sinima fi Misr*, 1:268–69.

48. American Cosmograph, "Program for Thursday 19 to Wednesday 25 February 1931."

49. Nicole Angel McManamny and Maureen McManamny, correspondence with author, 11–12 December 2016.

50. Hadari, *Tarikh al-sinima fi Misr*, 1:365.

51. McManamny and McManamny, correspondence.

52. *Annuaire des juifs d'Égypte*, 269–70.

53. *Cocaine, or the Abyss* also screened at the Crystal Cinema in Beirut in 1933. Edward Asswad, "Times Square: Chatter—Egypt," *Variety*, 6 June 1933.

54. Advertisement for *Anshuda al-fu'ad*, *Al-Ahram*, 13 April 1932, 8.

55. Ahmad al-Hadari, *Tarikh al-sinima fi Misr*, vol. 2, *Min bidayat 1931 ila akhir 1940* (Cairo: Al-Hay'a al-misriyya al-'ama li-l-kitab, 2007), 33.

56. Advertisement, *Al-Ahram*, 11 April 1932, 9.

57. Awad and Hamouda, *Birth of the Seventh Art*, 313.

58. "Sharit al-usbu': Awlad Misr," *Al-Kawakib*, 15 May 1933, 15.

59. Fahmi, "Sinima Tugu Mizrahi," 157–60.

60. Most of the later nostalgia literature about cosmopolitan Alexandria, by contrast, largely represents the foreign-minority bourgeoisie; see Deborah A. Starr, *Remembering Cosmopolitan Egypt: Literature, Culture, and Empire* (London: Routledge, 2009).

61. L. Abou-Saif, "Najib Al-Rihani: From Buffoonery to Social Comedy," *Journal of Arabic Literature* 4 (1973): 45; the title *usatz* is an honorific.

62. "Salafini 3 gineh," *Al-Ithnayn wa-l-Dunya*, 9 October 1939, 46.

63. "Film al-usbu': Layla Mumtira," *Al-Ithnayn wa-l-Dunya*, 10 April 1939, 66–7.

64. "Film al-usbu': Al-Bashmaqawil," *Al-Ithnayn wa-l-Dunya*, 29 January 1940, 49.

65. Mursi, "Shawamikh 'alam al-sinima al-misriyya," 25.

66. "Al-Intaj al-sinima'i al-mahali: 100,000 gineh," *Al-Sabah*, 14 February 1936, 74.

67. "Wudu' shiq, mumumathilun akfa': Mukhrij qadir," *Al-Sabah*, 21 February 1936, 75.

68. "Al-Film al-jadid: Togo Mizrahi," review of *Mistreated by Affluence*, *Al-Sabah*, 29 January 1937, 71.

69. *Annuaire des juifs d'Égypte*, 269–70.

70. "Mukhrijuna wa-but' al-intaj," *Al-Ithnayn wa-l-Dunya*, 4 March 1940, 23; "Al-intaj al-sinima'i al-mahali."

71. "Al-Intaj al-sinima'i al-mahali."

72. "Wudu' shiq, mumumathilun akfa'."

73. "Ana tab'i kidda," *Al-Ithnayn*, 28 March 1938, 33–34.

74. "Salafini 3 gineh."

75. "Togo Mizrahi yuqadim 100,000 gineh," *Al-Sabah*, 13 March 1936, 82.

76. "Juhud al-ustaz Togo Mizrahi fi 'alam al-sinima," *Al-Sabah*, 8 October 1937, 67.

77. "Al-Intaj al-sinima'i al-mahali"; "Juhud al-ustaz Togo Mizrahi fi 'alam al-sinima."

78. Mursi may be referring to the whisper campaign, described in chap. 7, that attempted to dampen enthusiasm for *Sallama* (1945). Mursi, "Shawamikh 'alam al-sinima al-misriyya," 25.

79. Viola Shafik, "Badr Lama's Patterned Vest or the Challenges of Writing a 'National' Film History" (paper presented at the conference "Early Cinema in the Balkans and the Near East: Beginnings to Interwar Period," Athens, Greece, June 2015).

80. "Fawq al-sitar al-fiddi: Shabah al-madi," review of *Shabah al-madi*, *Al-Ithnayn*, 10 December 1934, 38.

81. Before this time, two brief items had appeared in *Al-Ithnayn*'s satirically minded gossip column about actors traveling to Alexandria to negotiate contracts with Mizrahi: "Al-Masrah wa-l-sinima: 'Abd al-Salam al-Nablusi," *Al-Ithnayn*, 17 December 1934, 36; and "Al-Masrah wa-l-sinima: Bi-l-tayara," *Al-Ithnayn*, 24 December 1934, 44.

82. Mursi, "Shawamikh 'alam al-sinima al-misriyya," 25.

83. "Sharikat al-aflam al-misriyya wa-l-ustaz Togo Mizrahi," *Al-Sabah*, 26 January 1940.

84. "Al-Ustaz Togo Mizrahi yujadid 'aqd ijar Studio Wahbi," *Al-Sabah*, 5 December 1941, 38. Some sources from the early 1940s continue to refer to the location as Studio Wahbi, listing Togo Mizrahi as studio director: "Film rabab," *Al-Lati'if al-musawwara*, 4 August 1941, 20.

85. "Film Togo al-jadid," *Al-Sabah*, 12 December 1941, 36.

86. *Al-Sabah* reported that Mizrahi's contract with Studio Wahbi ended in August 1945 and that he started construction on a new studio. "Studiyu Jadid," *Al-Sabah*, 23 August 1945, 33. Ahmad Kamil Mursi also recalls that Mizrahi purchased land in Giza and built a studio. According to Mursi, the studio was later renamed Studio Giza, under the direction of 'Isa and Yusuf Karama. Mursi, "Shawamikh 'alam al-sinima al-misriyya," 24. Jacques Mizart, however, maintains not only that Togo continued to work in the studio on Husni Street, but that the offices of the Egyptian Films Company remained at that location until the company was sequestered in 1961. Jacques Mizart, correspondence with author, 16–17 October 2019.

87. Joel Gordon, *Revolutionary Melodrama: Popular Film and Civic Identity in Nasser's Egypt* (Chicago: Middle East Documentation Center, 2002).

88. "Ra'y l-il-ustaz Ahmad Badr Khan," *Al-Sabah*, 21 November 1941, 35; "Bayna raghbat al-fanan wa-miyul al-jumhur," *Al-Sabah*, 14 November 1941, 28.

89. Muhammad Amin, "Ila al-jumhur awalan thum ila Togo Mizrahi," *Al-Sabah*, 25 November 1943, 25.

90. "Togo Mizrahi: Doyen du cinéma en Egypte," *La tribune juive*, 17 June 1942.

91. Ibid.

92. "Layla," review of *Layla*, *Al-Ahram*, 8 April 1942.

93. "Safha min jihad Togo Mizrahi," *Al-Sabah*, 4 November 1943, 16–17.

94. "Togo Mizrahi yadrib raqam qiyasi fi al-intaj wa-l-ikhraj," *Al-Sabah*, 12 October 1944, 35.

95. Marku Ibrahim Kuhayn, "Al-Nijah al-'azim li-film Layla bint madaris," *Al-Shams*, 14 November 1941.

96. "Al-Najah al-bahir li-film Layla bint madaris," *Al-Shams*, 31 October 1941, 3.

97. Ibid.

98. Togo Mizrahi, "Kul aflami zift! Wa-lakin li-maza?," *Al-Sabah*, 9 October 1942, 32.

99. Ibid.

100. Robert Vitalis, "American Ambassador in Technicolor and Cinemascope: Hollywood and Revolution on the Nile," in *Mass Mediations: New Approaches to Popular Culture in the Middle East and Beyond*, ed. Walter Armbrust (Berkeley: University of California Press, 2000), 277, 289n16.

101. "Idarat Sinima Cosmo bayn filmay qalb imra'a wa-fata mutamarrida," *Al-Sabah*, 12 April 1940, 41. *Heart of a Woman* premiered a week late, on 11 April 1940, at Cinema Cosmo in Alexandria and opened in Cairo on 6 May 1940 at Cinema Royal. Al-Hadari, *Tarikh al-sinima fi Misr*, 2:403.

102. Cinema Studio Misr screened only Studio Misr films, and Studio Nahas signed a multifilm contract with Cinema Kursal. "Sharikat al-sinima wa-dur al-sinima," *Al-Sabah*, 7 September 1944, 27.

103. "Hal ta'lam," *Al-Sabah*, 16 December 1943, 26.

104. "Hal ta'lam?" *Al-Sabah*, 11 May 1944, 26.

105. "Kayfa wuzi'at al-aflam al-kham al-laty wasalat akhiran ila Misr?," *Al-Sabah*, 27 May 1943, 19.

106. It is not clear if the accusation refers to the two sound stages at the Giza studio, or if it refers to the studios in Giza and Alexandria. "Hal tunsha' studiyuhat jadida?," *Al-Sabah*, 17 February 1944, 26.

107. Cited in Mursi, "Shawamikh 'alam al-sinima al-misriyya," 55.

108. "Ra'y al-ustaz Togo Mizrahi fi film Ibn al-Haddad," *Al-Sabah*, 2 November 1944, 25.

109. "Mukhriju al-aflam al-misriyya, liman yakun al-tafawuq haza al-mawsum?," *Al-Sabah*, 18 January 1945, 23.

110. Togo Mizrahi, "Al-Muntij al-misri huwa al-muntij al-kamil fi al-'alam," *Al-Sabah*, 19 November 1942, 14.

111. Ibid.

112. The previous year, director Kamal Salim died suddenly during the production of *Qissat gharam* (*Love Story*). Mizrahi asked Muhammad 'Abd al-Gawad to complete the production, but contemporaneous sources suggest that Mizrahi also participated in directing the project. "Hal Ta'alim," *Al-Sabah*, 6 December 1945, 33.

113. Magdy Mounir el-Shammaa, "Shadows of Contemporary Lives: Modernity, Culture, and National Identity in Egyptian Filmmaking" (PhD diss., UCLA, 2007), 42.

114. "Togo Mizrahi wa-l-Gazayirli."; "Al-Ustaz Togo Mizrahi 'awdatihi min uruba," *Al-Sabah*, 15 October 1937, 67.

115. Samir W. Raafat, "From Badi'a to Abbas: Looking Back on Giza's Riverside Drive, Part VI, Francophile Copts," *Egyptian Mail*, December 1995, www.egy.com/giza/95–11–18.5.php; *Le mondain égyptien: The Egyptian Who's Who*, ed. E.J. Blatner (Alexandria: V. Lubisco and A. & O. Sisto, 1943), 9: 186.

116. Jacques Mizart, correspondence with author, 24 September 2013.

117. "Togo Mizrahi fi Italiya," *Al-Sabah*, 17 May 1945, 24.

118. Jacques Mizart, personal archive.

119. "'Nihna hinna' aflam sihyuniyya fi istudiyu Misri," *Al-Fanun*, no. 3 (1946), cited in Ahmad Ra'fat Bahjat, *Al-Yahud wa-l-sinima fi Misr* ([Cairo]: A.R. Bahjat, 2005), 59.

120. "Al-Sihyuni Togo Mizrahi yahawil al-aflam al-sihyuniyya ila al-'arabiyya," *Al-Misbah*, 24 December 1946, 4–5. Cited in el-Shammaa, "Shadows of Contemporary Lives," 29. I am very grateful to Madgy el-Shammaa for sharing this article with me.

121. el-Shammaa, "Shadows of Contemporary Lives," 29n19.

122. "Al-Sihyuni Togo Mizrahi."

123. Bosley Crowther, "Palestinian Film in Premiere Here," *New York Times*, 26 September 1947. *Adama* is a multilingual film featuring the immigrant residents of the Ben Shemen youth village speaking in their native languages, framed by voice-over narration in English. "Review of *Adamah*," *Palestine Post*, 29 September 1948, 2. Shooting for *My Father's House* was slated to finish in November 1946, after which it was reportedly to be sent to the United States for editing. "Shooting Local Film," *Palestine Post*, 25 October 1946, 4.

124. "Bet avi," *Davar ha-shavu'a*, 29 November 1946, 2.

125. Bahjat, *Al-Yahud wa-l-sinima fi Misr*, 60.

126. Ibid., 59.

127. "Aflam Italiya wa-Togo Mizrahi," *Al-Istudiyu*, 21 September 1949, 9.

128. Hasan Imam 'Amr, "Zikrayat faniyya: Togo Mizrahi," *Al-Wafd*, 6 November 1995, 12.

129. *Dunya al-fann*, 23 March 1948, cited in Bahjat, *Al-Yahud wa-l-sinima fi Misr*, 61.

130. Viola Shafik, *Popular Egyptian Cinema: Gender, Class, and Nation* (Cairo: American University in Cairo Press, 2007), 23.

131. An earlier (undated) statement of Mizrahi's was quoted at length in a 1949 interview celebrating his return to Egypt and his anticipated return to the film industry. "Interview with Togo Mizrahi," *Al-Istudiyu*, 15 December 1949, 4.

132. *Ciné-Film*, no. 15 (March 1949), 22, cited in Andrew Flibbert, "State and Cinema in Pre-Revolutionary Egypt, 1927–1952," in *Re-Envisioning Egypt 1919–1952*, ed. Arthur Goldschmidt, Amy J. Johnson, and Barak A. Salmoni (Cairo: American University in Cairo Press, 2005), 462n15.

133. Flibbert, "State and Cinema in Pre-Revolutionary Egypt," 451.

134. "Interview with Togo Mizrahi," 4.

135. Ibid. Mizrahi reports that Ahmad Badr Khan started shooting a film on this topic, but government support was withdrawn from the project. It is not clear if Badr Khan was shooting a film based on Mizrahi's scenario, or if it was a competing project.

136. *Al-Sabah*, 1948, cited in Bahjat, *Al-Yahud wa-l-sinima fi Misr*, 61.

137. *Al-Sabah*, 20 January 1949, cited in Bahjat, *Al-Yahud wa-l-sinima fi Misr*, 61.

138. *Al-Sabah*, 17 March 1949, cited in Bahjat, *Al-Yahud wa-l-sinima fi Misr*, 61.

139. "Aflam Italiya wa-Togo Mizrahi."

140. "Interview with Togo Mizrahi," 4.; "Togo Mizrahi: Hal ya'awad ila al-sinima?," *Akhir Sa'a*, 20 January 1950, 21.

141. "Interview with Togo Mizrahi," 6.

142. Kamal al-Shinawi, "Kamal al-Shinawi yahki 'an tajribatihi fi film 'Amir al-intiqam.'" in *Sultanat al-shasha: Ra'idat al-sinima al-misriyya*, ed. Muna Ghandur (Beirut: Riyad al-Rayyis li-l-kutub wa-l-nashr, 2005), 164.

143. Ibid.

144. Jacques Mizart, correspondence with author, 24 September 2013.

145. Mizrahi, "Togo Mizrahi, raconté par son frère," 21.

146. Passport issued to Togo Guiseppe Mizrahi by the Italian Consulate in Cairo on 8 February 1952. Courtesy of Jacques Mizart.

147. The Egyptian Films Company, Certificate of Employment for Alfred Mizrahi, signed by Togo Mizrahi, 10 May 1962. Courtesy of Jacques Mizart. The 1 January 1952 issue of Ciné-Film also reported on the transfer of the studio to Alfred. Bahjat, Al-Yahud wa-l-sinima fi Misr, 62.

148. Passport issued to Togo Guiseppe Mizrahi.

149. Passport issued to Togo Guiseppe Mizrahi.

150. Egyptian Films Company, Certificate of Employment. Courtesy of Jacques Mizart.

151. Letter reproduced in Awad and Hamouda, Birth of the Seventh Art, 42. According to John Waterbury, "over the period 1961–66 some 4000 families were affected by sequestration measures. Total assets seized during those years may have been worth EGP 100 million and included 122,000 feddans, 7,000 urban properties, about 1,00 business 'establishments.' And over EGP 30 million in stocks and bonds." John Waterbury, The Egypt of Nasser and Sadat: The Political Economy of Two Regimes (Princeton, NJ: Princeton University Press, 1983), 339. Behna Films was nationalized in 1961, and most of its assets were liquidated in 1969. El-Shimi Rowan, "Behna Films Re-opens after 50 Years in Alexandria," Ahram Online, 30 January 2013, http://english.ahram.org.eg/NewsContent/32/0/63527/Index.aspx.

152. Letter dated 18 August 1966, reproduced in Awad and Hamouda, Birth of the Seventh Art, 36.

153. According to Jacques Mizart, in the early 1960s, while Alfred was managing Togo's affairs in Egypt, Anwar Sadat resided at the Mizrahi villa in Giza near the Pyramids. Jacques Mizart, correspondence with author, 16 October 2019.

154. Jacques Mizart, interview with author, 16 May 2017.

155. Jacques Mizart, correspondence with author, 24 September 2013.

156. Shafik, Popular Egyptian Cinema, 23.

157. Jacques Mizart, interview with author, 12 October 2019.

158. Prof. Ahmed H. El Borai to Camille Ben Lassin, 23 June 1987. The letter appears on the letterhead of the Cultural Bureau of the Egyptian embassy in Paris. Courtesy of Jacques Mizart.

159. Bahjat, Al-Yahud wa-l-sinima fi Misr, 59–63.

160. Shafik, Popular Egyptian Cinema, 23.

3. CRIMES OF MISTAKEN IDENTITY

1. Under the terms of the Ottoman-era capitulations to foreign powers, citizens of capitulatory powers were subject to the laws of their states, and were tried in consular courts. Other courts, the "Mixed Courts," were established in 1875 to address civil and commercial disputes between foreigners and locals, and between foreigners of different nationalities. Domestic criminal cases were argued before still other courts, the "Native Courts." Religious personal status courts dealt with civil matters pertaining to members of the community.

The Montreux Convention of 1937 established a framework for reform, immediately abolishing Consular Courts and winding down the activities of both the Native Courts and the Mixed Courts by 1949. Their case load was rolled into a new set of courts, the "National Courts." Mark Hoyle, "The Mixed Courts of Egypt 1926–1937," *Arab Law Quarterly* 2, no. 4 (1987): 357–89.

2. *The Concise Oxford Companion to the Theatre,* ed. Phyllis Hartnoll and Peter Found, 2nd ed. (Oxford: Oxford University Press, 1996; repr., 2012), s.v. "farce."

3. Ibid.

4. "Wudu' shiq, mumumathilun akfa': Mukhrij qadir," *Al-Sabah,* 21 February 1936.

5. "Salafini 3 gineh," *Al-Ithnayn wa-l-Dunya,* 9 October 1939.

6. "Film al-usbu': Al-Bashmaqawil," *Al-Ithnayn wa-l-Dunya,* 29 January 1940.

7. "Remembering Ali Abu Shadi: One of Egypt's Pillars of Film Criticism," *Al-Ahram Weekly,* 24 February 2018.

8. 'Ali Abu Shadi, "Genres in Egyptian Cinema," in *Screens of Life: Critical Film Writing from the Arab World,* ed. Alia Arasoughly (Saint-Hyacinthe, Quebec: World Heritage Press, 1996), 91–92.

9. Ibid., 91.

10. Ibid., 85.

11. Ibid., 90.

12. Eric Bentley, *The Life of the Drama* (New York: Atheneum, 1964), 219–56.

13. M.M. Bakhtin, *The Dialogic Imagination: Four Essays,* trans. Caryl Emerson and Michael Holquist (Austin: University of Texas Press, 1981), 163.

14. See, e.g., Robert Stam, *Subversive Pleasures: Bakhtin, Cultural Criticism, and Film* (Baltimore: Johns Hopkins University Press, 1989); and Martin Flanagan, *Bakhtin and the Movies: New Ways of Understanding Hollywood Film* (Basingstoke, UK: Palgrave Macmillan, 2009).

15. M.M. Bakhtin, *Rabelais and His World,* trans. Helene Iswolsky (Cambridge, MA: MIT Press, 1968).

16. Stam, *Subversive Pleasures.*

17. Ibid., 114.

18. Iman Hamam makes a parallel argument about the subversive potential of twenty-first-century Egyptian *sha'abi* cinema. Like the Levantine films I am discussing, these contemporary *sha'abi* comedies, according to Hamam, feature "formulaic and fragmentary" plots "with awkward beginnings" and "abrupt endings," through which social mobility is affected through "physical transmutations, and the typical comedy 'body-swap' scenario." Hamam identifies 'Ali al-Kassar, Isma'il Yasin (who featured, early in his career, in films alongside al-Kassar), and Naguib al-Rihani as influences on the twenty-first-century comic idiom. Iman Hamam, "Disarticulating Arab Popular Culture: The Case of Egyptian Comedies," in *Arab Cultural Studies: Mapping the Field,* ed. Tarik Sabry (London: I.B. Tauris, 2011), 187–88.

19. Israel Gershoni and James Jankowski, *Redefining the Egyptian Nation, 1930–1945* (Cambridge and New York: Cambridge University Press, 1995).

20. Anat Lapidot-Firilla, editor's note in *Journal of Levantine Studies* 1, no. 1 (2011): 6.

21. Deborah A. Starr and Sasson Somekh, "Editors' Introduction: Jacqueline Shohet Kahanoff—a Cosmopolitan Levantine," in *Mongrels or Marvels: The Levantine Writings*

of Jacqueline Shohet Kahanoff, ed. Deborah A. Starr and Sasson Somekh (Stanford, CA: Stanford University Press, 2011), xi–xxiv.

22. When I discuss individuals hailing from the eastern Mediterranean or their spoken Arabic dialect, I use the Arabic term *"shami."*

23. Andrew Flibbert lists several notable examples of this commonly accepted claim. Andrew Flibbert, "State and Cinema in Pre-Revolutionary Egypt, 1927–1952," in *Re-Envisioning Egypt, 1919–1952,* ed. Arthur Goldschmidt, Amy J. Johnson, and Barak A. Salmoni (Cairo: American University in Cairo Press, 2005), 461n3.

24. Joel Gordon, *Revolutionary Melodrama: Popular Film and Civic Identity in Nasser's Egypt* (Chicago: Middle East Documentation Center, 2002).

25. Sawsan el-Messiri, *Ibn Al-Balad: A Concept of Egyptian Identity* (Leiden: Brill, 1978).

26. Ibid., 74.

27. Al-Kassar had tried his hand at cinema early in the silent era, appearing in a short, *Al-Khala al-amrikiyya (The American Aunt,* Bonvilli, 1920), an adaptation of Brandon Thomas's popular farce *Charley's Aunt* (1892). In 1935, in *Bawwab al-'imara (The Doorman,* Alexander Farkas), al-Kassar made his first screen appearance as the character 'Usman 'Abd al-Basit.

28. For more on the involvement of al-Rihani and his troupe in shaping national discourses during the 1919 Revolution, see Ziad Fahmy, *Ordinary Egyptians: Creating the Modern Nation through Popular Culture* (Stanford, CA: Stanford University Press, 2011), 134–66.

29. A brief discussion of Naguib al-Rihani's film *Salama fi khayr (Salama Is Fine,* 1937) appears in chap. 5. A longer analysis of the film as an articulation of Levantine cinema can be found in Deborah A. Starr, "Masquerade and the Performance of National Imaginaries: Levantine Ethics, Aesthetics, and Identities in Egyptian Cinema," *Journal of Levantine Studies* 1, no. 2 (2011): 31–57.

30. The latter bears no relation to the novel by Alexandre Dumas père.

31. Nicole Angel McManamny and Maureen McManamny, correspondence with author, 11–12 December 2016.

32. "Chalom Al-Turguman," *Al-Sabah,* 18 January 1935, 39; "Ce qui se passe dans nos studios," *Variétés,* 27 January 1935.

33. As director of *The Athlete,* Leon Angel is credited as L. Nagel. Ibrahim Dasuqi and Sami Hilmi report that Angel signed an exclusive contract with Orfanelli. As a result, he could not be credited by his full name on a production with another studio. Dasuqi and Hilmi, *Madrasat al-Iskandariyya li-l-taswir al-sinima'i* (Alexandria: Maktabat al-Iskandariyya, 2013).

34. Gudrun Krämer, *The Jews in Modern Egypt, 1914–1952* (Seattle: University of Washington Press, 1989), 28.

35. Dario Miccoli, *Histories of the Jews of Egypt: An Imagined Bourgeoisie, 1880s–1950s* (London and New York: Routledge, 2015). Reuven Snir, "'A Carbon Copy of Ibn Al-Balad'? The Participation of Egyptian Jews in Modern Arab Culture," *Archiv Orientální* 74, no. 1 (2006).

36. Raphael Bakhur Mosseri, "Togo Mizrahi yashuh sam'atna fi sharit Al-'Izz bahdala," *Al-Shams,* 4 March 1937. Mosseri somewhat cryptically holds up another film—which he refers to as "Rothschild"—as an example of how to respectfully portray Jewish characters. It is not clear if he means the French comedy *Rothchild* (Marco de Gastyne, 1933), in which a

tramp is mistaken for a member of the banking family, or the Hollywood drama *The House of Rothschild* (Alfred Werker, 1934).

37. ʿAdalat's identity was confirmed by Nicole Angel McManamny and Maureen McManamny. Correspondence with author, 11–12 December 2016.

38. For a study of the emergence of bourgeois aspirations among Jews in early-twentieth-century Egypt, see Miccoli, *Histories of the Jews of Egypt*.

39. Lucie Ryzova, *The Age of the Efendiyya: Passages to Modernity in National-Colonial Egypt* (Oxford: Oxford University Press, 2014).

40. Gabriel Rosenbaum, "Elements and Evidence of Spoken Judeo-Egyptian Arabic in Old Egyptian Movies," in *Jewish Languages—Languages in Contact Conference* (The Hebrew University of Jerusalem2016); Gabriel Rosenbaum, "The Arabic Dialect of Jews in Modern Egypt," *Bulletin of the Israeli Academic Center in Cairo*, no. 25 (December 2002): 38–46.

41. Mosseri, "Togo Mizrahi."

42. In what becomes established as a trope in Egyptian cinema, Greeks, unlike Arabized Jews, speak Greek among themselves and heavily accented Arabic with other interlocutors. In *The Two Delegates*, the waiters in a restaurant from which Chalom steals food all speak Greek. Chalom is able to replicate the sounds convincingly enough to trick the kitchen staff into putting up an order.

43. Some of the gags in the treatment rooms, shot without dialogue, resemble scenes in Charlie Chaplin's *The Cure* (1917).

44. *Mistreated by Affluence* features a similar gag. A local banker, wishing to spy on the competition, Bank Chalom, assumes the identity of Dr. Farti, the director of Banque Europa. This Alexandria resident masquerading as the representative of a foreign company also speaks gibberish.

45. For more on the emergence of the *effendiyya* in this period, see Ryzova, *Age of the Efendiyya*; and Wilson Chacko Jacob, *Working Out Egypt: Effendi Masculinity and Subject Formation in Colonial Modernity, 1870–1940* (Durham, NC: Duke University Press, 2011).

46. Ryzova, *Age of the Efendiyya*, 57n35.

47. Ziad Fahmy, *Street Sounds: Listening to Everyday Life in Modern Egypt* (Stanford, CA: Stanford University Press, forthcoming).

48. Sami Zubaida, *Islam, the People and the State: Essays on Political Ideas and Movements in the Middle East* (London and New York: Routledge, 1989), 106–16.

49. For a discussion of marriage as a reflection of the modern and bourgeois aspirations of Egyptian Jewry at this time, see Miccoli, *Histories of the Jews of Egypt*. Other scholars have also looked at transformations of marriage practices and wedding ceremonies as articulations of modernity or reflections on social changes affected by modernization. See, e.g., Zubaida, *Islam, the People and the State*, 116–17; and Hanan Kholoussy, *For Better, for Worse: The Marriage Crisis That Made Modern Egypt* (Stanford, CA: Stanford University Press, 2010).

50. In the Islamic tradition, the ceremony of Katib al-kitab, at which the Fatiha is recited, may precede the communal wedding celebrations by days or weeks.

51. For a longer discussion of the parallel depiction of Jewish and Muslim weddings in *Mistreated by Affluence*, see Deborah A. Starr, "Chalom and ʿAbdu Get Married: Jewishness and Egyptianness in the Films of Togo Mizrahi," *Jewish Quarterly Review* 107, no. 2 (Spring 2017): 209–30.

52. In chap. 5, I unpack the significance of race in al-Kassar's performance. See also Eve Troutt Powell, *A Different Shade of Colonialism: Egypt, Great Britain, and the Mastery of the Sudan* (Berkeley: University of California Press, 2003).

53. Ba'za' is a comic, made-up name. There was already a long-standing tradition of comedians assigning comic names to their characters. For example, see Ziad Fahmy's discussion of 'Abdallah Nadim in Fahmy, *Ordinary Egyptians*.

54. Abu Shadi, "Genres in Egyptian Cinema," 90–91.

55. Bakhtin, *Rabelais and His World*, 370.

56. Ibid.

4. QUEERING THE LEVANTINE

1. Steven Cohan, "Queering the Deal: On the Road with Hope and Crosby," in *Out Takes: Essays on Queer Theory and Film*, ed. Ellis Hanson (Durham, NC: Duke University Press, 1999), 25.

2. Judith Butler, *Gender Trouble: Feminism and the Subversion of Identity* (New York: Routledge, 1990).

3. Richard Thompson Ford, "What's Queer about Race?," in *After Sex?: On Writing since Queer Theory*, ed. Janet Halley and Andrew Parker (Durham, NC: Duke University Press, 2011), 123.

4. I do not assume in my analysis that queerness need align with progressive or radical politics. While Mizrahi's queer Levantine disrupts emerging parochial ethnoreligious nationalisms in 1930s Egypt, his liberal, pluralist ethics of coexistence could hardly be termed radical.

5. Ellis Hanson, "Introduction," in *Out Takes: Essays on Queer Theory and Film*, ed. Ellis Hanson (Durham, NC: Duke University Press, 1999), 4.

6. Wilson Chacko Jacob, *Working Out Egypt: Effendi Masculinity and Subject Formation in Colonial Modernity, 1870–1940* (Durham, NC: Duke University Press, 2011). See also Luci Ryzova, *The Age of the Efendiyya: Passages to Modernity in National-Colonial Egypt* (Oxford: Oxford University Press, 2014).

7. A film Togo Mizrahi produced, *Al-Riyadi* (*The Athlete*, 1937), garners brief mention in Jacob's discussion of the place of sport and fitness in the emergence of what he terms "effendi masculinity." The film, starring Chalom, was directed by Leon Angel (credited as L. Nagel) and Clément Mizrahi. Jacob, *Working Out Egypt*, 156.

8. Israel Gershoni and James Jankowski, *Redefining the Egyptian Nation, 1930–1945* (Cambridge and New York: Cambridge University Press, 1995). In the American literary and film vernacular in the same period, Dashiell Hammett's Joel Cairo offers a notable example of the slipperiness attributed both to the Levantine and to queerness. I am not suggesting that Hammett's novel *The Maltese Falcon* (1929) or its 1930s film adaptations—*The Maltese Falcon* (Roy Del Ruth, 1931) and *Satan Met a Lady* (William Dieterle, 1936)—should be read as direct intertexts for Mizrahi's work. Rather, I wish to point out the parallel associations between queerness and what I have termed "Levantine" identities in Mizrahi's films.

9. Vito Russo lists legions of examples from Hollywood cinema from the 1910s through the 1930s in which homoerotic innuendo between men was played comically. The American press, which took issue with more directly subversive characters and plots, tended not to

comment on "open signs of homosexuality in a comic context." Vito Russo, *The Celluloid Closet: Homosexuality in the Movies* (New York: Harper & Row, 1987), 37.

10. Off-screen, Fawzi and Ihsan al-Gazayirli were father and daughter. Onstage and on-screen, they regularly played opposite one another as a married couple or as one another's love interest. It is beyond the scope of my analysis to unpack the signification of this relationship. But it is worth noting the inherent queerness underpinning the "restoration of heteronormativity" in this scene.

11. Although polygamy is permitted by Islam and remains legal in Egypt, it was not commonly practiced in interwar Alexandria and Cairo. Hanan Kholoussy, *For Better, for Worse: The Marriage Crisis That Made Modern Egypt* (Stanford, CA: Stanford University Press, 2010), 83.

12. I am thinking here of Eric Bentley's contention about the centrality of violence to farce, and the inherent dialectic within the genre between gentleness and violence. Eric Bentley, *The Life of the Drama* (New York: Atheneum, 1964), 219–56.

13. For more on female same-sex desire in the Middle East and its representation in literature and film, see Stephen O. Murray, "Woman–Woman Love in Islamic Societies," in *Islamic Homosexualities: Culture, History, and Literature*, ed. Stephen O. Murray and Will Roscoe (New York: New York University Press, 1997), 97–104; and Samar Habib, *Female Homosexuality in the Middle East: Histories and Representations*, Routledge Research in Gender and Society 13 (New York: Routledge, 2007).

14. In his 2002 novel 'Imarat Ya'qubiyan (*The Yacoubian Building*), 'Ala al-Aswani returns to roof dwellers to reflect anew upon Egypt's multicultural past and its bearing on the present and future of Egyptian society. 'Ala al-Aswani, 'Imarat Ya'qubiyan (Cairo: Mirit li-l-nashr wa-al-ma'lumat, 2002); *The Yacoubian Building*, trans. Humphrey T. Davies (New York: Harper Perennial, 2006). For analyses of the signification of the homosexual relationship between a resident of the building and a roof dweller in *The Yacoubian Building*, see Hanadi al- Samman, "Out of the Closet: Representation of Homosexuals and Lesbians in Modern Arabic Literature," *Journal of Arabic Literature* 39, no. 2 (2008). Also see Khalid Hadeed, "Homosexuality and Epistemic Closure in Modern Arabic Literature," *International Journal of Middle East Studies* 45, no. 2 (2013): 271–91.

15. Deborah A. Starr, "Masquerade and the Performance of National Imaginaries: Levantine Ethics, Aesthetics, and Identities in Egyptian Cinema," *Journal of Levantine Studies* 1, no. 2 (2011): 31–57.

16. Rebecca Bryant, "Everyday Coexistence in the Post-Ottoman Space," in *Post-Ottoman Coexistence: Sharing Space in the Shadow of Conflict*, ed. Rebecca Bryant (New York: Berghahn Books, 2016), 2.

17. Viola Shafik, *Popular Egyptian Cinema: Gender, Class, and Nation* (Cairo: American University in Cairo Press, 2007), 31.

18. For more on popular assumptions about this association in the Egyptian context, see Karin van Nieuwkerk, *A Trade Like Any Other: Female Singers and Dancers in Egypt* (Austin: University of Texas Press, 1995).

19. Chalom's expressive whistling in this scene is reminiscent of Harpo Marx. *Mistreated by Affluence* appears to reference Marx Brothers movies at other junctures as well.

20. The Arabic "ta'ali ya ruhi" plays on Ruhiya's name.

21. The quotation in the heading just above is the tagline for an advertisement for *The Pasha Director's Daughter. Al-Ithnayn,* 3 January 1938, 40.

22. Advertisement for *The Pasha Director's Daughter. Al-Ithnayn,* 15 November 1937, 47.

5. JOURNEYS OF ASSUMED IDENTITY: SEVEN O'CLOCK (1937)

1. Anouchka Lazarev, "Italians, Italianity and Fascism," trans. Colin Clement, in *Alexandria 1860–1960: The Brief Life of a Cosmopolitan Community,* ed. Robert Ilbert and Ilios Yannakakis (Alexandria: Harpocrates Press, 1997), 80. For a lengthier discussion of the statue and its significance, see Deborah A. Starr, *Remembering Cosmopolitan Egypt: Literature, Culture, and Empire* (London: Routledge, 2009), 31–36.

2. The Hollywood adaptation of Mark Twain's 1881 novel *The Prince and the Pauper,* directed by William Keighley and starring Errol Flynn and Claude Rains, was released in the United States in May 1937 and opened in Cairo in January 1938.

3. Viola Shafik, *Arab Cinema: History and Cultural Identity* (Cairo: American University in Cairo Press, 1998), 46, 92.

4. Ibid., 72.

5. Ibid.

6. Starr, *Remembering Cosmopolitan Egypt.*

7. Magdy Mounir el-Shammaa, "Shadows of Contemporary Lives: Modernity, Culture, and National Identity in Egyptian Filmmaking" (PhD diss., UCLA, 2007), 49n71. According to el-Shammaa, in addition to self-promotional gestures, Mizrahi used product placement, like the Philips radio that figures prominently in what I describe as the "third movement" of *Seven O'Clock,* to help finance film production.

8. For more on *Salama Is Fine,* see Walter Armbrust, "The Ubiquitous Nonpresence of India: Peripheral Visions from Egyptian Popular Culture," in *Global Bollywood: Travels of Hindi Song and Dance,* ed. Sangita Gopal and Sujata Murti (University of Minnesota Press, 2008), 200–220; and Deborah A. Starr, "Masquerade and the Performance of National Imaginaries: Levantine Ethics, Aesthetics, and Identities in Egyptian Cinema," *Journal of Levantine Studies* 1, no. 2 (Winter 2011): 31–57.

9. Eve Troutt Powell, "Burnt Cork Nationalism: Race and Identity in the Theater of 'Ali Al-Kassar," in *Colors of Enchantment: Theater, Dance, Music, and the Visual Arts of the Middle East,* ed. Sherifa Zuhur (Cairo: Amiercan University in Cairo Press, 2001), 21.

10. Ibid.

11. Ibid.

12. Ibid., 36.

13. Ibid.

14. Advertisement for *Al-Abyad wa-l-aswad, Al-Sabah,* 1 January 1937, 28.

15. "Al-Ustaz Togo Mizrahi 'awdatihi min uruba," *Al-Sabah,* 15 October 1937, 57.

16. "Manazir fakahiyya kassariyya: Bayn al-Kassar al-abyad wa-l-Kassar al-aswad," *Al-Ithnayn,* 15 March 1937.

17. Arthur Goldschmidt, *Historical Dictionary of Egypt,* 4th ed. (Lanham, MD: Scarecrow Press, 2013), 47.

18. "Un thé," *La tribune juive,* 14 October 1936.

19. Scheherazade Qassim Hassan, "Musical Instruments in the Arab World," in *Garland Encyclopedia of World Music*, vol. 6, *The Middle East*, ed. Virginia Danielson, Scott Marcus, and Dwight Reynolds (London: Routledge, 2001), 429–53. A *manjur* is a percussion instrument that is worn around the waist, and dancing produces the rhythm.

20. I am very grateful to Ahmed El Maghraby and Michael Frishkopf for their insights on *zar*.

21. See, e.g., fig. 6, a photo of the cast and crew of *Layla the Country Girl*.

22. Eve Troutt Powell, *A Different Shade of Colonialism: Egypt, Great Britain, and the Mastery of the Sudan* (Berkeley: University of California Press, 2003), 194.

23. Michael Rogin, *Blackface, White Noise: Jewish Immigrants in the Hollywood Melting Pot* (Berkeley: University of California Press, 1996).

24. *Roman Scandals* premiered at Cinema Royal in Cairo on 21 January 1935. Advertisement for *Roman Scandals*, *Al-Sabah*, 18 January 1935, 40.

25. Ahmad al-Hadari, *Tarikh al-sinima fi Misr*, vol. 1, *Min bidayat 1896 ila akhir 1930* (Cairo: Nadi al-sinima bil-qahirah, 1989), 148–49.

26. See, e.g., the seduction of a maid in *Al-Bab al-maftuh* (*The Open Door*, Henri Barakat, 1963).

27. The sanitarium scenes are reminiscent of the Marx Brothers' *A Day at the Races* (Sam Wood, 1937).

6. TRAVELING ANXIETIES

1. Ahmad al-Hadari, *Tarikh al-sinima fi Misr*, vol. 2, *Min bidayat 1931 ila akhir 1940* (Cairo: Al-Hay'a al-misriyya al-'ama li-l-kitab, 2007), 366.

2. Togo Mizrahi directed *A Rainy Night* and shares writing credits with Stephan Rosti, who also plays the villain in the film.

3. Hadari, *Tarikh al-sinima fi Misr*, 2:365–69.

4. "Yusuf Wahbi yahraj film," *Al-Ithnayn*, 5 October 1936.

5. Togo Mizrahi also maintained the studio in Alexandria. The pressbook for *Al-Bashmaqawil* (*The Chief Contractor*, 1940), starring Fawzi al-Gazayirli, indicates that the film was developed and printed in Alexandria. Mahmoud Qassim Cinema Collection, Rare Books and Special Collections Library, American University in Cairo.

6. Pressbook for *A Rainy Night*, Mahmoud Qassim Cinema Collection, Rare Books and Special Collections Library, American University in Cairo.

7. "Amina Rizq wa-Mahmud Dhu al-Faqar ba'd Yusuf Wahbi wa-Fatima Rushdi," *Al-Sabah*, 28 January 1943, 16.

8. "Yusuf Wahbi wa-Togo Mizrahi," *Al-Sabah*, 4 February 1943, 30.

9. "Min huna wa-hunak," *Al-Sabah*, 20 January 1944, 28.

10. Moshe Behar and Zvi Ben-Dor Benite, "The Possibility of Modern Middle Eastern Jewish Thought," *British Journal of Middle Eastern Studies* 41, no. 1 (2014): 43–61.

11. Pressbook for *A Rainy Night*.

12. In the social norms reflected in prerevolutionary cinema, as articulated by Joel Gordon, Ahmad's lineage and education make him a suitable mate for Saniya, even if her family is unaware of that lineage at the time of their marriage. According to Gordon, by the mid-1950s Egyptian cinema no longer relied on the revelation of obscured high-class lineage to make cross-class marriage socially acceptable. Joel Gordon, "Class-Crossed

Lovers: Popular Film and Social Change in Nasser's New Egypt," *Quarterly Review of Film and Video* 18, no. 4 (2001): 385–96.

13. *A Rainy Night* conforms to the conventions of the remarriage plot, a device common in Hollywood romantic comedies of the 1930s and 1940s. Stanley Cavell, *Pursuits of Happiness: The Hollywood Comedy of Remarriage* (Cambridge, MA: Harvard University Press, 1981).

14. For a wide-ranging, incisive discussion of the technology and discourses of modernity in Egypt, see Timothy Mitchell, *Rule of Experts: Egypt, Techno-Politics, Modernity* (Berkeley: University of California Press, 2002).

15. Albert Hourani, *Arabic Thought in the Liberal Age, 1798–1939* (London: Oxford University Press, 1962), 27–28.

16. One of the films Ryzova analyzes in this vein is Wahbi's *Ibn al-haddad* (*Son of a Blacksmith*, 1944), produced by Mizrahi's Egyptian Films Company. Lucie Ryzova, *The Age of the Efendiyya: Passages to Modernity in National-Colonial Egypt*, (Oxford: Oxford University Press, 2014).

17. The film *Al-'Azima* (*Determination*, Kamal Salim), released several months later, also features an unemployment montage.

18. Michele Sarfatti, "Characteristics and Objectives of the Anti-Jewish Racial Laws in Fascist Italy, 1938–1943," in *Jews in Italy under Fascist and Nazi Rule, 1922–1945*, ed. Joshua D. Zimmerman (Cambridge and New York: Cambridge University Press, 2005), 74.

19. Wilson Chacko Jacob, *Working Out Egypt: Effendi Masculinity and Subject Formation in Colonial Modernity, 1870–1940* (Durham, NC: Duke University Press, 2011); Ryzova, *Age of the Efendiyya*.

20. Robert O. Collins and Robert L. Tignor, *Egypt & the Sudan* (Englewood Cliffs, NJ: Prentice-Hall, 1967), 126–27.

21. Eve Troutt Powell, *A Different Shade of Colonialism: Egypt, Great Britain, and the Mastery of the Sudan* (Berkeley: University of California Press, 2003).

22. Pierre Crabites, "The Nile Waters Agreement," *Foreign Affairs* 8, no. 1 (1929): 145–49.

23. Robert O. Collins, *A History of Modern Sudan* (Cambridge and New York: Cambridge University Press, 2008), 44.

24. David Eugene Mills, "Dividing the Nile: The Failure to Strengthen Egyptian–Sudanese Economic Bonds, 1918–1945" (PhD Diss., University of Utah, 1997), 46.

25. Ibid., 57.

26. Ibid., 56.

27. Harold Shepstone, "Conquest of the Desert (Part 1)," *Wonders of World Engineering*, 27 April 1937, 289–92; Shepstone, "Conquest of the Desert (Part 2)," *Wonders of World Engineering*, 4 May 1937, 293–95. See also Mills, "Dividing the Nile," 57.

28. Mills, "Dividing the Nile," 57.

29. Ibid., 61.

30. Powell, *Different Shade of Colonialism*, 5.

31. Aaron Gillette, *Racial Theories in Fascist Italy* (London: Routledge, 2002), 57.

32. Sarfatti, "Anti-Jewish Racial Laws," 74.

33. Robert L. Tignor, "Bank Misr and Foreign Capitalism," *International Journal of Middle East Studies* 8, no. 2 (1977): 161–81; Eric Davis, *Challenging Colonialsm: Bank Misr and Egyptian Industrialization* (Princeton, NJ: Princeton University Press, 1983).

34. Joel Beinin, "Egypt: Society and Economy, 1923–1952," in *The Cambridge History of Egypt*, ed. M.W. Daly (Cambridge: Cambridge University Press, 1998), 325.

35. Najat Abdulhaq, *Jewish and Greek Communities in Egypt: Entrepreneurship and Business before Nasser* (London: I.B. Tauris, 2016).

36. Tignor, "Bank Misr and Foreign Capitalism," 178.

37. Robert Vitalis, *When Capitalists Collide: Business Conflict and the End of Empire in Egypt* (Berkeley: University of California Press, 1995), 27–28.

38. Ibid., 27.

39. In 1951 Leon and Esther Angel left Egypt and immigrated to Melbourne, Australia, to join their daughter, who had married an Australian and was already living there. Angel went on to found a Sephardi synagogue in Melbourne, and rose to a leadership position in the local Masonic lodge. Maureen McManamny (Leon and Esther's granddaughter), correspondence with author, December 11, 2015.

40. Joel Beinin, *The Dispersion of Egyptian Jewry: Culture, Politics, and the Formation of a Modern Diaspora* (Berkeley: University of California Press, 1998), 46. For a parallel example from Iraq, see Menahem Salih Daniel, "Letter to Chayyim Weitzmann," in *Modern Middle Eastern Jewish Thought: Writings on Identity, Politics, and Culture, 1893–1958*, ed. Moshe Behar and Zvi Ben-Dor Benite (Waltham, MA: Brandeis University Press, 2013), 109–13.

41. Eyal Sagui-Bizawe, "Yehudim ba-ta'asiyat ha-qolno'a ba-mitsrayim," *Ha-kayvun mizrah*, Fall 2003, 90.

7. COURTESAN AND CONCUBINE

1. Walter Armbrust, "Long Live Patriarchy: Love in the Time of Abd Al-Wahhab," *History Compass* 7, no. 1 (2009): 251–81.

2. Hanan Kholoussy, *For Better, for Worse: The Marriage Crisis That Made Modern Egypt* (Stanford, CA: Stanford University Press, 2010), 56.

3. Ibid., 60.

4. Female seclusion, while widely accepted, had been practiced only among "urban middle and upper classes and rural gentry." Ibid., 51.

5. Hanan Hammad and Francesca Biancani also note the presence of *farangi* (European) girls and women in the sex trade. Hammad and Biancani, "Prostitution in Cairo," in *Selling Sex in the City: A Global History of Prostitution, 1600s–2000s*, ed. Magaly Rodríguez Garcia, Lex Heerma van Voss, and Elise van Nederveen Meerkerk (Leiden: Brill, 2017), 238.

6. Khaled Fahmy, "Prostitution in Egypt in the Nineteenth Century," in *Outside In: On the Margins of the Modern Middle East*, ed. Eugene L. Rogan (London: I.B. Tauris, 2001).

7. Liat Kozma, *Policing Egyptian Women: Sex, Law, and Medicine in Khedival Egypt* (Syracuse, NY: Syracuse University Press, 2011), 52–53.

8. Ibid.

9. Ibid., 65.

10. Ibid., 67.

11. Gabriel Baer, "Slavery in Nineteenth Century Egypt," *Journal of African History* 8, no. 3 (1967): 417–41.

12. The Comprehensive Law on Brothels was passed 15 July 1896. Hammad and Biancani, "Prostitution in Cairo," 246. The invitation for the opening party of the film is dated 3 June 1896.

13. Ibid.

14. Hammad and Biancani, "Prostitution in Cairo," 252.

15. Cathlyn Mariscotti, *Gender and Class in the Egyptian Women's Movement, 1925–1939: Changing Perspectives* (Syracuse, NY: Syracuse University Press, 2008), 107–8.

16. Beth Baron, *Egypt as a Woman: Nationalism, Gender, and Politics* (Berkeley: University of California Press, 2005), 51.

17. Hammad and Biancani, "Prostitution in Cairo," 250–51.

18. Hanan Hammad, *Industrial Sexuality: Gender, Urbanization, and Social Transformation in Egypt* (Austin: University of Texas Press, 2016), 205.

19. Hammad and Biancani, "Prostitution in Cairo," 253–54.

20. Haytham Bahoora, "The Figure of the Prostitute, Tajdid, and Masculinity in Anticolonial Literature of Iraq," *Journal of Middle East Women's Studies* 11, no. 1 (2015): 47.

21. Hammad and Biancani, "Prostitution in Cairo," 248.

22. Jacob M. Landau, *Studies in the Arab Theater and Cinema* (Philadelphia: University of Pennsylvania Press, 1958), 182. Consider also that after *Layla*'s success, 'Abd al-Wahab approached Murad to costar in another film, but they determined it was not financially feasible. Hanan Mufid, *Layla Murad: Sayyidat qitar al-ghina'* (Cairo: Al-Hay'a al-misriyya al-'ama li-l-kitab, 2003), 81.

23. Mufid, *Layla Murad*, 81.

24. Ibid., 77–79. By 1947 Murad commanded 10,000 to 12,000 Egyptian pounds per film. Landau, *Studies in the Arab Theater*, 181.

25. Mufid, *Layla Murad*, 79–80.

26. Ibid.

27. *La dame aux camélias* (Abel Gance and Fernand Rivers, 1934). The film starred Yvonne Printemps and Pierre Fresnay.

28. Layla Murad, "Adwar uhibbtuha," in *Al-Watha'iq al-khassa li-Layla Murad*, ed. Ashraf Gharib (Cairo: Dar El Shorouk, 2016), 138–39. First published in 1956 in *Al-Kawakib*.

29. Tuberculosis was a familiar scourge in Egypt, "feared by rich and poor alike throughout the first half of the twentieth century." Hammad, *Industrial Sexuality*, 183.

30. In a nod to the original, Layla's Greek seamstress in the film is named Marguerite.

31. Viola Shafik, "Prostitute for a Good Reason," *Women's Studies International Forum* 24, no. 6 (2001): 715. Landau, *Studies in the Arab Theater*, 68.

32. Viola Shafik, *Popular Egyptian Cinema: Gender, Class, and Nation* (Cairo: American University in Cairo Press, 2007), 208–9. Shafik notes that dancers also experienced a boost in reputability at the same time (208). However, the profession still carries the stigma of its former association with prostitution. See also Karin van Nieuwkerk, *A Trade Like Any Other: Female Singers and Dancers in Egypt* (Austin: University of Texas Press, 1995).

33. Sherifa Zuhur, *Asmahan's Secrets: Woman, War and Song* (Austin: Center for Middle Eastern Studies, University of Texas at Austin, 2000), 12. For the specific cultural valences of the bodies of women performers in Egypt, see ibid. Also see Nieuwkerk, *A Trade Like Any Other*, 179–84.

34. Baron, *Egypt as a Woman*.

35. Lina Khatib, "The Orient and Its Others: Women as Tools of Nationalism in Egyptian Political Cinema," in *Women and Media in the Middle East: Power through Self-Expression*, ed. Naomi Sakr (London: I.B. Tauris, 2004), 82.

36. Gillian Vogelsang-Eastwood and Willem Vogelsang, *Covering the Moon: An Introduction to Middle Eastern Face Veils* (Leuven: Peeters, 2008), 60–64, 96–98.

37. At her wedding and other festive occasions, Farida wore a tiara. In other photographs of the family taken inside the palace, Farida is pictured without any head covering.

38. Another picture of the queen similarly attired, attending a public function, appeared on the front page of *Al-Ahram*, 15 April 1942.

39. "[Title illegible]," *Al-Ithnayn*, 6 April 1942, 14–15.

40. The ad also ran in *Ruz al-yusuf*, 2 April 1942, 21.

41. According to Samir Raafat, the ballooning membership of the Royal Automobile Club of Egypt from 1927 on indicates that by that date cars had become a status symbol among the elites. Samir W. Raafat, "History of Motoring in Egypt," *Egyptian Gazette*, 2 March 1997, www.egy.com/historica/97-03-02.php.

42. *King Farouk's Investiture in Cairo* (British Pathé, 1937), newsreel, https://www.britishpathe.com/video/king-farouks-investiture-in-cairo/query/Farouk.

43. *Alexandria Bombed* (British Pathé, 1941), newsreel, https://www.britishpathe.com/video/alexandria-bombed/query/alexandria+bombed. A few days after *Layla's* release, Alexandria was bombarded again from the air. "Ghara jawiyya jadida ʿala Al-Iskandariyya," *Al-Ahram*, 9 April 1942, 4. The first battle of El Alamein was fought three months later. Alexandria and Egypt's northern coast remained at risk until the decisive second battle of El Alamein, in November 1942.

44. "Cairo Parliament Opens," *New York Times*, 31 March 1942.

45. I thank Walter Armbrust for this insight.

46. "Layla," *Al-Ithnayn*, 13 April 1942.

47. Farida reported that she and Farouk were already estranged even before they made a final attempt to produce a male heir. Farouk Hashem, *Farida, the Queen of Egypt: A Memoir of Love and Governance*, trans. Morad Abou-Sabe (Bloomington, IN: AuthorHouse, 2014), 65.

48. I would like to thank Ziad Fahmy and Munther Younes, who assisted me with the translation of this song.

49. Ali Jihad Racy, *Making Music in the Arab World: The Culture and Artistry of Tarab* (Cambridge: Cambridge University Press, 2003), 83. The lyricist for both *Layla* and *Sallama*, Ahmad Rami, was extremely prolific, composing over three hundred songs, among them songs for thirty musical films (171).

50. "Raʾy al-anisa Umm Kulthum fi film Layla," *Rose al-Yusuf*, 23 April 1942.

51. Viola Shafik, "Egyptian Cinema," in *Companion Encyclopedia of Middle Eastern and North African Film*, ed. Oliver Leaman (London: Routledge, 2001), 125.

52. Virginia Danielson, *The Voice of Egypt: Umm Kulthum, Arabic Song, and Egyptian Society in the Twentieth Century* (Chicago: University of Chicago Press, 1997), 88.

53. Ifdal Elsaket, "The Star of the East: Umm Kulthum and Egyptian Cinema," in *Stars in World Cinema: Screen Icons and Star Systems across Cultures*, ed. Andrea Bandhauer and Michelle Royer (London: I.B. Tauris, 2015), 39.

54. Ibid., 40.

55. Danielson, *Voice of Egypt*, 89. See also Hasan Imam ʿAmr, "Zikrayat faniyya: Togo Mizrahi," *Al-Wafd*, 1995.

56. The credits identify the full title of Badr Khan's film as *Harun al-Rashid: Qissat Dananir* (*Harun al-Rashid: The Story of Dananir*).

57. Danielson, *Voice of Egypt,* 90.

58. Ibid.

59. Within the diegeses, Umm Kulthum's character is referred to as *jariya.* I use the more specific term *"qayna"* in order to signal the specific role these women historically played in court life.

60. *Women in World History: A Biographical Encyclopedia,* ed. Anne Commire and Deborah Klezmer (Waterford, CT: Yorkin Publications, 1999), s.v. "Dananir Al-Barmakiyya," 294–95.

61. *The Oxford Encyclopedia of Islam and Women,* ed. Natana J. DeLong-Bas (Oxford: Oxford University Press, 2013), s.v. "Qur'an."

62. Fuad Matthew Caswell, *The Slave Girls of Baghdad: The Qiyan in the Early Abbasid Era* (London: I.B. Tauris, 2011), 240.

63. Of this plot development, Ifdal Elsaket writes: "In a particularly conservative fashion, *Widad* articulates a capitalist narrative of merchant struggles and chattel sacrifices." Elsaket, "Star of the East," 48.

64. Virginia Danielson identifies it as thirteenth-century Egypt, although it is not clear on what basis she makes this claim. Danielson, *Voice of Egypt,* 88.

65. As a point of contrast, *Dananir* includes a scene featuring a delegation from Charlemagne to Harun al-Rashid.

66. Elsaket, "Star of the East," 45.

67. In addition to its obvious benefit of concealment for a character attempting to escape unnoticed in the dark of night, the act of veiling could also be read as an expression of Widad's newfound status as a free woman. The introduction of the hijab in the Abbasid era was "likely intended to protect the free woman from unwelcome attention and molestation resulting from her being mistaken for a woman slave." Caswell, *Slave Girls of Baghdad,* 48. As such, Widad's veiling could be interpreted as an expression of her freedom, as well as a sign of the cost of achieving it.

68. Shafik, *Popular Egyptian Cinema,* 256. Shafik points to Umm Kulthum's last film, *Fatima* (Ahmad Badr Khan, 1947), to illustrate the prevalence of the seduction narrative in 1940s Egyptian cinema.

69. Ibid.

70. Baron, *Egypt as a Woman,* 49.

71. Kay Dickinson, "'I Have One Daughter and That Is Egyptian Cinema': 'Aziza Amir amid the Histories and Geographies of National Allegory," *Camera Obscura* 22, no. 1 (64) (2007): 137–77.

72. Studio Misr continued to push its nationalist agenda. Umm Kulthum's second film with Studio Misr, *Nashid al-amal* (*Anthem of Hope,* Ahmad Badr Khan, 1937), set in the present, espoused overtly nationalist themes. *Lashin* (Fritz Kramp, 1938) ran afoul of the censors for its representation of a corrupt despot.

73. Viola Shafik, *Arab Cinema: History and Cultural Identity* (Cairo: American University in Cairo Press, 1998), 166.

74. "God does not love arrogant or boastful people," Qur'an 31:18. All Qur'an citations are from *The Qur'an,* trans. M.A. Abdel Haleem (New York: Oxford University Press, 2005).

75. Shafik, *Arab Cinema,* 167.

76. Ibid., 82.

77. Ibid.

78. The serialization in *Al-Thaqafa* ran from 3 June to 14 October 1941. *Sallamat al-Qass* won first prize in a competition held by the journal *Al-Nil* for the best Arabic story on the subject of Islamic history. The serialized novel that preceded *Sallamat al-Qass* in the pages of *Al-Thaqafa—Zanubiya*, by Muhammad Farid Abu Hadid—dealt with a pre-Islamic female figure. ʿAli Ahmad Ba Kathir, "Sallamat al-Qass," *Al-Thaqafa*, no. 127 (1941): 26.

79. Muhammad Abu Bakr Hamid, introduction to *Al-ʿAmal al-riwaʾiyya*, by ʿAli Ahmad Ba Kathir, ed. Muhammad Abu Bakr Hamid (Cairo: Al-Majlis al-aʿla li-l-thaqafa, 2010).

80. Marlé Hammond, "The Morphing of a Folktale: Sallama and the Priest," *Middle Eastern Literatures* 15, no. 2 (2012): 117n16.

81. Ibid.

82. The previous year, *Habbaba* (Niyazi Mustafa, 1944), a film about Habbaba (ʿAziza ʿAmir) was released. In 1953, Jacob M. Landau deemed it an excellent historical film, "remembered for its able presentation of life and manners at the Court of the Caliph Yazid II." Landau, "The Arab Cinema," *Middle Eastern Affairs* 4 (November 1953): 355.

83. Hammond, "Morphing of a Folktale," 123.

84. Ibid., 124.

85. Ibid., 127.

86. Ibid., 128–29.

87. Ibid., 131.

88. This verse also appears in the novel *Sallamat al-Qass*. ʿAli Ahmad Ba Kathir, *Al-ʿAmal al-riwaʾiyya*, ed. Muhammad Abu Bakr Hamid, vol. 1 (Cairo: Al-Majlis al-aʿla li-l-thaqafa, 2010), 138; Hamid, introduction to *Al-ʿAmal al-riwaʾiyya*.

89. Hammond, "Morphing of a Folktale," 120.

90. Qurʾan 14:38–41.

91. Hammond notes the substitution of one *aya* for another, but declines to interpret the significance. She cites a blog that claims that Mizrahi himself was responsible for selecting the verses Umm Kulthum recites in the film. Hammond, "Morphing of a Folktale," 130.

92. Bankole Ajibabi Omotoso, "Ali Ahmad Ba-Kathir, a Contemporary Conservative Arab Writer: An Appraisal of His Main Novels and Plays" (PhD diss., University of Edinburgh, 1972), 37. For more on Ba Kathir's identification with Islamist movements in Egypt, see Mohammad Salama, *Islam and the Culture of Modern Egypt from the Monarchy to the Republic* (Cambridge: Cambridge University Press, 2018).

93. Eeqbal Hassim, "The Significance of Qurʾanic Verses in the Literature of Ali Ahmad Bakathir," *NCEIS Research Papers* 1, no. 3 (2009).

94. "Film Sallama li-anisa Umm Kulthum," *Al-Sabah*, 8 March 1945; ʿAmr, "Zikrayat faniyya: Togo Mizrahi."

95. Ba Kathir expressed displeasure about the film adaptation. Ahmad Raʾfat Bahjat, *Al-Yahud wa-l-sinima fi Misr* ([Cairo]: A.R. Bahjat, 2005), 208.

96. Several key scenes in *Fatima* (Ahmad Badrkhan, 1947) also revolve around the title character (Umm Kulthum) guarding her honor. Fatima is a modern, educated woman employed as a nurse. Fathi Bey (Anwar Wagdi) tries to seduce her and she refuses. After much discussion—and Fatima's appeal, rendered in the song "Wa-asun karamati" ("I Maintain My Honor")—Fathi offers to marry her in a civil ceremony (*zawag ʿurfi*).

97. The character of Shawq does not appear in Ba Kathir's novel. For a description of the differences between the novel and film, see Rida al-Tayyar, *Al-Riwaya al-ʿarabiya fi-l-sinima* (Baghdad: Wizarat al-thaqafa wa-l-iʿlam, 1983), 102–6.

98. As Everett Rowson notes, in early Islamic history effeminate men (*mukhannathun*)— "men who resembled women," not castrates—were permitted into the female domestic sphere "on the assumption that they lacked sexual interest in women." Rowson, "The Effeminates of Early Medina," *Journal of the American Oriental Society* 111, no. 4 (1991): 675. Thus, whether or not one assumes the servant in *Sallama* is a eunuch, the character indexes a nonbinary sexuality. For more on the history of eunuchs in the employ of imperial Islamic courts, see David Ayalon, *Eunuchs, Caliphs and Sultans: A Study in Power Relationships* (Jerusalem: Hebrew University Magnes Press, 1999); Nadia Maria El-Cheikh, "Servants at the Gate: Eunuchs at the Court of Al-Muqtadir," *Journal of the Economic & Social History of the Orient* 48, no. 2 (2005): 234–52; and Shaun Elizabeth Marmon, *Eunuchs and Sacred Boundaries in Islamic Society* (New York: Oxford University Press, 1995).

99. 'Ali Ahmad Ba Kathir, *Al-'Amal al-riwa'iyya*, ed. Muhammad Abu Bakr Hamid, vol. 1. (Cairo: Al-Majlis al-a'la li-l-thaqafa, 2010), 83–84.

100. Umm Kulthum, "Togo Mizrahi bi-qalam Umm Kulthum," *Al-Sabah*, 19 April 1945, 23.

101. Umm Kulthum's first film, *Widad* (1936), was directed by Fritz Kramp, a German-born filmmaker who directed another early production by Studio Misr, *Lashin* (1938). Kramp's whereabouts in 1945 are unknown, and Umm Kulthum's comments may not have reached him.

102. "Umm Kulthum wa-Togo Mizrahi mu'amarat wa-isha'at," *Al-Sabah*, 19 April 1945, 23.

103. Ibid.

104. "Kayfa iktashafat thum fashalat mu'amarat mudiri al-sharikat al-sinima'iyya didd film Salama wa-Umm Kulthum," *Al-Sabah*, 26 April 1945.

105. Togo Mizrahi, letter cited in "Mawqif Istudiyu Misr min film Umm Kulthum," *Al-Sabah*, 10 May 1945, 26–7.

106. "Hal ta'lam?" *Al-Sabah*, 11 May 1944, 26.

107. "Umm Kulthum fi Sallama ma'a Husni Bey Naguib," *Al-Sabah*, 19 April 1945, 19; "Sahib al-jalala al-malik yushaid film Sallama fi sinima Istudiyu Misr," *Al-Sabah*, 17 May 1945, 24.

108. 'Amr, "Zikrayat faniyya: Togo Mizrahi."

109. "Bayn Studiyu Misr wa-film Umm Kulthum," *Al-Sabah*, 24 May 1945, 24.

110. "Irad film Sallama," *Al-Sabah*, 8 November 1945, 21.

111. Mizrahi, letter cited in "Mawqif Istudiyu Misr min film Umm Kulthum."

112. Ibid.

113. "Bayan min itihad al-muntijin," *Al-Sabah*, 24 May 1945, 23.

114. "[Untitled]," *Al-Sabah*, 25 July 1945, 24.

115. 'Amr, "Zikrayat faniyya: Togo Mizrahi."

116. "Hal ta'lam," *Al-Sabah*, 6 December 1945, 33.

8. FRAMES OF INFLUENCE

1. Paula Jacques, *Kayro Jacobi, juste avant l'oubli* (Paris: Mercure de France, 2010), 22–23.

2. Association pour la sauvegarde du patrimoine culturel des Juifs d'Egypte, "Paula Jacques," www.aspcje.fr/nos-activites/comptes-rendus-cercles-de-lecture/93-090310-paula-jacques.html.

3. Jacques, *Kayro Jacobi*, 11. The term *khawalat* had historically referred to male dancers who dressed as women—a practice that became common in Egypt in the early nineteenth century when women were prohibited from dancing in public. Garay Menicucci, "Unlocking the Arab Celluloid Closet: Homosexuality in Egyptian Film," *Middle East Report* 206 (Spring 1998): 32.

4. Jacques, *Kayro Jacobi*, 11.

5. Aimée Israel-Pelletier, *On the Mediterranean and the Nile: The Jews of Egypt* (Bloomington: Indiana University Press, 2018).

6. Zein Nassar, "A History of Music and Singing on Egyptian Radio and Television," in *Music and Media in the Arab World*, ed. Michael Frishkopf (Cairo and New York: American University in Cairo Press, 2010), 72.

7. Ahmad Kamil Mursi, "Shawamikh 'alam al-sinima al-misriyya Togo Mizrahi," *Al-Sinima wa-l-nas*, no. 11 (1979): 25.

8. Ibid.

9. Ibid.

10. Per Walter Armbrust, *munulugat* ("monologues") were "aria-like pieces—expressions of a single person's thoughts, though in tremendously varied forms. Yasin's monologues were comic and often topical." Walter Armbrust, "Ismail Yasin in the Coloring Book," *Arte East Quarterly*, Fall 2007, http://arteeast.org/quarterly/ismail-yasin-in-the-coloring-book/?issues_season = fall&issues_year = 2007.

11. Radio listings, *Al-Ithnayn*, 15 April 1935, 46.

12. Both Chalom and Isma'il Yasin play eponymous translators, in *Chalom al-turguman* (Leon Angel, 1935) and *Al-Turguman Isma'il Yasin* (Hasan al-Sayfi, 1961), respectively.

13. Menicucci, "Unlocking the Arab Celluloid Closet," 33.

14. Joel Gordon, "*Hasan and Marika*: Screenshots from a Vanishing Egypt," *Journal of Levantine Studies* 7, no. 1 (2017): 46; Alexander Kazamias, "The 'Purge of the Greeks' from Nasserite Egypt: Myths and Realities," *Journal of the Hellenic Diaspora* 35, no. 2 (2009): 13–34.

15. Gordon, "*Hasan and Marika*," 46–47.

16. For more about Israeli television's weekly broadcasts of Arabic movies, see *Seret 'aravit* (*Arab Movie*, Eyal Sagui-Bizawi and Sara Tsifroni, 2015).

17. Samirah Alkassim, *The Cinema of Muhammad Malas: Visions of a Syrian Auteur* (New York: Palgrave Macmillan, 2018), 118.

18. Five years earlier, Malas produced a documentary, *Halab, maqamat al-masra* (*Aleppo, Maqams of Pleasure*, 1999), about the elderly musician Sabri Mudallal, a disciple the Aleppan musicians featured in the photographs. *Tarab* has a number of meanings; here I am referring to a traditional genre of music popular in the eastern Mediterranean in the late nineteenth and early twentieth centuries.

19. Marlé Hammond, "The Morphing of a Folktale: Sallama and the Priest," *Middle Eastern Literatures* 15, no. 2 (2012): 113–36.

20. /www.youtube.com/watch?v = FrL4-Ny3UkI. Posted by Abdulrhman on 1 October 2018. Viewed 19,807 times as of 28 May 2019.

21. /www.youtube.com/watch?v = p9HNcBhMxlI&list = PLyPPHM8QeqICMq59av-tjSEzs17YdPfup. Posted by Yasir al-Bushi on 17 October 2017. Viewed 29,084 times as of 28 May 2019.

22. www.youtube.com/watch?v = EJS6hoGvNP8&t = 12s. Posted by Aflamna el Helwa on 9 December 2016. Viewed 142,645 times as of 28 May 2019.

23. Posted on the Aflam Zaman YouTube channel on 6 January 2016: www.youtube.com /watch?v = Ug3E1jUD_TE&t = 799s. Viewed 1,002,520 times as of 28 May 2019.

24. According to Samir Farid, a negative of Ibrahim Lama's film *Al-Dahaya* (*The Victims*, 1932) survived. Samir Farid, "Periodization of Egyptian Cinema," in *Screens of Life: Critical Film Writing from the Arab World*, ed. Alia Arasoughly (Saint-Hyacinthe, Quebec: World Heritage Press, 1996), 5. As of this writing, only a short clip from *The Victims*, under four minutes in length, has appeared streaming online.

25. The films that were lost to fire and then reshot were *Ibn al-sahra'* (*Son of the Desert*, Ibrahim Lama, 1942) and *'Asifa fi-l-rabi'* (*A Storm in the Spring*, Ibrahim Lama, 1951). "Seasons of Fires in the History of the Egyptian Cinema," *Al-Kawakib*, 1951. Translated and reproduced in Muhammad Awad and Sahar Hamouda, eds., *The Birth of the Seventh Art in Alexandria: Catalogue* (Alexandria: Bibliotheca Alexandrina, 2007), 374.

26. "Ihtiraq film al-manduban," *Al-Sabah*, 18 January 1935; "Ihtiraq film al-bashmaqawil," *Al-Sabah*, 16 May 1941.

27. Togo Mizrahi, "Bayan min al-ustaz Togo Mizrahi 'an al-aflam al-muhtariqa fi dur al-sinima," *Al-Sabah*, 1 August 1931.

28. Samir Farid, "Preservation and Archival Problems in the Cinema of Arab-Medi terranean Countiries," in *Le cineteche dei paesi arabo-mediterranei*, ed. Anna Di Martino (Naples: Magma Editions, 2004), 71–93, www.euromedi.org/home/azioni/pubblicazioni/art-edanza/cineteche/FARID.PDF.

29. *Saving Egyptian Film Classics* (Sayed Badreya, 2002).

30. Togo Mizrahi, "Tarikh al-sinima fi Misr," *Al-Sabah*, 17 April 1942, 24.

31. Ibid. The address Mizrahi provides appears to refer to the studio of 'Aziz Bandarli and Umberto Dorés, which another source locates at 3 Greek Hospital Street. Bibliotheca Alexandrina, "Cinema Industry: Studios," www.bibalex.org/alexcinema/industry/studios.html.

32. He also cryptically credits "Darwish"—presumably composer Sayyid Darwish (1892–1923)—but it is not clear what role he played, if any, in the establishment of silent cinema.

33. Mizrahi, "Tarikh al-sinima fi Misr."

34. Bibliotheca Alexandrina, "Historical Background: A Chronology of Firsts in Alexandria," www.bibalex.org/alexcinema/historical/chronology.html.

35. Mizrahi, "Tarikh al-sinima fi Misr."

APPENDIX: TOGO MIZRAHI FILMOGRAPHY

1. Many of Mizrahi's films included credits in both Arabic and French, and many of the pressbooks were published bilingually. I provide the French titles when they appear in the film or the promotional materials at the time of release.

2. For information about Mizrahi's Greek films, see the website of the Greek Film Archive Foundation: www.tainiothiki.gr.

3. *Doctor Epaminondas* is an adaptation of Mizrahi's 1935 Arabic film, *Dr. Farahat*.

4. *The Refugee Girl* is the only Greek film of Mizrahi's known to have survived.

5. *Captain Scorpion* is an adaptation of Mizrahi's 1935 Arabic film *The Sailor*.

WORKS CITED

EGYPTIAN PERIODICALS

Al-Ahram
Akhir sa'a
Fann al-sinima
Al-Istudiyu
Al-Ithnayn (published as *Al-Ithnayn wa-l-Dunya* beginning with issue 239, 9 January 1939)
Al-Kawakib
Al-Lata'if al-musawwara
Al-Misbah
Rose al-Yusuf
Al-Sabah
Al-Shams
La tribune juive

BOOKS, ESSAYS, JOURNAL ARTICLES, AND ARCHIVES

'Abd al-Fatah, Wa'il. "Mukhrij min Misr, am qanbala yahudiyya mufakhakha?" *Al-Mustaqbil*, 10 November 2005, 20.

Abdulhaq, Najat. *Jewish and Greek Communities in Egypt: Entrepreneurship and Business before Nasser*. London: I.B. Tauris, 2016.

Abou-Saif, L. "Najib Al-Rihani: From Buffoonery to Social Comedy." *Journal of Arabic Literature* 4 (1973): 1–17.

Abu Shadi, 'Ali. "Genres in Egyptian Cinema." In *Screens of Life: Critical Film Writing from the Arab World*, edited by Alia Arasoughly, 84–129. Saint-Hyacinthe, Quebec: World Heritage Press, 1996.

Aciman, André. *Out of Egypt: A Memoir*. New York: Farrar Straus Giroux, 1994.

Alkassim, Samirah. *The Cinema of Muhammad Malas: Visions of a Syrian Auteur*. New York: Palgrave Macmillan, 2018.

'Amr, Hasan Imam. "Zikrayat faniyya: Togo Mizrahi." *Al-Wafd*, 6 November 1995, 12.

'Amr, Iman. "Al-Taghyirat al-tarikhiyya wa-atharha 'ala sinima al-thalathiniyat." In *Al-Sinima al-misriyya: Al-Nash'a wa-l-takwin*, edited by Hashim al-Nahhas, 53–102. Cairo: Al-Majlis al-a'la li-l-thaqafa, 2008.

Anderson, Benedict. *Imagined Communities: Reflections on the Origin and Spread of Nationalism*. London: Verso, 1983.

Annuaire des juifs d'Égypte et du Proche-Orient (Cairo: Société des éditions historiques juives d'Égypte, 1942)

Armbrust, Walter. "The Golden Age before the Golden Age: Commercial Egyptian Cinema before the 1960s." In *Mass Mediations New Approaches to Popular Culture in the Middle East and Beyond*, edited by Walter Armbrust, 292–327. Berkeley: University of California Press, 2000.

————. "Ismail Yasin in the Coloring Book." *Arte East Quarterly*, Fall 2007, http://arteeast.org/quarterly/ismail-yasin-in-the-coloring-book/?issues_season=fall&issues_year=2007.

————. "Long Live Patriarchy: Love in the Time of Abd Al-Wahhab." *History Compass* 7, no. 1 (2009): 251–81.

————. *Mass Culture and Modernism in Egypt*. Cambridge and New York: Cambridge University Press, 1996.

————. "The Ubiquitous Non-presence of India: Peripheral Visions from Egyptian Popular Culture." In *Global Bollywood: Travels of Hindi Song and Dance*, edited by Sangita Gopal and Sujata Murti, 200–220. Minneapolis: University of Minnesota Press, 2008.

Association pour la sauvegarde du patrimoine culturel des Juifs d'Egypte, "Paula Jacques," www.aspcje.fr/nos-activites/comptes-rendus-cercles-de-lecture/93-090310-paula-jacques.html.

Aswani, 'Ala al-. 'Imarat Ya'qubiyan. Cairo: Mirit li-l-nashr wa-al-na'lumat, 2002.

————. *The Yacoubian Building*. Translated by Humphrey T. Davies. New York: Harper Perennial, 2006.

Awad, Muhammad, and Sahar Hamouda, eds. *The Birth of the Seventh Art in Alexandria: Catalogue*. Alexandria: Bibliotheca Alexandrina, 2007.

Ayalon, David. *Eunuchs, Caliphs and Sultans: A Study in Power Relationships*. Jerusalem: Hebrew University Magnes Press, 1999.

Ba Kathir, 'Ali Ahmad. *Al-'Amal al-riwa'iyya*. Edited by Muhammad Abu Bakr Hamid. Vol. 1. Cairo: Al-Majlis al-a'la li-l-thaqafa, 2010.

————. "Sallamat al-Qass." *Al-Thaqafa*, no. 127 (3 June 1941): 26–29.

Baer, Gabriel. "Slavery in Nineteenth Century Egypt." *Journal of African History* 8, no. 3 (1967): 417–41.

Bahjat, Ahmad Ra'fat, ed. *Misr: Mi'at sana sinima*. Cairo: Mahrajan al-Qahira al-sinima'i al-dawli al-'ishrun, 1996.

————. *Al-Yahud wa-al-sinima fi Misr*. [Cairo]: A.R. Bahjat, 2005.

Bahoora, Haytham. "The Figure of the Prostitute, Tajdid, and Masculinity in Anticolonial Literature of Iraq." *Journal of Middle East Women's Studies* 11, no. 1 (2015): 42–62.

Bakhtin, M.M. *The Dialogic Imagination: Four Essays.* Translated by Caryl Emerson and Michael Holquist. Austin: University of Texas Press, 1981.

——. *Rabelais and His World.* Translated by Helene Iswolsky. Cambridge, MA: MIT Press, 1968.

Baron, Beth. *Egypt as a Woman: Nationalism, Gender, and Politics.* Berkeley: University of California Press, 2005.

Behar, Moshe, and Zvi Ben-Dor Benite, eds. *Modern Middle Eastern Jewish Thought: Writings on Identity, Politics, and Culture, 1893–1958.* Waltham, MA: Brandeis University Press, 2013.

——. "The Possibility of Modern Middle Eastern Jewish Thought." *British Journal of Middle Eastern Studies* 41, no. 1 (2014): 43–61.

Beinin, Joel. *The Dispersion of Egyptian Jewry: Culture, Politics, and the Formation of a Modern Diaspora.* Berkeley: University of California Press, 1998.

——. "Egypt: Society and Economy, 1923–1952." In *The Cambridge History of Egypt,* edited by M.W. Daly, 309–33. Cambridge: Cambridge University Press, 1998.

Ben-Dor Benite, Zvi. "Global Experiments in Mizrahi Thought: 'Asia,' 'Europe' and the 'East' in the Writings of Hayyim Ben-Kiki." Paper presented at conference "Symposium on Jewish Thought in Arab Societies, 1880–1960," Beersheba, Israel, May 2014.

Bentley, Eric. *The Life of the Drama.* New York: Atheneum, 1964.

Bhabha, Homi K. *The Location of Culture.* London and New York: Routledge, 1994.

Bibliotheca Alexandrina. "Alex Cinema: The Birth of the Seventh Art in Alexandria." www.bibalex.org/alexcinema/index.html.

——. "Cinema Industry: Studios." www.bibalex.org/alexcinema/industry/studios.html.

——. "Historical Background: A Chronology of Firsts in Alexandria." https://www.bibalex .org/alexcinema/historical/chronology.html.

Brock, Cutler. "Aghion Family." In *Encyclopedia of Jews in the Islamic World.* Leiden: Brill, 2010.

Bryant, Rebecca. "Everyday Coexistence in the Post-Ottoman Space." In *Post-Ottoman Coexistence: Sharing Space in the Shadow of Conflict,* edited by Rebecca Bryant, 1–40. New York: Berghahn Books, 2016.

Bunis, David, Joseph Chetrit, and Haideh Sahim. "Jewish Languages Enter the Modern Era." In *The Jews of the Middle East and North Africa in Modern Times,* 113–41. New York: Columbia University Press, 2003.

Butler, Judith. *Gender Trouble: Feminism and the Subversion of Identity.* London and New York: Routledge, 1990.

Caswell, Fuad Matthew. *The Slave Girls of Baghdad: The Qiyan in the Early Abbasid Era.* London: I.B. Tauris, 2011.

Cavell, Stanley. *Pursuits of Happiness: The Hollywood Comedy of Remarriage.* Cambridge, MA: Harvard University Press, 1981.

Cohan, Steven. "Queering the Deal: On the Road with Hope and Crosby." In *Out Takes: Essays on Queer Theory and Film,* edited by Ellis Hanson, 23–45. Durham, NC: Duke University Press, 1999.

Cohen, Mark. "The Neo-Lachrymose Conception of Jewish-Arab History." *Tikkun* 6 (1991): 55–60.

Cole, Juan. *Colonialism and Revolution in the Middle East: Social and Cultural Origins of Egypt's 'Urabi Movement.* Princeton, NJ: Princeton University Press, 1993.

Collins, Robert O. *A History of Modern Sudan.* Cambridge and New York: Cambridge University Press, 2008.

Collins, Robert O., and Robert L. Tignor. *Egypt & the Sudan.* Englewood Cliffs, NJ: Prentice-Hall, 1967.

The Concise Oxford Companion to the Theatre. Edited by Phyllis Hartnoll and Peter Found. Oxford: Oxford University Press, 1996.

Crabites, Pierre. "The Nile Waters Agreement." *Foreign Affairs* 8, no. 1 (1929): 145–49.

Crowther, Bosley. "Palestinian Film in Premiere Here." *New York Times,* 26 September 1947.

Daniel, Menahem Salih. "Letter to Chayyim Weitzmann." In *Modern Middle Eastern Jewish Thought: Writings on Identity, Politics, and Culture, 1893–1958,* edited by Moshe Behar and Zvi Ben-Dor Benite, 109–13. Waltham, MA: Brandeis University Press, 2013.

Danielson, Virginia. *The Voice of Egypt: Umm Kulthum, Arabic Song, and Egyptian Society in the Twentieth Century.* Chicago: University of Chicago Press, 1997.

Dasuqi, Ibrahim, and Sami Hilmi. *Madrasat al-Iskandariyya li-l-taswir al-sinima'i.* Alexandria: Maktabat al-Iskandariyya, 2013.

Davis, Eric. *Challenging Colonialism: Bank Misr and Egyptian Industrialization.* Princeton, NJ: Princeton University Press, 1983.

Dickinson, Kay. "'I Have One Daughter and That Is Egyptian Cinema': 'Aziza Amir Amid the Histories and Geographies of National Allegory." *Camera Obscura* 22, no. 1 (64) (2007): 137–77.

El-Cheikh, Nadia Maria. "Servants at the Gate: Eunuchs at the Court of Al-Muqtadir." *Journal of the Economic & Social History of the Orient* 48, no. 2 (2005): 234–52.

Elsaket, Ifdal. "Jungle Films in Egypt: Race, Anti-Blackness, and Empire." *Arab Studies Journal* 25, no. 2 (Fall 2017): 8–32.

———. "The Star of the East: Umm Kulthum and Egyptian Cinema." In *Stars in World Cinema: Screen Icons and Star Systems across Cultures,* edited by Andrea Bandhauer and Michelle Royer, 36–50. London: I.B. Tauris, 2015.

Fahmi, Mahmud 'Ali. "Sinima Togo Mizrahi (1930–1946): Dirasa Naqdiyya." In *Al-Sinima al-misriyya: Al-Nash'a wa-al-takwin,* edited by Hashim al-Nahhas, 153–209. Cairo: Al-Majlis al-a'la li-l-thaqafa, 2008.

Fahmy, Khaled. "Prostitution in Egypt in the Nineteenth Century." In *Outside In: On the Margins of the Modern Middle East,* edited by Eugene L. Rogan, 77–103. London: I.B. Tauris, 2001.

Fahmy, Ziad. "Jurisdictional Borderlands: Extraterritoriality and 'Legal Chameleons' in Precolonial Alexandria, 1840–1870." *Comparative Studies in Society and History* 55, no. 2 (2013): 1–25.

———. *Ordinary Egyptians: Creating the Modern Nation through Popular Culture.* Stanford, CA: Stanford University Press, 2011.

———. *Street Sounds: Listening to Everyday Life in Modern Egypt.* Stanford, CA: Stanford University Press, forthcoming.

Farid, Samir. "Periodization of Egyptian Cinema." In *Screens of Life: Critical Film Writing from the Arab World,* edited by Alia Arasoughly, 1–18. Saint-Hyacinthe, Quebec: World Heritage Press, 1996.

———. "Preservation and Archival Problems in the Cinema of Arab-Mediterranean Countiries." In *Le cineteche dei paesi arabo-mediterranei*, edited by Anna Di Martino, 71–93. Naples: Magma Editions, 2004, www.euromedi.org/home/azioni/pubblicazioni /artedanza/cineteche/FARID.PDF.

Flanagan, Martin. *Bakhtin and the Movies: New Ways of Understanding Hollywood Film.* Basingstoke, UK: Palgrave Macmillan, 2009.

Flibbert, Andrew. *Commerce in Culture: States and Markets in the World Film Trade.* New York: Palgrave Macmillan, 2007.

———. "State and Cinema in Pre-Revolutionary Egypt, 1927–1952." In *Re-Envisioning Egypt, 1919–1952,* edited by Arthur Goldschmidt, Amy J. Johnson, and Barak A. Salmoni, 448–60. Cairo: American University in Cairo Press, 2005.

Ford, Richard Thompson. "What's Queer about Race?" In *After Sex?: On Writing since Queer Theory,* edited by Janet Halley and Andrew Parker, 121–29. Durham, NC: Duke University Press, 2011.

Gellner, Ernest. *Nations and Nationalism.* Ithaca, NY: Cornell University Press, 1983.

Gershoni, Israel, and James Jankowski. *Redefining the Egyptian Nation, 1930–1945.* Cambridge and New York: Cambridge University Press, 1995.

Ghanamaweh, Mohannad. "Entrepreneurship in a State of Flux: Egypt's Silent Cinema and Its Transition to Synchronized Sound, 1896–1934." PhD diss., UCLA, 2020.

Ghandur, Muna. *Sultanat al-shasha: Ra'idat al-sinima al-misriyya.* Beirut: Riyad al-Rayyis li-l-kutub wa-l-nashr, 2005.

Gillette, Aaron. *Racial Theories in Fascist Italy.* London and New York: Routledge, 2002.

Ginat, Rami. *A History of Egyptian Communism: Jews and Their Compatriots in Quest of Revolution.* Boulder, CO: Lynne Rienner Publishers, 2011.

Goldschmidt, Arthur. *Historical Dictionary of Egypt.* 4th ed. Lanham, MD: Scarecrow Press, 2013.

Gordon, Joel. "Class-Crossed Lovers: Popular Film and Social Change in Nasser's New Egypt." *Quarterly Review of Film and Video* 18, no. 4 (2001): 385–96.

———. "*Hasan and Marika*: Screenshots from a Vanishing Egypt." *Journal of Levantine Studies* 7, no. 1 (Summer 2017): 35–56.

———. *Revolutionary Melodrama: Popular Film and Civic Identity in Nasser's Egypt.* Chicago: Middle East Documentation Center, 2002.

Habib, Samar. *Female Homosexuality in the Middle East: Histories and Representations.* Routledge Research in Gender and Society 13. London and New York: Routledge, 2007.

Hadari, Ahmad al-. "Istudiyu Misr . . . Madrasa sinima'iyya fi al-thalathiniyat." In *Al-Sinima al-misriyya: Al-Nash'a wa-l-takwin,* edited by Hashim al-Nahhas, 129–51. Cairo: Al-Majlis al-a'la li-l-thaqafa, 2008.

———. *Tarikh al-sinima fi Misr.* Vol. 1, *Min bidayat 1896 ila akhir 1930.* Cairo: Nadi al-sinima bil-Qahira, 1989.

———. *Tarikh al-sinima fi Misr.* Vol. 2, *Min bidayat 1931 ila akhir 1940.* Cairo: Al-Hay'a al-misriyya al-'ama li-l-kitab, 2007.

Hadeed, Khalid. "Homosexuality and Epistemic Closure in Modern Arabic Literature." *International Journal of Middle East Studies* 45, no. 2 (2013): 271–91.

Hafez, Sabry. "The Quest for / Obsession with the National in Arabic Cinema." In *Theorising National Cinema,* edited by Valentina Vitali and Paul Willemen, 209–25. London: British Film Institute, 2006.

Hamam, Iman. "Disarticulating Arab Popular Culture: The Case of Egyptian Comedies." In *Arab Cultural Studies: Mapping the Field*, edited by Tarik Sabry, 186–213. London: I.B. Tauris, 2011.

Hamid, Muhammad Abu Bakr. Introduction to *Al-'Amal al-riwa'iyya*, by 'Ali Ahmad Ba Kathir, edited by Muhammad Abu Bakr Hamid, 7–21. Cairo: Al-Majlis al-a'la li-l-thaqafa, 2010.

Hammad, Hanan. *Industrial Sexuality: Gender, Urbanization, and Social Transformation in Egypt*. Austin: University of Texas Press, 2016.

Hammad, Hanan, and Francesca Biancani. "Prostitution in Cairo." In *Selling Sex in the City: A Global History of Prostitution, 1600s–2000s*, edited by Magaly Rodríguez Garcia, Lex Heerma van Voss, and Elise van Nederveen Meerkerk, 233–60. Leiden: Brill, 2017.

Hammett, Dashiell. *The Maltese Falcon*. New York: Vintage Books, 1984.

Hammond, Marlé. "The Morphing of a Folktale: Sallama and the Priest." *Middle Eastern Literatures* 15, no. 2 (2012): 113–36.

Hanley, Will. *Identifying with Nationality: Europeans, Ottomans, and Egyptians in Alexandria*. New York: Columbia University Press, 2017.

Hanson, Ellis. Introduction to *Out Takes: Essays on Queer Theory and Film*, edited by Ellis Hanson, 1–19. Durham, NC: Duke University Press, 1999.

Hashem, Farouk. *Farida, the Queen of Egypt: A Memoir of Love and Governance*. Translated by Morad Abou-Sabe. Bloomington, IN: AuthorHouse, 2014.

Hassan, Scheherazade Qassim. "Musical Instruments in the Arab World." In *Garland Encyclopedia of World Music*, vol. 6, *The Middle East*, ed. Virginia Danielson, Scott Marcus, and Dwight Reynolds, 429–53. London and New York: Routledge, 2001.

Hassim, Eeqbal. "The Significance of Qur'anic Verses in the Literature of 'Ali Ahmad Bakathir." *NCEIS Research Papers* 1, no. 3 (2009): 1–27.

Hayward, Susan. "Framing National Cinemas." In *Cinema and Nation*, edited by Mette Hjort and Scott MacKenzie, 88–102. London and New York: Routledge, 2000.

Hilmi, Sami. *Al-Shakhsiya al-sakandariyya fi al-sinima al-misriyya*. Alexandria: Maktabat al-Iskandariyya, 2007.

Hjort, Mette, and Scott MacKenzie. Introduction to *Cinema and Nation*, edited by Mette Hjort and Scott MacKenzie, 1–16. London and New York: Routledge, 2000.

Hourani, Albert. *Arabic Thought in the Liberal Age, 1798–1939*. London: Oxford University Press, 1962.

Hoyle, Mark. "The Mixed Courts of Egypt, 1926–1937." *Arab Law Quarterly* 2, no. 4 (1987): 357–89.

Ibrahim, Munir Muhammad. *Al-Sinima al-misriyya fi al-thalathiniyat (1930–1939)*. Cairo: Wizarat al-thaqafa, sunduq al-tanmiya al-thaqafiyya, 2002.

Israel-Pelletier, Aimée. *On the Mediterranean and the Nile: The Jews of Egypt*. Bloomington: Indiana University Press, 2018.

Jacob, Wilson Chacko. *Working Out Egypt: Effendi Masculinity and Subject Formation in Colonial Modernity, 1870–1940*. Durham, NC: Duke University Press, 2011.

Jacques, Paula. *Kayro Jacobi, juste avant l'oubli*. Paris: Mercure de France, 2010.

Jarvie, Ian. "National Cinema: A Theoretical Assessment." In *Cinema and Nation*, edited by Mette Hjort and Scott MacKenzie, 75–87. London and New York: Routledge, 2000.

Kahanoff, Jacqueline. "Childhood in Egypt." In *Mongrels or Marvels: The Levantine Writings of Jacqueline Shohet Kahanoff*, edited by Deborah A. Starr and Sasson Somekh, 1–13. Stanford, CA: Stanford University Press, 2011.

Karim, Muhammad, and Mahmud Ali. *Mudhakkirat Muhammad Karim: 50 sana sinima*. Cairo: Kitab al-idha'a wa-al-tilifizyun, 1972.

Kazamias, Alexander. "The 'Purge of the Greeks' from Nasserite Egypt: Myths and Realities." *Journal of the Hellenic Diaspora* 35, no. 2 (2009): 13–34.

Khatib, Lina. "The Orient and Its Others: Women as Tools of Nationalism in Egyptian Political Cinema," in *Women and Media in the Middle East: Power through Self-Expression*, ed. Naomi Sakr (London: I.B. Tauris, 2004), 72–88.

Kholoussy, Hanan. *For Better, for Worse: The Marriage Crisis That Made Modern Egypt*. Stanford, CA: Stanford University Press, 2010.

Kozma, Liat. "White Drugs in Interwar Egypt: Decadent Pleasures, Emaciated Fellahin, and the Campaign against Drugs." *Comparative Studies of South Asia, Africa and the Middle East* 33, no. 1 (2013): 89–101.

———. *Policing Egyptian Women: Sex, Law, and Medicine in Khedival Egypt*. Syracuse, NY: Syracuse University Press, 2011.

Krämer, Gudrun. *The Jews in Modern Egypt, 1914–1952*. Seattle: University of Washington Press, 1989.

Kulthum, Umm. "Togo Mizrahi bi-qalam Umm Kulthum." *Al-Sabah*, 19 April 1945, 1.

Landau, Jacob M. "The Arab Cinema." *Middle Eastern Affairs* 4 (November 1953): 349–58.

———. *Jews in Nineteenth-Century Egypt*. New York: New York University Press, 1969.

———. *Studies in the Arab Theater and Cinema*. Philadelphia: University of Pennsylvania Press, 1958.

Lapidot-Firilla, Anat. Editor's note in *Journal of Levantine Studies* 1, no. 1 (2011): 5–12.

Laura, Lohman, Davary Bahar, Lohman Laura, Ayubi Zahra, and Cannon Byron. "Qur'ān." In *The Oxford Encyclopedia of Islam and Women*, edited by Natana J. DeLong-Bas. Oxford: Oxford University Press, 2013.

Lazarev, Anouchka. "Italians, Italianity and Fascism." Translated by Colin Clement. In *Alexandria 1860–1960: The Brief Life of a Cosmopolitan Community*, edited by Robert Ilbert and Ilios Yannakakis. Alexandria: Harpocrates Press, 1997.

Le mondain égyptien: The Egyptian Who's Who. Edited by E.J. Blatner. Vol. 9. Cairo: F.E. Noury et Fils, 1943.

Mabro, Robert. "Nostalgic Literature on Alexandria." In *Historians in Cairo: Essays in Honor of George Scanlon*, edited by George T. Scanlon and Jill Edwards, 237–65. Cairo: American University in Cairo Press, 2002.

Mahmoud Qassim Cinema Collection, Rare Books and Special Collections Library, American University in Cairo.

Mar'i, Diya'. "Al-Ajanib fi al-sinima al-misriyya." In *Al-Sinima al-misriyya: Al-Nash'a wa-l-takwin*, edited by Hashim al-Nahhas, 211–96. Cairo: Al-Majlis al-a'la li-l-thaqafa, 2008.

Mariscotti, Cathlyn. *Gender and Class in the Egyptian Women's Movement, 1925–1939: Changing Perspectives*. Syracuse, NY: Syracuse University Press, 2008.

Marmon, Shaun Elizabeth. *Eunuchs and Sacred Boundaries in Islamic Society*. New York: Oxford University Press, 1995.

Mejri, Ouissal. "The Birth of North African Cinema." In *Africa's Lost Classics: New Histories of African Cinema*, edited by Lizelle Bisschoff and David Murphy, 24–34. London: Legenda, 2014.

Menicucci, Garay. "Unlocking the Arab Celluloid Closet: Homosexuality in Egyptian Film." *Middle East Report* 206 (Spring 1998): 32–36.

Messiri, Sawsan el-. *Ibn Al-Balad: A Concept of Egyptian Identity*. Leiden: Brill, 1978.

Miccoli, Dario. *Histories of the Jews of Egypt: An Imagined Bourgeoisie, 1880s–1950s*. London and New York: Routledge, 2015.

Mills, David Eugene. "Dividing the Nile: The Failure to Strengthen Egyptian–Sudanese Economic Bonds, 1918–1945." PhD diss., University of Utah, 1997.

Mitchell, Timothy. *Rule of Experts: Egypt, Techno-Politics, Modernity*. Berkeley: University of California Press, 2002.

Mizrahi, Alfred. "Togo Mizrahi, raconté par son frère, Alfred Mizrahi." In *La sortie au cinéma: Palaces et ciné-jardins d'Égypte, 1930–1980*, edited by Marie-Claude Bénard, 19–23. Marseille and Aix-en-Provence: Éditions Parenthèses-MMSH, 2016.

Mizrahi, Togo. "Al-Muntij al-Misri huwa al-muntij al-kamil fi al-'alam." *Al-Sabah*, 19 November 1942, 14.

———. "Bayan min al-ustaz Togo Mizrahi 'an al-aflam al-muhtariqa fi dur al-sinima." *Al-Sabah*, 1 August 1941, 1.

———. "Khitab maftuh min al-ustaz Togo Mizrahi ila nujum wa-kawakib aflamuh al-misriyya." *Al-Sabah*, 17 January 1941, 32.

———. "Kul aflami zift! Wa-lakin li-maza?" *Al-Sabah*, 29 October 1942, 32.

———. "Tarikh al-sinima fi Misr." *Al-Sabah*, 17 April 1942, 1.

Mufid, Hanan. *Layla Murad: Sayyidat qitar al-ghina'*. Cairo: Al-Hay'a al-misriyya al-'amma li-l-kitab, 2003.

Murad, Layla. "Adwar uhibbtuha." In *Al-Watha'iq al-khassa li-Layla Murad*, edited by Ashraf Gharib, 138–41. Cairo: Dar El Shorouk, 2016.

Murray, Stephen O. "Woman–Woman Love in Islamic Societies." In *Islamic Homosexualities: Culture, History, and Literature*, edited by Stephen O. Murray and Will Roscoe, 97–104. New York: New York University Press, 1997.

Mursi, Ahmad Kamil. "Shawamikh 'alam al-sinima al-misriyya: Togo Mizrahi." *Al-Sinima wa-l-nas*, no. 11 (1979): 24–25, 55.

Nahhas, Hashim al-. *Al-Huwiya al-qawmiyya fi al-sinima al-'arabiyya: Dirasa istitla'iyya mustaqbaliyya*. Cairo: Al-Hay'a al-misriyya al-'ama li-l-kitab, 1986.

Nassar, Zein. "A History of Music and Singing on Egyptian Radio and Television." In *Music and Media in the Arab World*, edited by Michael Frishkopf, 67–76. Cairo and New York: American University in Cairo Press, 2010.

Nieuwkerk, Karin van. *A Trade Like Any Other: Female Singers and Dancers in Egypt*. Austin: University of Texas Press, 1995.

Omotoso, Bankole Ajibabi. "Ali Ahmad Ba-Kathir, a Contemporary Conservative Arab Writer: An Appraisal of His Main Novels and Plays." PhD diss., University of Edinburgh, 1972.

Poffandi, Stefano, ed. *Indicateur égyptien administratif et commercial*. Alexandria: A. Moures, 1904.

Powell, Eve Troutt. "Burnt Cork Nationalism: Race and Identity in the Theater of 'Ali Al-Kassar." In *Colors of Enchantment: Theater, Dance, Music, and the Visual Arts of the Middle East*, edited by Sherifa Zuhur, 27–38. Cairo: American University in Cairo Press, 2001.

———. *A Different Shade of Colonialism: Egypt, Great Britain, and the Mastery of the Sudan*. Berkeley: University of California Press, 2003.

Prager, Leonard. "Yiddish Theater in Egypt." *Bulletin of the Israeli Academic Center in Cairo* 15 (1992): 73–81.

Qalyubi, Muhammad Kamil al-. *Muhammad Bayumi al-ra'id al-awwal li-l-sinima al-misri-yya.* [Cairo]: Akadimiyat al-funun, Wahdat al-isdarat, 1994.

The Qur'an. Translated by M.A. Abdel Haleem. New York: Oxford University Press, 2005.

Raafat, Samir W. "From Badi'a to Abbas: Looking Back on Giza's Riverside Drive, Part VI, Francophile Copts." *Egyptian Mail,* December 1995, http://www.egy.com/giza/95–11–18.5.php.

———. "History of Motoring in Egypt." *Egyptian Gazette,* 2 March 1997, www.egy.com/historica/97–03–02.php.

Racy, Ali Jihad. *Making Music in the Arab World: The Culture and Artistry of Tarab.* Cambridge: Cambridge University Press, 2003.

Rekabtalaei, Golbarg. "Cinematic Governmentality: Cinema and Education in Modern Iran, 1900s–1930s." *International Journal of Middle East Studies* 50, no. 2 (2018): 247–69.

Rogin, Michael. *Blackface, White Noise: Jewish Immigrants in the Hollywood Melting Pot.* Berkeley: University of California Press, 1996.

Rosen, Philip. "History, Textuality, Nation: Kracauer, Burch and Some Problems in the Study of National Cinemas." In *Theorising National Cinema,* edited by Valentina Vitali and Paul Willemen, 17–28. London: British Film Institute, 2006.

Rosenbaum, Gabriel. "The Arabic Dialect of Jews in Modern Egypt." *Bulletin of the Israeli Academic Center in Cairo,* no. 25 (December 2002): 38–46.

———. "'Aravit yehudit meduberet ba-mitzrayim ha-modernit: Marhivim 'Ivriyim ve-lo-takaniyim." *Massorot* 12 (2002): 117–48.

———. "Elements and Evidence of Spoken Judeo-Egyptian Arabic in Old Egyptian Movies." Paper presented at the conference "Jewish Languages: Languages in Contact," Hebrew University of Jerusalem, June 2016.

Rowson, Everett K. "The Effeminates of Early Medina." *Journal of the American Oriental Society* 111, no. 4 (1991): 671–93.

Russo, Vito. *The Celluloid Closet: Homosexuality in the Movies.* New York: Harper & Row, 1987.

Ryzova, Lucie. *The Age of the Efendiyya: Passages to Modernity in National-Colonial Egypt.* Oxford: Oxford University Press, 2014.

Sagui-Bizawe, Eyal. "Yehudim ba-ta'asiyat ha-qolno'a ba-mitsrayim." *Ha-kayvun mizrah,* Fall 2003, 83–98.

Salama, Mohammad. *Islam and the Culture of Modern Egypt from the Monarchy to the Republic.* Cambridge: Cambridge University Press, 2018.

Samman, Hanadi al-. "Out of the Closet: Representation of Homosexuals and Lesbians in Modern Arabic Literature." *Journal of Arabic Literature* 39, no. 2 (2008): 270–310.

Sarfatti, Michele. "Characteristics and Objectives of the Anti-Jewish Racial Laws in Fascist Italy, 1938–1943." In *Jews in Italy under Fascist and Nazi Rule, 1922–1945,* edited by Joshua D. Zimmerman, 71–80. Cambridge and New York: Cambridge University Press, 2005.

Shafik, Viola. *Arab Cinema: History and Cultural Identity.* Cairo: American University in Cairo Press, 1998.

———. "Badr Lama's Patterned Vest or the Challenges of Writing a 'National' Film History." Paper presented at the conference "Early Cinema in the Balkans and the Near East: Beginnings to Interwar Period," Athens, Greece, June 2015.

———. "Egyptian Cinema." In *Companion Encyclopedia of Middle Eastern and North African Film*, edited by Oliver Leaman, 23–129. London and New York: Routledge, 2001.

———. *Popular Egyptian Cinema: Gender, Class, and Nation*. Cairo: American University in Cairo Press, 2007.

———. "Prostitute for a Good Reason." *Women's Studies International Forum* 24, no. 6 (2001): 711–25.

Shamir, Shimon. "The Evolution of the Egyptian Nationality Laws and Their Application to the Jews in the Monarchy Period." In *The Jews of Egypt: A Mediterranean Society in Modern Times*, edited by Shimon Shamir, 33–67. Boulder, CO: Westview Press, 1987.

Shammaa, Magdy el-. "Shadows of Contemporary Lives: Modernity, Culture, and National Identity in Egyptian Filmmaking." PhD diss., UCLA, 2007.

Shemer, Yaron. "From Chahine's *al-Iskandariyya . . . leh* to *Salata baladi* and '*An Yahud Misr*: Rethinking Egyptian Jews' Cosmopolitanism, Belonging and Nostalgia in Cinema." *Middle East Journal of Culture and Communication* 7, no. 3 (2014): 351–75.

Shepstone, Harold. "Conquest of the Desert (Part 1)." *Wonders of World Engineering*, 27 April 1937, 289–92.

———. "Conquest of the Desert (Part 2)." *Wonders of World Engineering*, 4 May 1937, 293–95.

Shinawi, Kamal al-. "Kamal al-Shinawi yahki 'an tajribatihi fi film Amir al-intiqam." In *Sultanat al-shasha: Ra'idat al-sinima al-misriyya*, by Muna Ghandur, 164. Beirut: Riyad al-Rayyis li-l-kutub wa-l-nashr, 2005.

Snir, Reuven. "'A Carbon Copy of Ibn Al-Balad'? The Participation of Egyptian Jews in Modern Arab Culture." *Archiv Orientální* 74, no. 1 (2006): 37–64.

Somekh, Sasson. "Farag, Murad." In *Encyclopedia of Jews in the Islamic World*. Leiden: Brill, 2010.

———. "Participation of Egyptian Jews in Modern Arabic Culture, and the Case of Murad Farag." In *The Jews of Egypt: A Mediterranean Society in Modern Times*, edited by Shimon Shamir, 130–40. Boulder, CO: Westview Press, 1987.

Stam, Robert. *Subversive Pleasures: Bakhtin, Cultural Criticism, and Film*. Baltimore: Johns Hopkins University Press, 1989.

Starr, Deborah A. "Chalom and 'Abdu Get Married: Jewishness and Egyptianness in the Films of Togo Mizrahi." *Jewish Quarterly Review* 107, no. 2 (Spring 2017): 209–30.

———. "In Bed Together: Coexistence in Togo Mizrahi's Alexandria Films." In *Post-Ottoman Co-Existence: Sharing Space in the Shadow of Conflict*, edited by Rebecca Bryant, 129–56. Oxford: Berghan Books, 2016.

———. "Masquerade and the Performance of National Imaginaries: Levantine Ethics, Aesthetics, and Identities in Egyptian Cinema." *Journal of Levantine Studies* 1, no. 2 (Winter 2011): 31–57.

———. *Remembering Cosmopolitan Egypt: Literature, Culture, and Empire*. London and New York: Routledge, 2009.

Starr, Deborah A., and Sasson Somekh. "Editors' Introduction: Jacqueline Shohet Kahanoff—a Cosmopolitan Levantine. In *Mongrels or Marvels: The Levantine Writings of Jacqueline Shohet Kahanoff*, ed. Deborah A. Starr and Sasson Somekh (Stanford, CA: Stanford University Press, 2011), xi–xxix.

Stein, Sarah Abrevaya. *Extraterritorial Dreams: European Citizenship, Sephardi Jews, and the Ottoman Twentieth Century*. Chicago: University of Chicago Press, 2016.

Tayyar, Rida al-. *Al-Riwaya al-'arabiyya fi al-sinima*. Baghdad: Wizarat al-thaqafa wa-l-i'lam, 1983.

"Timeline of Egyptian Cinema, 1896–1980s," *Rawi: Egypt's Heritage Review*, no. 9 (2018): 86–87.

Thomas, Brandon. *Charley's Aunt*. Cambridge: Proquest LLC, 2007. Accessed November 13, 2019, https://cornell.on.worldcat.org/oclc/300059307. Originally published 1892.

Tignor, Robert L. "Bank Misr and Foreign Capitalism." *International Journal of Middle East Studies* 8, no. 2 (1977): 161–81.

Viscomi, Joseph. "Out of Time: History, Presence, and the Departure of the Italians of Egypt, 1933–Present." PhD diss., University of Michigan, 2016.

Vitali, Valentina, and Paul Willemen, eds. *Theorising National Cinema*. London: British Film Institute, 2006.

Vitalis, Robert. "American Ambassador in Technicolor and Cinemascope: Hollywood and Revolution on the Nile." In *Mass Mediations: New Approaches to Popular Culture in the Middle East and Beyond*, edited by Walter Armbrust. Berkeley: University of California Press, 2000, 269–89.

——. *When Capitalists Collide: Business Conflict and the End of Empire in Egypt*. Berkeley: University of California Press, 1995.

Vogelsang-Eastwood, Gillian, and Willem Vogelsang. *Covering the Moon: An Introduction to Middle Eastern Face Veils*. Leuven: Peeters, 2008.

Waterbury, John. *The Egypt of Nasser and Sadat: The Political Economy of Two Regimes*. Princeton, NJ: Princeton University Press, 1983.

Willemen, Paul. "The National Revised." in *Theorising National Cinema*, edited by Valentina Vitali and Paul Willemen, 29–43. London: British Film Institute, 2006.

Williams, Alan Larson. *Republic of Images: A History of French Filmmaking*. Cambridge, MA: Harvard University Press, 1992.

Women in World History: A Biographical Encyclopedia, edited by Anne Commire and Deborah Klezmer, 294–95. Waterford, CT: Yorkin Publications, 1999.

Youssef, Mary. *Minorities in the Contemporary Egyptian Novel*. Edinburgh: Edinburgh University Press, 2019.

Zubaida, Sami. *Islam, the People and the State: Essays on Political Ideas and Movements in the Middle East*. London and New York: Routledge, 1989.

Zuhur, Sherifa. *Asmahan's Secrets: Woman, War and Song*. Austin: Center for Middle Eastern Studies, University of Texas at Austin, 2000.

FILMS

Here I list films by filmmakers other than Togo Mizrahi. For a Mizrahi filmography, see the appendix.

'Abd al-Wahab, Fatin. *Al-Anisa Hanafi (Miss Hanafi)*. 1954.

Abu Sayf, Salah. *Raya wa-Sakina (Raya and Sakina)*. 1953.

Angel, Leon. *Chalom al-turguman (Chalom the Dragoman)*. 1935.

Badreya, Sayed. *Saving Egyptian Film Classics*. 2002.

Badr Khan, Ahmad. *Dananir*. 1940.

——. *Fatima*. 1947.

———. *Nashid al-amal* (*Anthem of Hope*). 1937.

Barakat, Henri. *Amir al-intiqam* (*Prince of Vengeance*). 1950.

———. *Al-Bab al-maftuh* (*The Open Door*). 1963.

Bayumi, Muhammad. *Al-Khatib raqam 13* (*The Thirteenth Fiancé*). 1933.

Bonvilli. *Al-Khala al-amrikiyya* (*The American Aunt*). 1920.

Butler, David. *Ali Baba Goes to Town*. 1937.

Capra, Frank. *Mr. Deeds Goes to Town*. 1936.

Chaplin, Charlie. *The Cure*. 1917.

Crosland, Alan. *The Jazz Singer*. 1928.

Cukor, George. *Camille*. 1936.

Del Ruth, Roy. *The Maltese Falcon*. 1931.

Dieterle, William. *Satan Met a Lady*. 1936.

Farkas, Alexander. *Bawwab al-'imara* (*The Doorman*). 1935.

Galal, Ahmad. *Bint al-basha al-mudir* (*The Pasha Director's Daughter*) 1938.

———. *Fata mutamarrida* (*Rebellious Girl*). 1940.

———. *Shagarat al-Durr*. 1935.

———. *Zawja bi-l-niyaba* (*Wife by Proxy*). 1936.

Gance, Abel. *La fin du monde* (*The End of the World*). 1931.

Gance, Abel, and Fernand Rivers. *La dame aux camélias* (*Camille*). 1934.

Gastyne, Marco de. *Rothchild*. 1933.

Gazayirli, Fu'ad al-. *Al-Abyad wa-l-aswad* (*The White and the Black*). 1936.

Hafiz, Bahiga. *Layla al-badawiyya* (*Layla the Bedouin*). 1944.

———. *Layla bint al-sahra'* (*Layla Daughter of the Desert*). 1937.

Halbawi, Hasan, al-. *Mukhadarat* (*Drugs*). 1930.

Karim, Muhammad *Awlad al-zawat* (*Children of the Aristocracy*). 1932.

———. *Yahya al-hubb* (*Long Live Love*). 1938.

Keighley, William. *The Prince and the Pauper*. 1937.

Kimchi, Rami. *Sinema mitsrayim* (*Cinema Egypt*). 1998.

Kline, Herbert. *My Father's House*. 1947.

Kramp, Fritz. *Lashin*. 1938.

———. *Widad*. 1936.

Lama, Ibrahim. *'Asifa fi-l-rabi'* (*A Storm in the Spring*). 1951.

———. *Al-Dahaya* (*The Victims*). 1932.

———. *Ibn al-sahra'* (*Son of the Desert*). 1942

———. *Qubla fi al-sahra'* (*A Kiss in the Desert*), 1928.

———. *Salah al-Din*. 1941.

———. *Shabah al-madi* (*Ghost from the Past*). 1934.

Laricci, Leonard. *Madame Loretta*. 1919.

Lerski, Helmar. *Adama* (*Tomorrow's a Wonderful Day*). 1948.

Malas, Muhammad. *Bab al-maqam* (*Passion*). 2005.

———. *Halab, maqamat al-masra* (*Aleppo, Maqams of Pleasure*). 1999.

McCarey, Leo. *The Kid from Spain*. 1932.

McLoed, Norman. *Monkey Business*. 1931.

Melford, George. *The Sheik*. 1921

Mustafa, Niyazi. *Salama fi khayr* (*Salama Is Fine*). 1937

———. *Habbaba*. 1944.

Örfi, Vedat (Wedad), and Stefan Rosti. *Layla*. 1927.

Qaliyubi (El-Kalioubi), Muhammad al-. *Muhammad Bayumi, waqa'i' al-zaman al-da'i' (Mohamed Bayumi, Chronicle of a Lost Time)*. 1991.

Rafla, Hilmi. *Al-'Aql fi igaza (The Mind Is on Vacation)*. 1947.

Rosito, Victor. *Fi bilad Tut Ankh Amun (In the Land of Tutankhamun)*. 1923.

Sagui-Bizawi, Eyal, and Sara Tsifroni. *Seret aravit (Arabic Movie)*. 2015.

Salim, Kamal. *Al-'Azima (Determination)*. 1939.

Sayfi, Hasan, al-. *Hasan wa-Marika (Hasan and Marika)*. 1958.

———. *Al-Turguman Isma'il Yasin (Isma'il Yasin the Translator)*. 1961.

Schenck, Harry. *Beyond Bengal*. 1934.

Sutherland, Edward. *Palmy Days*. 1931.

Taurog, Norman. *Strike Me Pink*. 1935.

Tuttle, Frank. *Roman Scandals*. 1933.

Volpe, Mario. *Anshuda al-fu'ad (Songs of the Heart)*. 1932.

Von Sternberg, Josef. *The Blue Angel*. 1930.

Wagdi, Anwar. *Layla bint al-aghniya' (Layla the Rich Girl)*. 1946.

———. *Layla bint al-akabir (Layla the Aristocratic Girl)*. 1953.

———. *Layla bint al-fuqara' (Layla the Poor Girl)*. 1945.

Werker, Alfred. *The House of Rothschild*. 1934.

Wood, Sam. *A Day at the Races*. 1937.

NEWSREELS

Alexandria Bombed. British Pathé, 1941. https://www.britishpathe.com/video/alexandria-bombed/query/alexandria+bombed.

King Farouk's Investiture in Cairo. British Pathé, 1937. https://www.britishpathe.com/video/king-farouks-investiture-in-cairo/query/Farouk.

INDEX

'Abd al-Gawad, Muhammad, 156, 177, 191n112
'Abd al-Wahab, Fatin, 160
'Abd al-Wahab, Muhammad, 15, 25, 40, 126, 130
'Abdu, Hasan Muhammad, 35
Abu Shadi, 'Ali, 52–53, 55, 66
Abyss, or Cocaine, The (Mizrahi), 31, 34–35, 170
Abyss, The (Taymur), 34
'Adalat. *See* Angel, Esther Cohen
Abu Sayf, Salah, 21, 50
Abyad, Dawlat, 28, 173
Aciman, André, 6–7
Ahmad, 'Abd al-'Aziz, 110, 113*fig.*
Ahmad, 'Abd al-Gawad, 156, 177
Ahmad, Zakariya, 28, 170, 173–175
Alexandria: cinema houses in, 14, 15, 36, 107, 170–175; cinematographic "school" of, 21–22, 160, 161; coexistence in, 22, 55, 70, 84, 96, 101; corniche of, 1, 77, 78, 92; diversity of, 25, 50, 51, 91, 93, 94; film industry in, 10, 12, 20, 166–167; Greeks of, 61, 118; in *Cinema Egypt*, 161–162; in *Doctor Farahat*, 75; in *It's My Nature*, 105; in *Mistreated by Affluence*, 1–2, 73, 84; in *Neighborhood Watchman, The*, 50, 54; in *Seven O'Clock*, 25, 54, 91–92, 93–96, 100, 104, 105; in *Two Delegates, The*, 50, 54, 63; Italians of, 91; Jews of, 6, 28, 30, 122, 161; Nubians of, 50, 101; World War II in, 139
'Alam, Salwa, 28
'Ali Baba and the Forty Thieves (Mizrahi), 40, 152, 160, 174

Ali Baba Goes to Town (Butler), 102
American Aunt, The (Bonvilli), 103
American Cosmograph Theaters (Cinema Cosmo), 14–15, 34, 42, 107, 130, 155–6, 170–177
Amir, 'Aziza, 11–13, 16, 145, 167
'Amr, Hasan, 156
Angel, Esther Cohen ('Adalat), 58, 59, 59*fig.*, 83, 119, 171
Angel, Leon, 55, 57–58, 59, 60, 73, 119, 170–171, 177; pictures of, 59*fig.*, 60*fig.*, 74*fig.*, 85*fig.*, 88*fig.*; as Chalom (character), 3, 24, 50, 51, 54, 56–64, 73, 83–87, 119–120, 165; as Chalom (screen name), 3, 8, 35, 36, 160, 170–171
Anglo-Egyptian Treaty (1936), 15, 20–21, 98–99, 113–114, 139. *See also* Montreux Convention (1937)
'Arafa, Ibrahim, 104, 171
Armbrust, Walter, 19, 126
Asmahan, 131, 163
Association of Cinema Critics, 40
Athlete, The (Angel and Mizrahi), 57, 177, 187n19
Awad, Muhammad, 22, 35
awlad al-balad, See ibn al-balad

Ba Kathir, 'Ali Ahmad, 25, 126, 146–7, 148, 149, 154, 175
Badr Khan, Ahmad, 15, 21, 40, 127, 142, 145, 155
Bahjat, Ahmad, 49
Bahoora, Haytham, 129
Bakhtin, Mikhail, 52–53, 65, 66–67

225

Founded in 1893,
UNIVERSITY OF CALIFORNIA PRESS
publishes bold, progressive books and journals
on topics in the arts, humanities, social sciences,
and natural sciences—with a focus on social
justice issues—that inspire thought and action
among readers worldwide.

The UC PRESS FOUNDATION
raises funds to uphold the press's vital role
as an independent, nonprofit publisher, and
receives philanthropic support from a wide
range of individuals and institutions—and from
committed readers like you. To learn more, visit
ucpress.edu/supportus.